Transport Geography

Transport geography

H. P. White, M.A., M.C.I.T.,
Professor of Geography,
University of Salford

and

M. L. Senior, B.A., Ph.D.,
Lecturer in Geography
University of Salford

Longman
London and New York

Longman Group Limited
Longman House, Burnt Mill, Harlow
Essex CM20 2JE, England
Associated companies throughout the world

*Published in the United States of America
by Longman Inc., New York*

First published 1983

British Library Cataloguing in Publication Data

White, H. P.

Transport geography.
1. Transportation
I. Title II. Senior, M. L.
380.5′09   HE151

ISBN 0-582-30025-8

Library of Congress Cataloging in Publication Data

White, H. P. (Henry Patrick), 1920–
Transport geography.

Bibliography: p.
Includes index.
1. Transportation–Great Britain.
2. Transportation.
I. Senior, M. L., 1947– II. Title.
HE243.W475   380.5′0941   82-15332
ISBN 0-582-30025-8 (pbk.)

Set in 10/12 pt Linotron 202 Times Roman
Printed in Singapore by
Singapore National Printers (Pte) Ltd.

Contents

List of Figures

List of Tables

Preface

This book provides an introduction to transport geography from three viewpoints. In Part I Professor White takes first a systematic approach to the subject, devoting separate chapters to a consideration of the basic factors which shape and change transport systems. *The Historical Factor* deals with the consequences of past decision making, while the essential technological differences between transport modes are discussed in *The Technological Factor*, which in turn leads on naturally to a consideration of the relationship between these technological characteristics and the physical environment in *The Physical Factor*. The influence of technological attributes is further considered in *The Economic Factor*, which deals with the variations in costs and pricing methods of the different transport modes. Because decisions about transport investment and operation are not made solely on the narrow economic grounds of profit maximisation, some other influences on transport provision, notably the intervention of government bodies, are discussed in *The Political and Social Factor*. The final chapter in Part I, *The Morphological Factor*, considers the appearance of the various transport modes in their physical and locational setting.

In Part II a more overtly locational and areal view of transport geography is adopted by Professor White. Chapters 8 and 9 deal respectively with the role of transport in the location of economic activity and locational features of transport nodes, while Chapters 10 and 11 focus on the particular transport issues and problems facing urban areas and Third World countries respectively. Finally Chapter 12 concentrate on changes in the patterns of transport and their wider geographical effects.

In Part III Dr. Senior provides an applied and quantitative approach to some of the transport problems identified in Parts I and II, in which transport geographers and transport planners have mutual interests. He provides an introduction to some of the methods used for representing and forecasting travel demands, structuring the presentation around the elements of the trip decision-making process, namely the choices of trip frequency, vehicle ownership, trip destination, transport mode and network route.

It is suggested that Parts I and II provide suitable material for an introductory transport geography course at undergraduate level and for professional courses. Indeed some of this material could be selected for use in "A-level" and equivalent courses. The contents of Part III, if they are to be treated as a whole, require some previous training in quantitative methods up to the level of multivariate statistical analysis, and should, therefore, be reserved for second or third year undergraduate courses which seek to introduce transport planning methods.

Acknowledgements

The authors would like to record their gratitude to Mrs Jean Bateson for typing the manuscript and to Mr Reg Oliver (formerly Chief Cartographer) and Mrs Christine Warr (presently Chief Cartographer) for drawing the line diagrams and maps. All of them are past and present members of the Geography Department, University of Salford. We would also like to thank Mr Peter Grimshaw for preparing the map (Fig. 8.5) of cement movements from data he had collected for his own published work. Figures 3.1, 4.3, 4.7, and 7.1 are based on Ordnance Survey maps (50 000 series) and are reproduced with the permission of the Controller of Her Majesty's Stationery Office, Crown copyright reserved. Figure 13.8 is reproduced from *Progress in Human Geography* (From gravity modelling to entrophy maximising: a pedagogic guide), Vol. 3, No. 2, 1979 (fig. 2 on p. 183) by permission of Edward Arnold. Whilst every effort has been made to trace the owners of copyright material, in some cases this has proved impossible and we take this opportunity to apologise to any copyright holders whose rights we may unwittingly have infringed.

To our students, from whom we have learned so much.

Chapter 1
Introduction

The nature and function of transport

The essential importance and function of transport was admirably summarised by the economist Marshall (Milne & Laight 1965: 1): 'The transport industries, which undertake nothing more than the mere movement of persons from one place to another, have constituted one of the most important activities of man in every stage of advanced civilization.' It is not only a basic human activity, but is also movement in space. For these two reasons the study of transport is of great importance to geographers, not only for its own interest, but as an explanatory factor in the spatial patterns assumed by the human activities which are basic to geography.

For the most part the demand for transport is *derived*. With exceptions such as motorists who simply drive into the country, passengers on cruise liners and 'railfans', transport is used as a means to an end: the movement of people and goods from where they are to another place where, for the time being at any rate, their satisfaction or value will be enhanced. Transport creates *utilities of place*.

This concept can be expressed in monetary terms. Many years ago one of the authors bought more bananas than two could eat for a penny. But that was in West Cameroon, where the utility of bananas is low. If they could have been transported to Great Britain, where their utility was much higher, they would have been sold for at least 12 times as much, an increase far greater than accounted for by the cost of transport.

But the concept is also a spatial one. The main motivation in the demand for transport is economic. Surpluses and deficits of commodities or services arise over space and are necessary: (i) to inform interested parties of the existence and volume of supply and demand and of the price which must be paid to ensure exchange will take place; and (ii) for the surplus commodities or the people to be *transported* or moved physically. It will also be seen that (i) may also involve the transport of persons, letters or newspapers as well as the non-physical transfer of information by phone or radio.

So communications involve the transfer of people, commodities and information over space. This transfer takes place along a *line of communication* between two places. Along the line will be a number of different modes involving telecommunications, including telephone, telex and v.h.f. radio-telephone. Physical transfer is performed by a number of *transport modes* including, roads, railways and airlines. These modes will not necessarily run parallel to each other and sometimes it may be more correct to refer to a *corridor* rather than a line. Thus the corridor of movement between Manchester and Liverpool, some 50 km apart, is 13 km wide at one point, the distance separating the A580 East Lancs Road from the railway running via Warrington. Between these two are the M62 and the other railway route via St Helens Junction.

Lines of communication are relatively very stable, but over time new transport modes come into being and old ones decay, unless rejuvenated by technological advance. Thus there is a long-standing line of communication extending north-westward from London through the West Midlands. During the eighteenth century expanding trade led to the construction of a turnpike road (now the A5) more or less along the line of the Roman Watling Street. Then came the canal, and in turn it and the road gave way to the railway. During the present century the road revived with the coming of motor transport, which eventually led to the building of the M1/M6. The railway has been further developed by technological advance (electrification) and carries a frequent service of 160 kph (100 mph) trains. But the canal has not been improved and it now functions only as a cruise-way. But all these are part of the same line or corridor of communication.

The functions of transport

Even at the simplest level of economic development surpluses and deficits create a demand for transport. In Stone Age times there was a widespread demand for flint, as one of the few rocks suitable for making tools. But in southern Britain it occurs only in outcrops of Middle and Upper Chalk. So there was a widespread dissemination of flint tools from centres of production such as Grime's Graves near Brandon (Suffolk) over a rudimentary but effective transport network. Again, in early medieval North Africa Trans-Saharan trade developed salt and swords moving southward, good and leather northwards. This network depended on the widespread introduction of the pack-camel.

Clearly, as the economy develops the need for transport becomes more vital. The factors underlying economic development are themselves dependent on transport to bridge gaps in physical space. The four most important are:

1. *Division of labour* – The classical economists from Adam Smith onwards have shown how division of labour, as opposed to individual or group self-sufficiency, is the key to economic progress. But as soon as a group,

2

family, village, town or region comes to specialise in a limited range of activities, it becomes dependent on other groups to meet the consequent deficits and thus on transport to bridge the gap between the groups.

2. *Areal specialisation* – In the same way economic advance of an area of land is specialisation in the activities most closely adapted to the environment and resources. Thus, hill farmers in the British Isles no longer need battle against the adverse climate to raise food crops, but can concentrate on the raising of grass-fed livestock. But such specialisation means greater interdependence between areas and upon transport to bridge the gap.

3. *Extension of the market* – These processes are limited by the extent of the market in which the production can be sold. It can be extended by increasing demand in volume, in variety and in the geographical area of sales. Again, transport, by bridging the gap between producer and consumer, is the means of extending the market.

4. *Optimisation of production units* – This depends both on size and on location. The ability of a firm or plant to minimise production costs by reaching optimal size is controlled by the extent of the market. If the cost of producing 1 tonne of steel in a plant with 2 m. tonnes capacity is less than in one of 1 m. tonnes, it is possible to increase capacity to take advantage of this economy of scale only if there is a market for the increased production and transport facilities to supply that market. Costs may also be reduced by locating the plant where it fits best in the spatial structure of processes from raw material to finished product. Thus our steel plant is within a chain of processes from iron ore to motor car, and transport is required to bridge gaps between the separately located processes.

Transport plays a necessary part, not only in facilitating the movement of goods but also in the development of *services*. These by their nature 'perish on the instant of their performance' so the customers must be transported to the place at which the service is performed or vice versa. The housewife must be transported to the shops, children to school or doctor to patient. As services become more specialised and the size of production units optimised the catchment area of the service (its market) must be extended. Again this is a function of transport. For instance, in English soccer a First Division football club has to pay its players more highly than a non-League club; it therefore needs larger crowds to provide a greater income, and thus a more extensive catchment area, with corresponding transport links.

Transport also has important social functions. A fundamental feature of social life which has developed during the last century is the separation of work and residence. This has been made possible by transport developments, enabling people to live in a better environment and at the same time allowing them to travel to a place where the reward for their labour is higher. Transport also allows people to travel for recreational purposes, to sporting fixtures on Saturdays, to the sea on Sundays and to the mountains or foreign beaches for holidays.

Finally, transport has strategic importance. The ability to transport men and materials to a point where force is most effective is an age-old factor in warfare.

The function of transport, therefore, is to close the spatial gap between producer and consumer, using both these words in the widest sense possible.

We are inclined to think mainly of transport closing a physical gap and, therefore, to think in terms of distance. We say that Manchester is 307 km from London, or New York 5,557 km. But time can be of equal importance. In fact it may sometimes override distance in the view of the transport user. We can say that Manchester is 30 minutes by air from London, 2 hours 35 minutes by train and 4 hours 30 minutes by car. British Rail took, quite correctly, this view in selling their faster electric trains by using the slogan 'we are moving Manchester nearer to London'.

Time is of greater importance than distance to the commuter, who will say he lives 30 minutes from his city office, whether he comes in by bus from Peckham or train from Purley. In this sense Rugby, 133 km from Euston, is now nearer to London than Herne Bay, 101 km from Victoria, as the former can be reached by fast train in 65 minutes and compared with a fastest time to the latter of 80 minutes (1978 timetables).

Technological innovations over the years reduces journey times between two points, a process known as *time–space convergence*. Table 1.1 shows time-

Table 1.1 Travel time London to Edinburgh (629 km)

Date	Mode	Time
1754	Coach	10 days
1776	Stage coach	4 days
1836	Mail coach	42 hours 53 minutes
1854	Steam train	11 hours 25 minutes
1914	Steam train	8 hours 15 minutes
1955	Steam train	6 hours 30 minutes
1977	Diesel train	5 hours 27 minutes
1979	High-speed train	4 hours 37 minutes

After Janelle 1969 – based on time-tables, etc.

space convergence between London and Edinburgh in consequence of technological advance in surface transport.

We must also think of gaps being measurable in terms of cost. In 1968 British Rail introduced differential charges, raising fares more on popular routes than on the less popular. It now costs less to go from Manchester to Swansea (395 km) than to London (307 km). Again, since competition has led to market forces exerting a greater influence on air routes from the UK to North America than to Scandinavia, the cheapest fare to Los Angeles is now comparable with that to Copenhagen.

Transport as a system

Each mode of transport has differing technological characteristics. Some, such as road and rail, need special tracks; others, such as ocean shipping and airways, do not. Some modes, such as ocean shipping and railways require elaborate terminal facilities; others, road haulage particularly, do not. Aircraft require a very large expenditure of power per unit weight of payload carried, while large ships require a very small expenditure. This concept will be elaborated in Chapter 3.

Stemming from these technological differences, each mode has different economic characteristics. Because each road vehicle requires an engine which consumes fuel and a driver who requires wages, total costs of road haulage tend to rise in more or less direct proportion with the tonnage carried. Costs per tonne-km, therefore, tend to remain constant and there is little economy of scale. In contrast, because the running of an extra wagon in a train or even the running of an extra train represents a very small addition to the very heavy fixed costs of track and signalling, there are very clear economies of scale with rail transport (Ch. 6).

Thus each mode has its own advantages and disadvantages in a particular situation. While there is considerable overlap in suitability, so that in some situations two modes may be highly competitive, they may also be complementary in others.

But in addition 'no industry that is as vital to society as this can be expected to function in a void' (Hibbs 1970: 21). Transport lines, networks and systems are brought into being only by the demand for transport generated by the economy and the society of the areas they serve. But, in turn, the provision of a transport net will alter the nature and distribution of the socio-economic system. Development and change in the transport system is inextricably linked with those of the whole socio-economic system, of which it is a part.

In short, human activity of a social and economic nature may be regarded as an ecosystem of almost infinite complexity (Wagner 1960). Transport can be regarded as a system within that ecosystem, affecting and affected by the greater whole. It has more measurable inputs than have many geographical systems: inputs of capital, fixed equipment in the form of track and terminals, mobile equipment in the form of vehicles, vessels or aircraft; the nature of the terrain traversed; and the demands for transport made by the area served. The outputs are also measurable, not only in the more obvious terms of passenger-km and freight-tonne-km created but also in the growth and decline of the industries and communities served and the changes in their spatial distribution.

A transport network may then be regarded as a sub-system. We may regard the system as being intermodal, for example the short sea routes linking Great Britain and Ireland together with their land feeders of road and rail. But we may also regard a transport system as being made up of a number of unimodal sub-systems which overlap and intersect. Greater London and the Home Counties have a system of public transport serving the demands for commuting. This is made up of a number of sub-systems, buses, underground and suburban railways and coaches. These overlap, being partly in competition, and intersect, being partly complementary. Where they intersect, interchange facilities or transport nodes are created. For example, Victoria Station is a node with interchange facilities between suburban rail, underground rail and buses.

Figure 1.1 shows a conceptual framework for a transport system. It will be seen that inputs into the system include the demand for transport services and

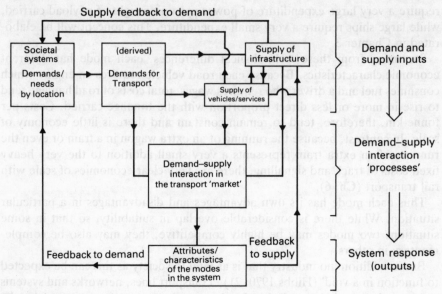

Fig. 1.1 A conceptual framework for a transport system

the supply of infrastructure, vehicles, fuel and operating staff. The output from the system, which satisfies the demand is the supply of transport in terms of vehicle-km, seat-km (for passengers) and capacity-tonne-km (for freight). The system therefore includes the vehicles, the infrastructure and the passengers and freight. You cannot have the one without the others. It is therefore incorrect to talk of a road system or a bus system, rather of a road or bus network. It should also be noted that the system is an open one. There are inputs from the environment and outputs back into it.

Transport geography

Geographers should be concerned with the study of transport for two main reasons. Firstly, transport is a significant human activity with a strong spatial component and is therefore a legitimate object of study in its own right, as much as agriculture, steel production or retailing. Secondly, it is an important factor influencing the spatial variation in many other social and economic activities.

Conversely, geographers, by virtue of their training and experience, have an important contribution to make to the development and the methodology of transport studies. In the first place they are concerned with the study of Man in relation to all aspects of the environment – physical, economic and social. This leads them to an interest in the interaction between the environmental factors and between the environmental factors and human activities. This has often been called the 'holistic' approach, but it can also be termed the 'systems approach' and in recent years geographers have become very much more concerned with developing this aspect of the discipline. As we have tried to show, the systems approach is also fundamental to the study of transport.

Secondly, geography is concerned with the organisation in space of environmental phenomena and with the variation over space of those phenomena. Because the causal environmental factors vary over space, the dependent human response also varies over space, and so too, in their turn, do the consequentials of that response. Geographers therefore approach the study of systems in terms of *spatial variables*. Each line of communication has specific location which is in some degree unique and distinguishable from other lines of transport in terms of environmental inputs to the system – physiography, traffic potential, past investment decisions and current managerial policies. It will therefore have a degree of uniqueness in terms of outputs such as the economic consequences on industry, commercial activity and land use. The M6 and the M2 are both motorways and thus have numerous aspects in common, such as limited access, restrictions on classes of users and possibility of being traversed at constant high speed. But there are other factors – morphology, gradients, traffic levels and periodic peaks among them – which differ, due to the two roads being located in different parts of the country. This also applies to networks as well as lines. Thus the network of rural roads in Norfolk is quite different from that of Mid Wales.

This contribution of geography is important, as other disciplines, notably economics, often eliminate the spatial variable in their search for meaningful generalisations (Chisholm 1970: Ch. 2). Others, history among them, sometimes merely ignore it. It is true that in the past, by insisting on uniqueness of place, geography was less able than economics to make meaningful generalisations or extrapolate future trends. But rapid advance in quantitative techniques has enabled it to do this, while at the same time to a great extent preserving its concern with uniqueness of place, a vital achievement for transport studies.

A third important contribution is the assumption, basic in geography, that it is through his technology that Man adapts himself to his environment and also succeeds in obtaining a measure of control over the environmental factors. The geographical approach thus creates an awareness of technological development as an input factor to transport systems (Ch. 3).

It is of course possible to adopt a modally based approach to the study of transport geography, analysing the characteristics, technology and spatial patterns of roads and road transport, then those of railways, ocean shipping, airways and so on. Alternatively, we can start with the various input factors to the transport systems and examine the consequences, selecting illustrations from all modes. This latter approach has been adopted here as transport systems are tending to become more intermodal and, as we have tried to show, the systems approach is best for the study of transport geography. But it is not without its drawbacks, as the causal factors are themselves parts of systems and there is much interaction between them.

In this book we are primarily concerned with the spatial patterns of transport systems. To provide an understanding of these the book has been divided into three parts. Part I deals in turn with each of the main causal factors and how they affect the various transport modes and systems. The first of these is the *historic factor*. This is important because the existing pattern of transport systems cannot be wholly explained without reference to the many past decisions which shaped it. We have already referred to the importance of the *technological factor*. Without some knowledge of the technological characteristics of a particular mode, we cannot judge the appropriateness of that mode for a particular situation. It is also a time of rapid technological change in transport and this has had basic repercussions on the transport system. Thus, while the consequences of the introduction of wide-body jet aircraft have been widely appreciated, those of widespread containerisation of seaborne general cargo have not. As geographers we are particularly concerned with the *physical factor*, which, even with advanced technology, still exerts control over route selection and operation. But equally important in route selection and operation, and vital in the choice between modes, is the *economic factor*. A study of the structure of transport costs and how these vary between modes, together with an appreciation of the relationship between cost and price, is necessary to an understanding of transport geography. Politics has been defined as 'the art of the possible'. Whatever may be the logic of a policy based on economic factors, its implementation is impossible if it is politically unacceptable. Politics is a reflection of social trends which themselves influence and are influenced by transport development. The *political and social factor* is therefore dealt with next. Finally, the *morphology* of the transport modes must be taken into account.

Having reviewed the basic causative factors in the evolution of transport systems, Part II consists of a series of *locational studies*. These focus in detail on representative aspects of the patterns to be found in transport systems. In Chapter 8 the relationship between transport and various aspects of *economic activity* is explored with the aid of specific case studies. Chapter 9 looks at *transport nodes*, which may be anything from a bus-stop to a major seaport, and the factors involved in their location. Of particular importance is the interconnection between transport and urban land use. Chapter 10, 'Transport in the urban scene', therefore deals with this and with some of the problems facing urban transport planners and operators. Chapter 11, 'Transport in the Third World', deals with another important aspect of transport geography, especially with the connection between transport and economic development. We have already noted that rapid change brought about by technological change has important consequences and Chapter 12, 'Recent geographical change in patterns of transport', considers some specific examples.

Finally, Part III deals with the various analytical methods by which the transport systems can be studied. We now have a number of powerful tools and an understanding of their uses and limitations is vital to the study of transport geography.

One last observation must be made: because of this particular approach and because of lack of space in the book, many factual details of the patterns of transport must be taken for granted. To derive full benefit from this book it should be used in conjunction with the background reading listed in the References, which have been made as full as reasonably possible.

Part I
The Basic Factors

Chapter 2
The historical factor

Even if not technologically minded, most people are aware of new developments in transport. Among these can be listed 'jumbo jet' and 'vertical take-off or landing' (VTOL) aircraft, 'super-tankers' (very large crude carriers) and the 'air-cushion vehicle' (ACV), popularly known as the hovercraft. All of these are now technologically feasible, though not all have become commercial successes.

One of the reasons for this, though obviously not the only one, is that many of them would entail entirely new systems. Basically the 'hovertrain' (tracked hovercraft) is a railway train (p. 24) running at speeds of 400 kph or more, not on wheels, but on an air cushion along a special concrete track which gives both support and guidance. One route proposed (Buchanan & Partners 1969) was between London and Manchester. Here demand, actual and potential, is very high. That demand can be expanded by the provision of better facilities was indicated by the upsurge of traffic after the 1966 railway electrification, which created new traffic as well as diverting some from competitors.

If a 'hover-rail' line were built, the heavy express passenger traffic on the orthodox railway would be completely diverted. But the present expresses from London to Manchester share the tracks, and therefore the heavy fixed costs (p. 46), all or part of the way with Inter-City expresses for other destinations, suburban services and freight trains. Unless, therefore, the surplus line capacity thus created could be soon reabsorbed, the loss of the Manchester traffic would have very serious repercussions on the whole electrified system between London, the Midlands and the North-West. Conversely, the immediate replacement of the whole existing rail system by hover-rail would be far too costly. The introduction of the 240 kph (150 mph) Advanced Passenger Train, which uses the orthodox railway track is, therefore, very much more feasible, though superficially less attractive.

The introduction of entirely new systems, especially when they require continuous infrastructure (see p. 71), as do road, rail and canal systems, are possible only if the existing facilities are hopelessly congested and where any increase in their capacity is very costly. An example of this situation can be taken from Japan. Along the 512 km 'corridor' between Tokyo and Osaka there is a very close concentration of population and industry. The existing electrified railway was, by the mid 1950s, becoming very congested. It was decided to build an entirely separate railway, on the broader gauge, serving only the major cities and allowing very high speeds. The 'Hikari' express trains were introduced averaging 168 kph with top speeds of 200 kph. The Tokaido Line was opened in 1964, and soon proved successful. By 1973 plans for extending the *Shin Kansen* system, as it is called, provide for a system of 6,000 km by 1985 which will link all the principal cities.

It is obviously a mistake to think that the slate can be wiped clean and a completely fresh start made with a transport system. Continual marginal changes can be made, but to change direction is much more difficult. Thus the shape and nature of a railway system is a legacy from the past. It can be adapted more closely to changing conditions by piecemeal changes, closing some lines, electrifying and resignalling others to increase capacity and building new ones. But we cannot, in a short space of time, change the gauge to which it is laid, or convert the whole system to tracked hovercraft. Marginal changes in a road network are being made continuously, so that after a period of time it may be drastically modified. Even a new motorway in fact provides only marginal change, while fundamental changes, such as a change in the rule of the road from left to right provided great difficulties in Sweden and would be virtually impossible in the United Kingdom. Continual marginal changes are, however, important in their cumulative effect and may be termed *incremental change* as opposed to measures entailing a fresh start which may be termed *green-field*.

But even airways and ocean transport are not entirely free from historical legacy. London and Liverpool, as a result of past investment decisions, were in the early 1970s so much the largest general cargo ports in Great Britain that despite their declining efficiency shipowners were unable to divert to other ports as much of their operations as they would wish. There was nowhere else for them all to go to. On the other hand, because airlines had invested so much in repair facilities at Heathrow, they were reluctant to move from the airport when it became congested in the 1950s to Gatwick where there was plenty of spare capacity.

Because of the nature of incremental change, the present shape of existing transport systems are fully explicable only in terms of historical processes, the result of the distribution of demand for transport as it existed in past periods. This demand was created by contemporary distributions of settlements and of economic activity, and it has resulted in innumerable past decisions as to the ways in which it could be satisfied. These decisions brought into being transport systems, which in their turn have modified the spatial distribution of demand. Some towns grew at the expense of others, entirely new settlements have been created, while the distribution of existing agricultural and commercial activity was modified and new activities emerged.

Historical development of transport systems can be considered under four interrelated headings:

1. The location and pattern of the systems
2. Technological development
3. Institutional development
4. Settlement and land-use patterns

1. The location and pattern of the systems

Differences between the road networks in England and in France are largely explicable in historical terms. Although both countries emerged early as nation-states, they had different systems of internal government. That of France was highly centralised, depending on an efficient postal service for government communication, while that of England was dependent more on a looser, more local structure.

The result was that from the seventeenth century onwards a network of *Routes Nationales* emerged in France, with trunk roads connecting the larger towns and ignoring the intermediate settlements. But England acquired no such system. There were few real trunk roads, only interconnected local networks which linked villages with market towns. Even after the increased traffic, resulting from the Industrial Revolution, began to be felt, this led not to a national network but to the upgrading of existing roads with capital put up by local landowners and businessmen (the turnpike system) (Copeland 1968; Albert 1972).

With the decline of long-distance road traffic after the Railway Age, the English turnpike trusts were bankrupted and the main roads passed to the local authorities. In France they remained the responsibility of the Central Government. By the early Motor Age the French trunk roads were good and the secondary system poor, while in Britain the secondary network was good while the main roads were inadequate. Desultory attempts were made to forge a national road system in Great Britain during the interwar years, but it was only increasing congestion after 1945 that forced the overall planning of motorways and trunk roads as a national system.

The introduction of entirely new systems, especially when they require continuous infrastructure (see p. 71), as do road, rail and canal systems, are decision is justified. Traffic on the new railway between Tokyo and Osaka exceeded expectations, as did the build-up of traffic on the M1 motorway. But not all decisions are justified. The 366 km Madeira–Marmoré railway was built between Porto Velho and Guajara Mirim through the tropical forest of the western part of the Amazon Basin. Its purpose was to connect two navigable stretches of the Upper Amazon and to promote traffic and economic development, not only in western Brazil, but also to and from Bolivia. Building the line was very costly in terms of both human life and of capital. But the traffic never came and a traveller's account indicated how few trains were run (Ibbotson 1954).

It is a matter of historical accident (in the sense that we do not know who made the decisions) that some countries adopted the left-hand rule of the road, while most countries keep to the right. Great Britain adopted the left-hand rule and so consequently did its overseas territories. Thus in West Africa, driving from say Accra to Lagos in 1960, one kept to the left as far as the Ghana frontier, crossed to the right to drive through Togo and Dahomey (now Benin), former French colonies, and recrossed to the left at the Nigerian frontier. Canada, however, in spite of its British connections adopted the right-hand rule because of its long frontier with the USA. The only 'left-hand' countries without British connections were Sweden, which changed over expensively in 1967, and Japan. Incidentally, early railways in Britain naturally used left-hand running. The first French railways were built by British engineers and to this day left-hand running is practised, except in Alsace and Lorraine, where most of the lines were built during the period of German occupation between 1870 and 1918. Belgian and Swiss railways also observe the left-hand rule, but Dutch and German railways keep to the right.

The historical factor in the shape of conscious investment decisions made in the past is particularly evident where the system requires a relatively elaborate and inflexible infrastructure. In Australia, with its federal system of government, railway construction was in the hands of the State Government, each of which selected a different gauge chosen in the light of contemporary economies and monetary resources. Obviously, this led to great difficulties as the networks reached the frontiers of their home states. It has only been since the late 1960s that all the State capitals (with the exception of Adelaide), have been linked by a uniform gauge system of 1,435 mm (4 ft $8\frac{1}{2}$ in) the world standard.

The British railway system, developed entirely on a commercial basis by private enterprise, has been characterised by the promotion of competing lines, though to a considerable extent their indiscriminate proliferation was controlled by Parliament, through the necessity of obtaining Private Acts to authorise new construction. Some companies were particularly aggressive in their intrusions into areas already served. The map (Fig. 2.1) shows the differing fate of two such networks.

In the latter part of the nineteenth century the Great Northern Railway was anxious to share in the heavy traffic of the West Riding industrial area. In the period 1854 to 1875 they had built a network serving all the major towns (Grinling 1903). But the area is hilly and the easier valley routes were pre-empted, so the lines suffered from heavy gradients. From 1920 onwards freight traffic was lost to road haulage, while the local passenger traffic was taken by buses. These losses continued at a greater rate after 1950 and the inconvenient GNR network became redundant and has been largely dismantled.

After 1859, Kent was served by two railway companies, the South Eastern and the London, Chatham and Dover (Fig. 2.2). These were bitter rivals and the situation was exacerbated by the personal enmity between Sir Edward Watkin, Chairman of the former and J. S. Forbes, General Manager of the latter. Rival lines were built to all the principal Kentish towns except Folkestone. But this fact has served the county and the nation in good stead. At the height of First World War, when Dover was the main embarkation point for the Western Front, the SER line was closed from 1915 to 1919 by a landslip

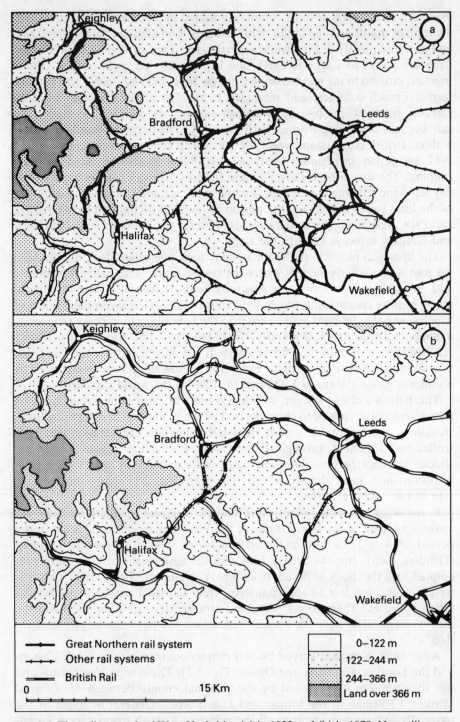

Fig. 2.1 The rail network of West Yorkshire (a) in 1923 and (b) in 1978. Note: (i) route duplication due to construction by the Great Northern; (ii) the heavy gradients incurred by having to avoid valleys already occupied; (iii) the almost complete elimination of the ex-GNR lines

Legend:
- ────── Great Northern rail system
- ┼┼┼┼┼┼ Other rail systems
- ══════ British Rail

- ☐ 0–122 m
- ░ 122–244 m
- ▒ 244–366 m
- ▓ Land over 366 m

0   15 Km

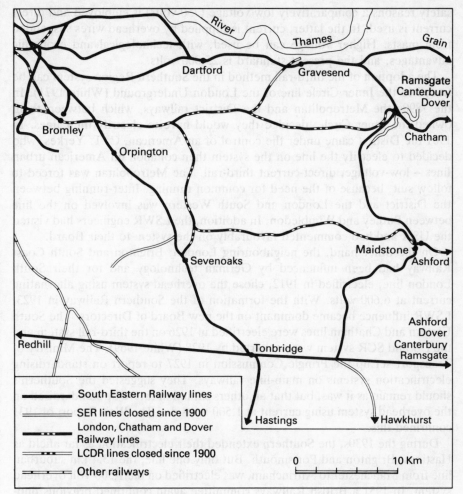

Fig. 2.2 The rail network of North-west Kent. Note that in contrast to Fig. 2.1, few of the duplicating lines have been closed

at Folkestone Warren, but the LCDR line remained. During the Second World War, the alternative routes enabled the railways to carry on in spite of extensive bomb damage. Between 1920 and 1939 the population of Kent increased rapidly, so too did commuting to London and expansion in Continental and Kentish holiday traffic. These trends continued after 1945 and there has been considerable industrial development. Not only have they been retained, but the rival networks have also been linked by new construction and electrified to deal with traffic increases (White 1969).

2. Technological development

As a case study, the story of railway electrification in Great Britain has been selected. There are two main systems in operation on British Rail: (i) the third-rail system employed on the Southern Region; and (ii) the overhead alternating-current system employed elsewhere. In the former, current is supplied to the trains by a third rail laid just outside the running rail. For safety reasons a comparatively low voltage (750 volts) is employed and direct current is used. In the latter, current is supplied by overhead wires suspended from masts. Higher voltage can be used, with technological and economic advantages, and the present standard is 25,000 volts.

The adoption of the third-rail method in the Southern Region system can be traced to the Inner Circle line of the London Underground (White 1971). In the 1890s the Metropolitan and the District railways, which between them owned the Inner Circle, decided they would have to electrify their lines. In 1901 the District came under the control of an American, C. T. Yerkes, who decided to electrify the line on the system then common on American urban lines – low-voltage, direct-current third-rail. The Metropolitan was forced to follow suit, because of the need for common running. Inter-running between the District and the London and South Western was involved on the line between Putney and Wimbledon. In addition, the LSWR engineers had visited the USA and had commented favourably on the system to their Board.

On the other hand, the neighbouring London, Brighton and South Coast Railway had been influenced by German technology and for their South London line, electrified in 1912, chose the overhead system using alternating current at 6,600 volts. With the formation of the Southern Railway in 1923, LSWR influence became dominant on the new Board of Directors. The South Eastern and Chatham lines were electrified in 1926 on the third-rail system and the LB and SCR system was converted by 1928 (White 1969). The Ministry of Transport set up the Pringle Commission in 1927 to report on standardising electrification systems on main-line railways. They suggested the Southern's should remain as it was, but that all others should in future be standardised on the overhead system using current at 1,500 volts d.c. The Weir Report of 1931 confirmed this.

During the 1930s, the Southern extended their electrification as far afield as Hastings, Brighton and Portsmouth. But only one line, the 13.4 km suburban line from Manchester to Altrincham, was electrified on the 1,500-volt overhead system. In 1951 a British Railways committee again confirmed previous findings, suggesting all electrification on the Southern Region east of Salisbury and Southampton should be third-rail and elsewhere it should be 1,500 volts overhead. Subsequently, a number of schemes using this system were opened. In 1956 because of technical advantages it was decided to employ high-voltage alternating current on all overhead systems, and since then all lines electrified at 1,500 volts have been converted, except that between Sheffield and Manchester, while all new electrification, including London to Glasgow, has been on the new a.c. system. Meanwhile, in 1967 third-rail electrification was extended through Southampton to Bournemouh. It was less costly to extend the Southern system than to adhere strictly to the 1951 decision. It is almost always easier to extend existing systems than to introduce new ones.

3. Institutional development

The present organisation of the bus network in England and Wales is also a historical legacy. Many people still travel to work in buses bearing time-honoured company names such as East Kent, Midland Red and Ribble. These are the *Territorial companies*, now wholly owned by the National Bus Company which was set up in 1969. Many more travel by buses operated by the transport department of the town in which they live. These are *Municipal operators*. A few people may travel in buses belonging to *Independent operators*.

Although many bus routes still being operated today were pioneered before the First World War, the route system of the local or stage-carriage bus service developed during the 1920s and was virtually completed by the mid-1930s. Capital for this rapid expansion came from a number of sources. The first and most important source was from local authorities. Most of them had already owned and operated tramway services and used buses to extend and eventually replace these. Eastbourne, which started bus operation in 1903, was one of the few to enter the Bus Age directly. Secondly, capital was put up by local businessmen, perhaps, though not necessarily, men who had previously been carriers or who had started a garage. Thirdly, the capital came from large established bus operators such as Crosville and Devon General. Fourthly, the railways began to put money into feeder bus routes. Working on a purely trial-and-error basis, the operators started up new services and modified existing ones wherever they felt there was a need. In this way a very stable system emerged which was not modified greatly between 1935 and 1970 (Hibbs 1968).

Gradually the larger operators took over the more remunerative routes of the smaller operators, and in their turn they were bought up by two large holding companies, Thomas Tilling and British Electric Traction. The Road Traffic Act of 1930 introduced a system of control which contributed greatly to the stability of the bus industry. A licensing system was set up to control the routes, schedules and fares. A tacit agreement then developed between the licensing authorities and the Territorial operators. The latter were given monopoly rights over the profitable inter-urban services, on condition that they used the profits to cross-subsidise the network of unprofitable rural services, which had become such a feature of Great Britain where virtually every village had a regular bus service. It is the decline in the money available for cross-subsidisation that has led to the present shrinkage of rural services. The Municipal operators were generally confined within the boundaries of the town. The railways were prevented by the 1930 Act from opening up new routes, but were given powers, of which they made full use, to invest in the Territorial companies. A few large Independents survived, notably Lancashire United and Barton Transport (Nottingham), but for the most part, the Independents were small firms operating a single route or a small network which the Territorials did not want.

Under the 1947 Transport Act the railway interests in buses were nationalised along with all the other railway assets, and soon after the Tilling interests were bought out by the State. In 1967 those of the British Electric Traction were also acquired, so that by 1968 all the Territorial systems were in fact nationalised. Under the 1968 Transport Act they were consolidated into the National Bus Company.

The Municipal operators for the most part survived unchanged. But in the four larger conurbations, the West Midlands, Merseyside, Greater Manchester and Tyne and Wear have been grouped together under the new Passenger Transport Executives (PTE), also set up by the 1968 Act. With the Local Government Reorganisation of 1974 PTE's have been set up in West Yorkshire and South Yorkshire Metropolitan Counties and Greater Glasgow.

London has always been a special case. By 1912 the buses were fully motorised and the largest fleet was operated by the London General Omnibus Company (LGOC). In 1907 the London Passenger Transport Conference was set up to consolidate the services and pricing policies of the LGOC and the Underground Group. All London buses, together with those operating in the inner parts of the Home Counties, were absorbed into the London Passenger Transport Board (LPTB) set up under an Act of 1933. There were now three fleets, the Red buses serving the inner areas, the Green buses the outer suburbs and the Green Line coach system. The LPTB was nationalised in 1947. But under the 1969 Transport (London) Act, the Red network was transferred to the Greater London Council and the other two to the National Bus Company.

4. Settlement and land-use patterns

Decisions to improve transport were usually based on estimates of the potential traffic between existing centres of economic activity. The Roman road network in Britain included a very important link (Watling Street) between London and the north-western frontiers of the province. There was also a lateral road (the Fosse Way) from Cirencester to York which crossed Watling Street at Wall near Lichfield. In the Middle Ages these particular roads fell into decay, though the growing towns of Lichfield and Coventry became road centres while Wall survived as an unimportant village. But during the eighteenth century both towns in turn were eclipsed by Birmingham. The latter therefore became successively the road, canal and rail centre of the West Midlands. Its importance, thus enhanced, has remained and it is not without significance that Birmingham and London were the first British cities to be linked by motorway (1961).

But the transport lines thus created or subsequently improved, in their turn, created entirely new towns. In Roman Britain the early roads were built for military purposes. But trade soon followed in the footsteps of the legions and towns grew up around the stations protecting the roads. Many of these had excellent geographical locations and have survived to this day, Dover, St Albans, Chichester, Leicester and Chester among them. Others such as Wall, already mentioned, Silchester (near Basingstoke) and Wroxeter (near Shrewsbury) once important road centres, have become deserted for more favoured sites which emerged in the Middle Ages.

It has been emphasised that the turnpikes were improvements of existing roads or short local diversions. Few new settlements were created by them. But towns such as Uxbridge, Slough and Daventry grew to importance as staging points along them. The Canal Age, however, did create some new settlements. Stoke Bruerne (near Northampton) grew up where the Grand Union Canal tunnelled under the oolitic cuesta. But it never became important. However, Stourport in Worcestershire, now a town of 13,500, owes its origin entirely to its being the point at which the Staffordshire and Worcestershire Canal (opened 1772) from the West Midlands entered the Severn.

The railways created many more entirely new settlements and transformed old villages. We can divide these into three classes.

1. Those which were selected as centres for railway workshops. Foremost among the new creations is, of course, Crewe, but there were many others, Eastleigh (Hants), Horwich (Lancs), Wolverton (Bucks), Earlestown (Lancs) and even the village of Melton Constable (Norfolk). Of the transformation, perhaps the best known is the small village of Swindon, but Ashford (Kent) and Doncaster are also of this class.
2. Ports selected as railway terminals. Sometimes these were insignificant fishing villages, occasionally they were completely new. Folkestone, Newhaven and Heysham are examples of the former and Immingham and Barry of the latter.
3. New seaside resorts also form a most important class. These grew by virtue of the Railway Age, the popularity of sea-bathing and the possibility of holiday excursions. The hamlet of Bournemouth originated as a coastguard station built in 1810. By 1851 it showed only modest growth and Holdenhurst Parish, in which it lay, numbered only 1,330 inhabitants. The first railway, a minor branch, reached Bournemouth in 1870, and four years later there was direct connection with the Midlands. Even so in 1891 Bournemouth's population numbered only 27,908. By that time, however, it was on a main line frrom London. By 1961, the built-up area stretched along the coast for 25 km and included over 300,000 people (White 1969). As a resort Bournemouth's growth was aided by the low land values of the sandy soils, the poverty of which had delayed the progress of the area before the Railway Age.

Bournemouth is by no means unique. In Lancashire, the Southport sands were favoured by Wigan miners, who during the later eighteenth century came with their families by canal and cart. But Southport owed its mushroom growth to the railway, while Blackpool and Morecambe were entirely creations of the Railway Age.

Such historical developments and the present patterns resulting from them are sometimes explicable only in terms of the actions and decisions of a single person. George Hudson, the 'Railway King', played a major part in promoting main-line railways during and after the 1845–46 'railway mania' (Lambert 1934). His efforts were directed at first creating and then maintaining his native town (York) as a railway centre. He supported two railway projects, the York and North Midland and the Great North of England, which ensured that York lay on the first through Anglo-Scottish rail route from London, which ran via Rugby, Derby and Newcastle. Later York became the junction between the original route and the direct one from London via Peterborough and Doncaster. Although this meant the decline of the York and North Midland as a route to London, the line gained added importance as part of the rail route from the North-East to Birmingham and the South-West and South Wales. York's position as a railway centre has been maintained ever since.

In contrast, no citizen of the old town of Nantwich in Cheshire took such pains to ensure it was served by the Grand Junction Railway, part of the route from London to the North-West and eventually on to Scotland. Instead the line passed 8 km to the east and a small station was provided where the line crossed the Nantwich–Congleton turnpike road. Although in the parish of Church Coppenhall, the station was called Crewe after Crewe Hall nearby. When Crewe became the junction for lines to Manchester and to North Wales, and later for those to Shrewsbury and to the Potteries, its future as a railway centre was assured and the new town soon outgrew Nantwich (Chaloner, 1973). Its 1961 population numbered 52,600 against 11,140 for that of Nantwich. As an urban service centre as well as an industrial town it now ranks higher than Nantwich, which exists largely as a residential and tourist centre, its numerous historic buildings surviving because of its stagnation during Victorian times. Today, as will be seen from Fig. 2.3, it is still Nantwich, not Crewe, that is the road centre, which has contributed to its revival in the last 30 years.

A diversion in a line of communication may occur when an existing line of transport is replaced by another on a different alignment. This may favour a settlement on the new line which grows at the expense of one on the old line. Fenny Stratford is an old settlement on the Roman Watling Street (the present

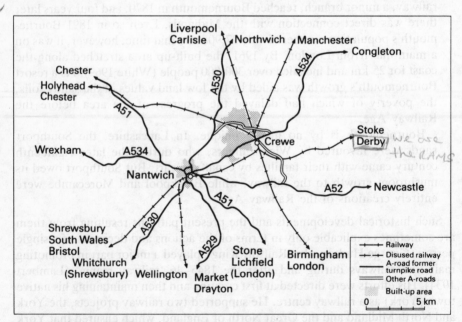

Fig. 2.3 Pattern of communications in South Cheshire. Note how the road system is concentrated on the old town of Nantwich and the railways on Crewe, which as a town dates only from the Railway Age

A5 trunk road). It is now a mere suburb of Bletchley, which grew to importance around the railway junction on the main line from Euston to the North-West. In the same way Wolverton, chosen in 1840 as the site for railway workshops, expanded at the expense of Stony Stratford on the A5 to the west and the market town of Newport Pagnell to the east. Similarly, Stamford (Lincs.) grew to importance through its position on the Great North Road (A1). Peterborough, an equally old town 19 km to the south-east, lay on the Great Northern Railway. During the nineteenth century it grew faster than Stamford, and in 1961 had a population of 64,770 against one of 12,650 for Stamford, though the latter experienced a revival of trade with the revival of traffic on the A1 in the Motor Age.

Lest it be thought these phenomena are confined to the British Isles, to conclude this historical chapter a few overseas examples may be selected. Nairobi, capital and largest town of Kenya, owes its origin to being a point at which locomotives were changed on the run from Mombasa to Kisumu, the original terminus of the Uganda Railway. Port Harcourt, the second port of Nigeria, was selected by a survey party as being a suitable point on the Bonny River for a coastal terminal of the proposed railway opened in 1916 from the Enugu coalfield. Examples can be multiplied to taste.

The historical factor also works indirectly through technological factors dealt with next. Past decisions, taken in the light of contemporary technology, will affect existing levels and layouts of transport systems.

Chapter 3
The technological factor

Each transport mode has its own technological characteristics. Thus a train needs a fixed track to run on, while a ship needs no such infrastructure. The latter requires a small expenditure of propelling power per unit of carrying capacity, in contrast with an aircraft which requires a heavy expenditure in order to keep aloft. The more power expended, the greater the cost involved. An appreciation of the basic technological characteristics of a transport mode is therefore necessary for full understanding. Upon them depends the economics of operation and, therefore, the suitability or otherwise of a transport mode for a particular situation. In order to examine this statement it is proposed to look at each of the principal modes in turn.

The road

The *trail*, a path worn by the constant passage of people, is the most ancient form of road. But human porterage is a very inefficient and costly means of transport. This is because not only is the weight a man can carry limited, but there is no economy of scale possible. An African porter can carry 27 kg on his head, so to carry 270 kg will need 10 men, and 2.7 tonnes 100 men. In 1898 it took 1,400 carriers to move 31.5 tonnes of rubber 208 km from Kumasi in Ghana to the port of Cape Coast at a cost of £700, which works out at 11p per tonne-km (White & Gleave 1971: 246). However, using a bicycle a man can convey a load of 100 kg, and in Eastern Nigeria and parts of South-East Asia much of the heavy short-distance traffic is carried in this way. If manpower is plentiful and personal needs are on a simple scale, it is possible to support modern armies solely by bicycle transport, as shown in Burma by the Japanese between 1942 and 1945 and subsequently during the Vietnam wars.

A pack-horse can carry much more than a man, some 320 kg, and can also use narrow trails, though again there is no economy of scale. But use of a wheeled vehicle can provide this. An eight-horse 'flying wagon', even on the poor eighteenth-century roads had a capacity of some 4 tonnes, or 500 kg per horse. However, the greater efficiency of motor vehicles has meant that animal traction has been superseded, not only in advanced countries but in much of the developing world as well.

In many parts of the world there is motor traffic without roads. The trails simply evolve by the constant passage of vehicles. But if traffic increases the trail must be improved, which converts it into a *road*. In 1954, the Public Works Department of Ghana assumed that if a trail was used by more than 5 vehicles per day, culverts and some surface would be needed, if more than 30 vehicles per day were expected a good gravel surface would be needed and if more than 150 vehicles, a bitumen seal. The need for a road also depends on climate. In tropical grasslands tracks are passable by vehicles, during the long dry season, but they cannot be used during the short rainy season.

A road system presupposes economic development, since it needs capital investment and political stability as it needs constant maintenance and freedom of passage. The level of road development in any country is therefore closely linked with its socio-economic development. In the United Kingdom, with dense population, high level of economic development and damp climate, the road network is close and virtually all roads, however minor, are surfaced.

As vehicles increase in size, speed and numbers the quality of the roads must be improved to match. Foundations must be strengthened (work has been done in the USA which tends to show the damage done to a road increases by the *fourth power* of the axle weight), surfaces improved, carriageway widths increased and curves and gradients reduced. The ultimate development is the segregation of motor traffic into motorways which have no 'grade' crossings with other roads and which have access limited to relatively few spur roads. These roads become very costly in terms of capital investment and land consumed, but probably still remain low cost in terms of cost per vehicle-km.

The road system cannot be considered apart from the vehicles using them. The dimensions, capacity and speed of the latter depends on the average road conditions met. But the great advantage of road vehicles is their flexibility in negotiating difficult and varied conditions of surface, gradient and curvature, even if these latter are very bad. Thus capital investment in road-building can be matched with the traffic levels. An adequate road can be built cheaply for limited traffic, but also the road network can be constantly upgraded as traffic expands.

The vehicle itself (or vehicle and trailer), while constantly tending to increase in size, has a limited capacity. Each vehicle needs an engine and a driver, so economy of scale is limited. This may be felt in very heavy traffic flows, but is no real drawback in most situations. In the same way, if traffic is very dense, as in large cities, the road space demanded by vehicles may become excessive.

Railways

Railways originated in an attempt to increase the hauling power of horses by providing a special track. The most efficient proved to be narrow iron rails on which wagons with flanged iron wheels were run. This reduced friction to a minimum, but meant the specialised vehicles were confined to the track. Between 1805 and 1830, steam locomotives replaced horses. There are three essential characteristics of a railway: (1) Vehicles are marshalled into *trains*; (2) The trains are run on fixed tracks, they are guided by the tracks and are incapable of moving off them. Normally, even on the most modern systems, the tracks are the familiar steel rails, but on a number of 'metro' systems, including those in Paris, Lyons, Montreal and Sapporo, rubber-tyred trains run on concrete beams. But these are still 'railways', as would be any monorail or guided hovercraft system (Kalla-Bishop 1972); (3) A rigid discipline is exercised over moving trains. A line is divided into sections, with only one train at a time allowed in each.

From this stems a number of consequences:

1. The great reduction in friction allows heavy loads to be moved at high speeds with small power expenditure. A 3,300 hp electric locomotive can haul a 500-tonne train at 160 kph between Euston and Crewe while developing less than half the power of one engine of a Boeing 707 jet aircraft.
2. However, this lack of friction prevents a locomotive from negotiating the gradients a road vehicle can ascend without difficulty. As a general rule, anything over 1 in 100 on a main line must be regarded as steep. The steepest gradients on motorways are 1 in 30, while 1 in 20 is not uncommon on main roads. This greatly increases the initial cost of rail transport by increasing the need for major earthworks in order to reduce gradients.
3. It is possible to combine speed, traffic density and safety in almost all weathers. Between Euston and Rugby passenger trains with a seating capacity of 500 to 600 can follow each other at 160 kph at $2\frac{1}{2}$-minute intervals. The 'Hikari' trains (p. 11) between Tokyo and Osaka run every 15 minutes and have 1,400 seats per train. In 1972 they had an average *load factor* of 67 per cent. So each train averages 950 passengers and some 55,000 passengers a day are carried. On the London Underground, passengers can be moved at the rate of 27,000 an hour per line of rail. But the potential for such heavy traffic flows is limited.
4. Because the trains are guided by the track, the scope for automation is much greater than with other means of transport. The Post Office has operated driverless trains on its mail-carrying railway in London for over 50 years. On the Victoria line of London Transport, opened in 1969, the passenger trains are automatically driven. The trunk route from the North-East of England to the South-West, with all its complex junctions, from just south of Chesterfield to beyond Bridgewater in Somerset, some 232 km, is now controlled by only five signal-boxes. at Derby, Saltley, Birmingham (New Street), Gloucester and Bristol. The complex Southern Region of British

Rail, with its very dense traffic, will eventually be controlled by only 13 signal-boxes, some of which are already built.

5. The fact that rail vehicles are tied to their tracks means a railway system is very much less flexible than is a road system. Again, even the most lightly used railway line must be maintained at a high standard, while a heavy capital investment is needed irrespective of the traffic expected. The railway becomes a most inefficient mode of transport where traffic flows are light (see p. 56–7 – fixed and variable costs).

Because of the heavy capital investment the railway must be used up to capacity if it is to be economic. Capacity depends on a combination of train load, average speed of the trains and the frequency of the service. Gradients are obviously a limiting factor upon the capacity of a railway line as they reduce the train loads and the speeds. There are other limiting factors. The sharper the curves, the greater the possible savings in earthworks. The narrower the gauge, the narrower the tops of embankments and the bottom of cuttings and the less earth to be moved. But on narrow-gauge lines speeds are lower, as is the carrying capacity of the wagons. Most important is the load permitted on each axle, a function of rail weight. On it depends the relationship of the tare weight or empty, non-revenue-earning, weight to the revenue-earning payload. (Table 3.1).

Table 3.1 Loads of four-axle wagons

Railway	Gauge	Axle load (tonnes)	All-up weight (tonnes)	Tare (tonnes)	Payload (tonnes)	Tare weight as % of all-up weight
Sierra Leone	2 ft 6 in (760 mm)	5	20	8	12	40
Nigeria	3 ft 6 in (1,067 mm)	8	32	11	21	33
Great Britain	4 ft 8½ in (1,435 mm)	25	100	21.5	78.5	21.5

Inland waterways

These depend either on natural waterways, rivers and lakes or on artificial waterways or on a combination of the two. Much capital must be spent on improving natural waterways and even more on building canals. The size of vessels used throughout a system is controlled by the shallowest point on a river or the smallest lock on a canal. The cost of a canal is also greatly increased by the irregularities in the terrain, for greatly increased earthworks and more frequent locks are required.

The vessels share the characteristics of all water transport, low power expenditure and slow average speeds. But if the former can be combined with a high capacity, operating costs are very low. The average 'boat and butty' on the English narrow canals had a capacity of no more than 30 tons each as against the 1,450-ton 'Spitzboot', the EEC standard, but required the same size crew.

If there is an adequate system of natural waterways, as in the case of the Great Lakes of North America, if the terrain enables canals to be built cheaply, as in The Netherlands and if there is a heavy traffic of bulky but low-value commodities, – petroleum, coal and steel – as there is available in the Rhine Valley, then inland waterways become very competitive (p. 80).

Ocean shipping

Ocean shipping is characterised by: (1) The large size of the transport units. A general cargo vessel averages 15,000 dead weight tons (dwt), a modern container ship 30,000 dwt, while petroleum tankers of over 300,000 dwt are in operation; (2) a comparatively small expenditure of power per unit weight carried; (3) Comparatively slow speeds. A cargo vessel will have a cruising speed of between 12 and 16 knots.[1]

A considerable economy of scale can be achieved by increasing the size of the vessel and this is the reason for the recent vast increase in the size of petroleum carriers. This economy of scale stems in the first place from the fact that a 25 per cent increase in dimensions (length, breadth and draught) results in a 95 per cent increase in capacity. Thus the larger the vessel the less constructional steel per capacity ton is needed. In 1955, a 20,000 dwt tanker cost up to £100 per ton to build. In 1965 a 100,000 dwt vessel cost only £30 per ton. Secondly, propulsion costs do not increase in proportion to size of vessel. To maintain 16 knots a 19,000 dwt tanker would need engines totalling 10,000 hp (1 hp per 1.9 tons). But a 100,000-tonner would need only 21,000 hp (1 hp per 4.76 tons). Similar economies can be obtained from crew numbers. Indeed, a fully automated 250,000 dwt tanker needs a crew of only about 30 men.

Ocean shipping, unlike the modes examined so far, does not need an infrastructure of track. Ships do, however, need elaborate terminal facilities in the shape of harbours and ports. A *harbour* is a place where vessels can shelter from storms and, if necessary, undergo repairs and revictualling. A *port* is the 'interface' at which water and land transport modes come into contact for the interchange of cargo and passengers.

Usually a port is also a harbour. But the two functions can be carried out separately. There are ports that are not harbours. At the surf-ports of West Africa and of Chile and Peru, the ships lie offshore without any shelter at all. There are harbours that are not ports, among them Scapa Flow in the Orkneys and Saldanha Bay (before the new iron-ore terminal was built), a better harbour than nearby Cape Town. Finally, there are great harbours with small importance as ports. The Sierra Leone River in West Africa has anchorage for '300 vessels of unrestricted draught' (*The Africa Pilot*), but the port of Freetown on its shores has berths for four ocean-going ships.

Some harbours are completely natural, such as San Francisco Bay and Milford Haven. In other cases protection from weather and waves is only partial and must be increased by partially closing up the entrance by the

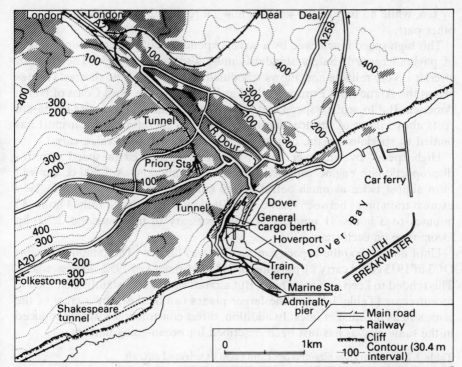

Fig. 3.1 The site of the port of Dover – an example of an artificial harbour and specialised ferry-port

construction of a mole or breakwater. But many harbours are completely artificial. Dover lies on a shallow bay completely open to Channel storms, and the large harbour is a sheet of water protected by three long moles (Fig. 3.1).

Ports where ships cannot *berth*, but must lie offshore and work cargo with boats or lighters, even if in a natural harbour, have a limited capacity and are therefore costly to work. At Colombo ships were protected by a long mole, but were unable to berth, and so had to work cargo to and from lighters.

Berths are normally provided at which ships can tie up and work their cargo directly to and from the shore. Ships require calm water if they are to be tied up to a quay, so the port must also be a harbour. If the tidal range is great, as it is in London with a range of 7.6 m at spring tides, the berths must be situated in enclosed *wet-docks*, which require elaborate entrance locks. A modern port, therefore, represents a very heavy capital investment, not only in the works needed to protect the berths but in dockside facilities. However, the morphology of ports is dealt with more fully later (p. 81).

The air

The fundamental contribution of the air as a mode of transport is the very high speeds which can be attained in everyday service. This has put a new dimension into travel. New York can be reached in $7\frac{1}{2}$ hours from London against 5 days by sea, while no part of the world is now more than 24 hours' flight from any other part.

This high speed is achieved by a lavish expenditure of power per unit weight of payload carried. Safety standards must also be very high. The modern aircraft is very reliable and allows scheduled Great Circle (the shortest) routes across the Arctic from Europe to the Far East and to the West Coast of North America. But to achieve speed and safety is costly and tends to raise tonne-km costs above those of surface transport. Hitherto, therefore, air transport has tended to specialise in the carriage of passengers and high-value cargo.

High speed, by whatever mode, is always costly. Extra speed requires disproportionate engine capacity and fuel consumption. A 1,500 cc car will burn almost twice as much petrol at 110 kph than at 80 kph. When in 1969 express train times between Crewe and Glasgow were reduced from 4 hours 45 minutes to 3 hours 41 minutes, it was necessary to use a second 2,700 hp locomotive on each train.

Until about 1960 the capacity of aircraft was limited. The famous Douglas DC3 of 1935 could carry 21 passengers and the Comet I of 1952, 40 passengers. This tended to keep unit costs high. But aircraft size has constantly increased in recent years (Table 3.2) and the larger planes can be flown by a crew of the same size as the smaller ones. In addition, direct construction costs are reduced in the same way as has just been described for ocean-going tankers.

Table 3.2 Comparative size and operating cost of selected aircraft

Aircraft type	Maximum payload (long tons)	Cost per capacity-tonne km (p)
DC3 – Dakota	3.5	84
Britannia turbo-prop	16.5	28
Boeing 707, jet	48.0	12.5
Boeing 747, jumbo jet	107.0	8

Like ocean shipping the air requires no continuous infrastructure of track, but it does need elaborate terminal facilities. Where surface routes are primitive and inadequate and where outlying airstrips without facilities can be constructed cheaply, the air can replace surface transport altogether. Even in the 1930s the goldfields in New Guinea were wholly supplied by air, so inefficient and costly was porterage, which was the only alternative.

In many ways the airport has similar functions to the seaport. It has harbour functions, for it is a place of shelter from adverse weather and for maintenance and refuelling. It also has port functions, being the interchange point between air and surface transport. An airport requires a considerable area of level land and a heavy capital investment in facilities (p. 82).

Other transport modes

For the transport of liquids, *pipelines* often represent least-cost modes. Large cities are supplied with water by pipeline. Los Angeles get its water from the

Colorado River 480 km away. Natural gas, now so important in Western Europe with the exploitation of the North Sea field, must be transported by land through pipes. Here, however, we must distinguish between *crude* and *product* transport. Crude oil and the lighter petroleum products can be pumped through pipes. But the heavier products, accounting for over 45 per cent of refinery output, are too viscous to flow at ambient temperatures. In Continental Europe refineries frequently have interior locations and are connected to the ports by pipeline. In Great Britain refineries tend to be coastal. Some of the lighter products are distributed by pipeline, but the heavier ones are transported by rail. Under certain circumstances, solids, suspended in water, can be transported. There is a pipeline for the conveyance of chalk from the quarries at Tottenhoe (Herts) to the factory at Rugby, 80 km away. In the USA coal is occasionally transported from mine to power station in this way. Altogether as the map (Fig. 3.2) shows, there is a considerable network of pipelines in many countries.

There are also attempts to combine the advantages of the aircraft and surface modes. The ACV, popularly called the *hovercraft*, floats on a pad of air about 305 mm thick, the maintenance of which requires only a fraction of the power required to keep an aircraft airborne. But the consequent lack of friction enables the hovercraft to maintain high speeds on both water and suitable level surfaces of 60 knots or so with small power expenditure. Though its chief use so far has been as a ferry on short sea routes (even in 1970, almost a third of the accompanied cross-Channel vehicles were moved by hovercraft) it can be used as an amphibious vehicle or a land vehicle in deserts or grasslands. The *hydrofoil*, in contrast, depends on high speed to raise itself out of the water on a very small 'foot', to reduce water resistance and, therefore, power expenditure (Jane's Surface Skimmers, see Jane's Yearbooks, annual).

Technological advance

Technological progress is constantly being made in all transport modes. But progress takes the form of significant 'break-throughs' made at irregular intervals. These can give a particular mode a comparative advantage, which may only be temporary. The balance of advantage is always changing, and these changes do have very considerable geographical consequences.

A good example is the change which took place in the economic geography of iron-ore transport in the 20 years after 1950. In that year long-distance flows of iron ore by sea were virtually confined to movement from Sweden and Algeria to Western Europe and from Sweden, Labrador and Venezuela to the USA (see Fig. 12.1). Most of the ore was transported in tramp ships of less than 10,000 dwt.

The next few years saw a rapid increase in size of ore carriers, which made possible, as we have seen with petroleum carriers, a decrease in costs. Further reductions were also made possible in the cost of construction by advances in shipyard technology. This and lower running costs of larger vessels, together

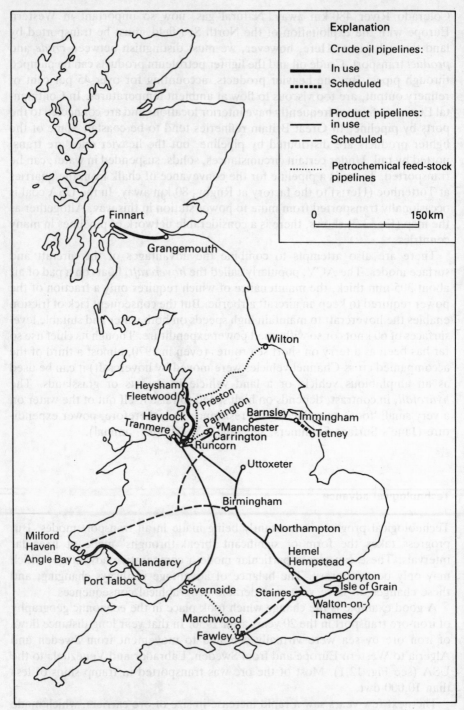

Fig. 3.2 Crude oil and product pipelines, Great Britain 1976. (After Foster 1969, with later additions)

with an increased supply of vessels greatly reduced freight rates. In 1950 rates between Brazil and Japan were betwen £5 and £7.50 per tonne. By 1965 they had fallen to £2.60 per tonne (Manners 1967). The geographical consequences are dealt with more fully in Chapter 12.

In the years after 1950 the increasing size and speed of lorries led to a reduction of costs (p. 64). This, together with increased flexibility and reliability of service, led to road transport making inroads into rail carryings. After 1960, developments in high-capacity railway wagons went a part of the way to redress the balance as far as bulk transport is concerned. Special wagons have been built for the carriage of petroleum, cement and aggregates. These are characterised by very large carrying capacity for small tare weight and capability of running at high speeds. The latest cement wagons in use in UK have a payload of 78.5 tonnes and a tare of only 21.5 tonnes, and can be run at 96 kph.

Technology as a factor has an important bearing on the comparative cost structure of various transport modes. But it also has an important bearing on the relationships between transport and the terrain and other physical features of the earth's surface. This will be dealt with in the next chapter.

Note

1. A knot is 1 nautical mile of 2,000 yards per hour.

Chapter 4
The physical factor

Few motorists escape the frustrating experience of having to follow a slow-moving lorry up a steep hill. Many holidaymakers suffer from delays at airports due to bad weather. Falling snow brings chaos to crowded city roads and late running to suburban trains. The traveller is being constantly made aware of the direct and indirect consequences of the physical environment upon transport.

Physiographic controls

We can divide the physical factor into physiographic controls and climatic controls. Obviously the nature of the terrain will affect the transport net in the area. But its effects will usually not be direct. To put it simply, the mere existence of a pass through a mountain range will not of itself mean that a routeway will follow it. The pass must lie on or near a potential line of communication connecting two places which generate a demand for transport between them. If that demand is sufficient, then sufficient capital will be found to build a transport line to connect the two places, utilising, other things being equal, the easiest routeway. It is not the ease of the routeway which, of itself, generates the demand.

The whole question of the relationship between terrain and transport is not a simple one and must be approached with caution. Because the St Gotthard Pass carried an important road, and underneath runs the most important railway crossing of the Alps in terms of tonnage handled, it must not be thought of as being the most convenient of the Alpine passes or even the most suitable as a route artery (Fig. 4.1). The St Gotthard (2,112 m) is only one of a

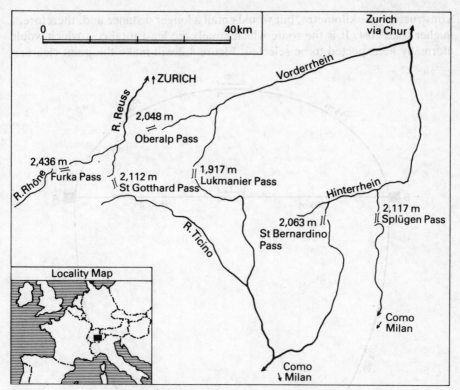

Fig. 4.1 Alpine passes in the St Gotthard area

group of north-south passes across the central part of the Alps and is neither the lowest nor the easiest. The others are the Lukmanier (1,917 m), San Bernardino (2,063 m) and Splügen (2,117 m). The Lukmanier was used in medieval times in preference to the St Gotthard as being easier, but to the north it leads to the east–west Vorderrhein (Further Rhine) Valley, whereas the St Gotthard leads to the north–south Reuss Valley. The San Bernardino has a road tunnel (opened in 1961) which is at only 1,644 m and, unlike the St Gotthard road, is open all the year. The Splügen was originally selected for the main railway line. But the St Gotthard route was finally preferred, though for political rather than engineering reasons. It meant the railway would traverse the Ticino Valley, thus a greater mileage would remain in Switzerland (the Splügen is on the frontier with Italy) and Canton Ticino would be provided with a good transport link with the rest of the country. The Splügen route has been selected for the new trans-Alpine motorway, not the St Gotthard (Rütz, 1969).

Route selection

The selection of a route for a line of transport through a mountain range is a matter of compromise. To choose an easier route might mean a lower cost of construction per kilometre, but would entail a longer distance and, therefore, a higher total cost. It is the route which entails the least total cost which would normally be expected to be selected. Figure 4.2 will make the point clearer.

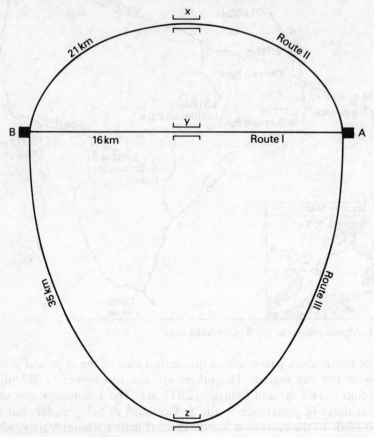

Fig. 4.2 Route selection: trade-off between length of route and cost of building. Route I is short but pass y has difficult approaches. Pass z would incur least costs but route III is long. Route II represents the least-cost compromise

The Canadian Pacific Railway, opened in 1886, was largely a political line, built as a condition of British Columbia's entry into the Canadian Confederation (p. 57)(Innes 1972). The line crosses the Rockies by the Kicking Horse Pass, which is higher and more difficult than the Yellowstone Pass to the north, now used by the Canadian National's line. Indeed, the Yellowstone was the original choice, but fear of a rival route to the south led to the choice of the Kicking Horse. There is now a more southerly route over the Crow's Nest Pass, but this involves crossing into the United States, to which the Canadian Government were opposed as far as the original CPR was concerned.

Expected traffic over the CPR was small, and to reduce capital cost the line was built over the shortest possible route between the summit station of Stephen (1,623 m above sea-level) down to Field 16.0 km to the west and 396 m lower. This section included 4.0 km inclined at 1 in 23 while the rest was at 1 in 40. The result was that eastbound trains required up to *five* locomotives, and as traffic grew Field Hill became very costly to work.

Eventually the section was relocated to bring the gradient down to an average of 1 in 52. This was done by increasing the length of the section from 16.0 to 20.8 km. The line was doubled back on itself, involving two spiral tunnels. As a result much heavier trains could be worked up Field Hill with only three steam locomotives.

Physiographic control in upland areas

The close connection between the physical features and the lines of communication are obvious enough in the case of mountain barriers such as the Alps and the Rockies. But equally, when looking at even a small-scale map of northern England, it is obvious the only practicable route for a south to north railway (or road) up the west side of the Pennines is over the col of *Shap Fell*, which links them with the massif of the Lake District. It is also obvious that the best route for a railway between Leeds and Carlisle is the one from Settle through Clapham and along the route of a line (now closed) to join the main line from Lancaster to Carlisle at Low Gill.

But given a further factor, the strife between the Midland and the London and North Western Railways, the decision of the former to build an independent line northward from Settle could be defended as logical. Here again the route taken is the best available. But because it was the second best to the Shap route, it necessitated much engineering ingenuity to minimise expenditure on earthworks while ensuring reasonable gradients.

Detailed examination shows adjustment of the line to the terrain is very close (Fig. 4.3). Use is made of a series of deep and narrow valleys penetrating the Pennine block and separated by narrow cols. For 20.8 km the line ascends the Ribble Valley at a continuous 1 in 100 (train crews call it 'The Long Drag'). At Ribblehead, the headwaters of the Greta, a tributary of the Lune, was captured by the Ribble, enabling the line to cross the marshy watershed by the Ribblehead viaduct. The line cuts through to Dentdale by the short Blea Moor tunnel. Now comes 6.5 km of all but level track and that through the main block of the Pennines *down* Dentdale and, therefore, rising rapidly above the valley floor. Rise Hill tunnel takes the line into the Upper Lune Valley, to run up it, so that at Garsdale station it is on the valley floor. Here there is a low watershed which allows the line to pass into Wensleydale. The line runs *up* the valley at 1 in 165 to the Ure/Eden watershed at the col of Ais Gill, which the line crosses into the open. The descent of Edendale is 1 in 100 for 25.8 km to Ormside viaduct (Jenkinson 1973).

Physiographic control in lowland areas

But even when we turn to lowland England we find that, though the relief is subdued and unspectacular, physical control over routes can still remain

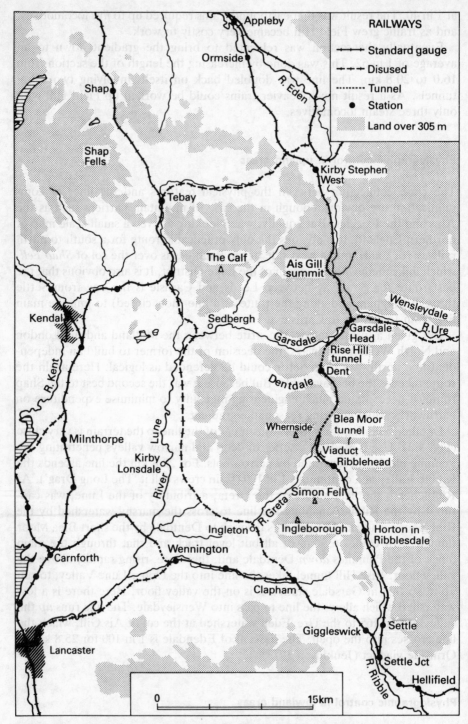

Fig. 4.3 Transport and terrain: the Settle and Carlisle Railway line

strong. A striking example is the Watford Gap through the oolitic limestone cuesta in Northamptonshire. Here, within a few hundred metres of each other along the floor of a wide, shallow valley run the M1 motorway, the main line railway from London to the north-west and the Grand Union Canal. A little further up the western side of the valley is the A5 trunk road, itself aligned along the Roman Watling Street. Finally, along the eastern slope runs the Northampton loop from the main railway. Here is a notable concentration of transport lines along a line of communication at least 1,800 years old.

Appleton (1960) has pointed out that the real significance of the Watford Gap, and of the valley by which the routes approach it up the oolitic dip slope, is its relationship to the whole extent of lowland England. A line drawn from London to South Lancashire passes through the Watford Gap, while concentrations of population in the West and East Midlands lie just off that line. In addition, similar gaps through the chalk cuesta to the south-east also lie alongside the line.

Watford Gap also provides an excellent example of physical considerations outweighing human. The main railway line, opened in 1838, traversed the Gap by Kilsby tunnel (2,218 m) approaching through Weedon, where the River Nene was crossed. For long it was thought the route was chosen because the important town of Northampton, lower down the Nene, refused to have the railway. Historical research (Hatley 1959) however, showed the citizens were anxious to have the railway. The Weedon route was selected because at that place the river was 21.3 m higher than at Northampton. Moreover, the valley is narrow and a short embankment carries the line 12.2 m above the river and 30.48 m higher than the lowest point on the Northampton loop, opened in 1878. The diagram (Fig. 4.4) shows the technical advantage of the Weedon route, especially in view of the small and underpowered locomotives of 1838.

There is another factor we must always take into consideration when studying the consequences of the physical environment, namely progress in technology. This works in two ways: by the introduction of new modes which have new relationships with the terrain, and by advances in existing modes, which result in readjustment of the transport line to the terrain.

The area of North Staffordshire/South Cheshire offers an excellent example of this continuous adjustment (Fig. 4.5). On the broad scale it is obvious that trunk routes northward from the West Midlands must pass through the Cheshire Gate between the Pennines and the hills of the Welsh Marches. On a local scale, however, there is something of a barrier at the entrance to the Cheshire Gate. A triangle of higher ground extends an apex south-westward from the Derbyshire Dome, made up of three triangular outcrops, Millstone Grit to the north-east, succeeded by the Lower Coal Measures and the Upper Coal Measures, the latter bordered by Bunter Sandstones.

The triangular upland has a steep north-western face, sloping from 320 m at the Cloud in the north-east to 90 m at the south-west near Market Drayton. Seen from the Cheshire Plain it is obviously quite a formidable barrier, but it has been modified by a series of gaps which are glacial overflow channels. These lead through to the valleys carved by the tributaries of the Upper Trent which seam the more gentle south-eastern slope.

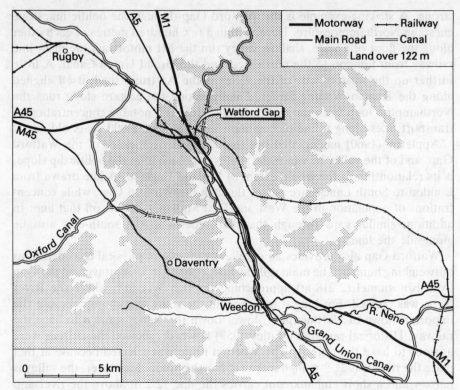

Fig. 4.4 Transport and terrain: the concentration of lines of transport through Watford Gap, Northamptonshire. (After Appleton 1960)

One of these spillways, the Bath Pool Gap at Kidsgrove (Fig. 4.6), provides a potential routeway from the Cheshire Plain to the Fowlea Valley leading down to Stoke-on-Trent. But there is a considerable 'lip' between the channel at 145 m and the general level of the plain at 90 m at Rode Heath, 3 km away. The A34 trunk road, turnpiked in 1743, avoids the gap, which in those days would have had a marshy floor. Instead it climbs the western side of the spillway to a height of 204 m.

The Trent and Mersey Canal also avoids the 'natural' route, being taken underneath the gap at 99 m through the 2,633 m Harecastle tunnel, built by James Brindley and opened in 1775. This proved inadequate and in 1827 a larger bore, constructed by Thomas Telford, was opened parallel to the original. The need for an adequate water supply would appear to have been the reason for the tunnel. By taking the canal through the ridge at a lower level than the spillway, the summit level could be extended to a length of 14.5 km, so that it could be fed from a series of reservoirs through the Caldon branch.

The railway also avoided the gap, negotiating the ridge by three tunnels, totalling 1,902 m and just above the canal tunnels. This allowed the line to fall at a steady 1 in 330 from the plain, through the tunnel and down the Fowlea Valley.

It was not until 1966 that the Bath Pool Gap was used. When the railway was

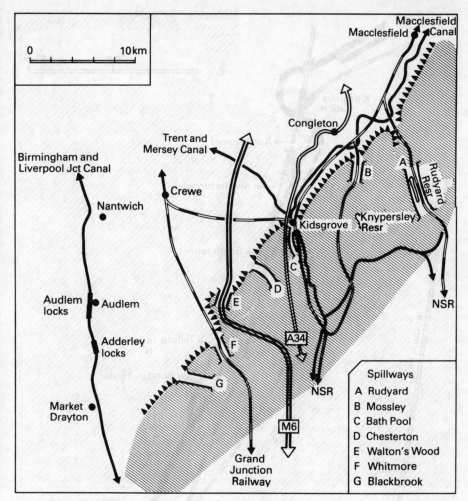

Fig. 4.5 Transport and terrain: North Staffordshire

to be electrified, there was insufficient room in the tunnels to take the traction wires. A 4.0 km diversion was, therefore, built along the floor of the gap. This entailed a 1 in 80 approach from the north. But this, which would have been a great obstacle to a mid-nineteenth-century steam locomotive, provides no difficulty for a modern electric locomotive.

The next spillway, the Chesterton Gap is 3.2 km south-westward. Similar in form to that at Bath Pool, it has never been used as a through routeway; 4.0 km beyond is the Walton's Wood spillway, which was also unused until in 1963 the M6 motorway was opened through it. Built to supersede the A34 and A50 trunk roads, a new alignment was sought, unlike that of the turnpike, one with the least gradients. The main cost of a motorway, apart from the land, is the earthworks needed to minimise gradients for the benefit of heavy lorries. Hence the use of the spillway. Even so, while the gradient through it is no obstacle to cars, it brings down the speed of big lorries to very low levels.

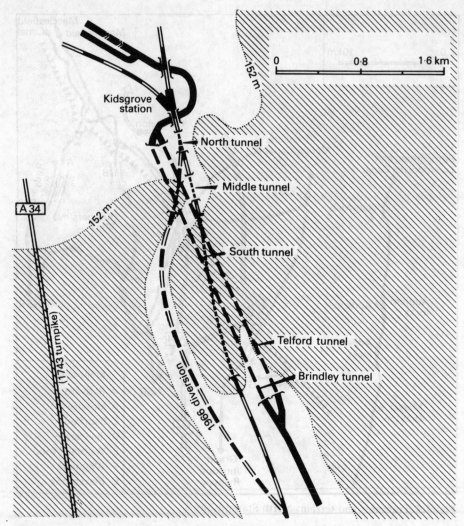

Fig. 4.6 The relationship of lines of transport to the Bath Pool Gap, North Stafford-shire

Technological advance, which permits steeper railway gradients, demands easier road gradients.

Adjacent to Walton's Wood is the Whitmore Gap, which carries the main line railway southward from Crewe across the high ground with gradients no steeper than 1 in 177, and that only for a short stretch. But though westward from this point the ridge becomes rapidly lower and less pronounced, there is no gap near Market Drayton. The Shropshire Union Canal, opened in 1835 as the Birmingham and Liverpool Junction Canal, is therefore carried up by two flights of locks. At Audlem there is a flight of 16 in 2.4 km with a rise of 28.3 m, and 1.6 km to the south of the uppermost lock there is another flight at Adderley, taking the canal up a further 9.4 m.

Consequences of other land forms

So far we have considered, through detailed examples, the relationship between mountain and lowland features on the one hand and upon transport
modes and lines on the other. Other land forms also affect transport lines. It is
not proposed to do more than mention some here, and the matter can easily be
pursued further in Appleton's book (1962).

Valleys, when incised into a plateau, may act as barriers rather than aids.
Some of the more spectacular bridges of the world are to be found in this
situation, notably those across the Niagara and Zambezi rivers below their
respective falls. On a much smaller scale, the only natural obstacles on the
49.2 km railway line between Manchester and Crewe are the crossings of the
seven valleys incised into the otherwise featureless Cheshire Plain. These are
crossed by a series of viaducts, the most striking being the one across the
Mersey at Stockport. There is also another fine one across the Dane near
Holmes Chapel. Similarly, the Shropshire Union Canal, running north and
south along the foothills of the Welsh hills, cuts across the 'grain' of the
country. It was taken by Telford across the valleys of the Dee and the Ceiriog
over two of the most impressive feats of eighteenth-century civil engineering,
the Pontcysyllte and Chirk aqueducts.

Rivers, whether incised or not, provide obstacles. The larger the river, the
fewer the crossing points, and routes are concentrated on the few bridges or
ferries as they are on the few passes across the mountain barriers. The notable
concentration of road and rail routes on the Mississippi crossings at St Louis
and Memphis provide an example. The special case of estuaries is also
important, especially in countries such as Great Britain which have a highly
irregular coastline (see Fig. 4.7). During the nineteenth century a number of
major railway bridges and tunnels were built to cross estuaries: well-known
examples are the Forth and Tay bridges and the Severn and Mersey tunnels.
Since 1950 most of these have been paralleled by road bridges or tunnels. In
1981, the Humber Estuary was finally crossed by a road bridge.

Geological controls

The consequences of the geological structure are both indirect, operating
through the physiography, and direct. The difference, however, is that the
physiographic influences must be studied in relation to the whole line of
communications or the whole network. Watford Gap is not important *per se*,
but in its relations with southern and midland England. The nature of the rock
outcrops encountered, on the other hand, have local rather than regional
consequences. The worst stretches on the road systems prior to 1800 were
always to be found on the clay outcrops (Fuller 1953). Water-bearing sands
in the Lias nearly defeated the builders of the Kilsby tunnel in the 1830s.
Geological knowledge has increased during the subsequent 130 years, but the
glacial deposits plastering the sides of Walton's Wood spillway tripled the cost

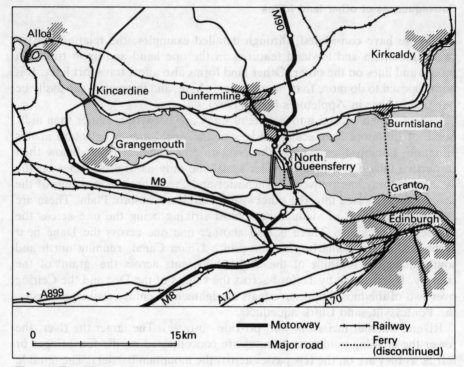

Fig. 4.7 The Firth of Forth as a barrier to communications

of the M6 in this section. It is widely rumoured that the contractors did not seek geological advice, as British Rail did do in connection with their nearby Bath Pool diversion.

Rail travellers from London Bridge to Brighton may contrast the wide, gently sloping cutting sides where the line traverses the London Clay up to Forest Hill, with the narrow, almost vertical sides of the cutting through the chalk up to Merstham Tunnel through the North Downs. Obviously the cost of earthworks through outcrops requiring a gentle angle of repose is increased by the need to excavate more 'spoil'.

Climatic consequences

The climatic influence must be seen from two aspects, the normal and the exceptional. Adjustments to the line of transport must be made for the normal and these are achieved at a price. The M62 trans-Pennine motorway is aligned at increased cost to reduce snow drifting and exposure to wind, while on the highest stretch lighting has been provided as the road is often above the cloud base. On the other hand it is very much more difficult, and therefore costly, to forestall the exceptional, though the effects of a catastrophe can be mitigated. In 1925 a narrow-gauge train was blown off the Owencarrow viaduct in County Donegal with consequent loss of life. Thereafter an anemometer was installed at a nearby station and when the wind exceeded a certain speed no train was allowed on to the viaduct.

A suitable point at which to start consideration of climatic influences is to look at the consequences for airport location and design. In the first place international regulations lay down there must be a 7 per cent increase in runway length for every 300 m of altitude to counteract decreased air pressure. This becomes highly significant at locations such as Nairobi (Kenya) at 1,675 m and at La Paz (Bolivia) 3,962 m above sea-level. Of more importance, however, is the expected number of days in the year when visibility is reduced dangerously by fog, smog and falling snow. This is perhaps becoming of less importance with the development of instrumental landing aids, but these are costly to install and operate. The number of days Heathrow and Gatwick are fogbound is relatively high. In the 1950s, when aircraft were smaller, diversionary fields with better fog records were available at Blackbushe and Hurn in Hampshire. With the growth of aircraft size, alternatives become more distant, Ringway (Manchester), Prestwick (Ayrshire) and Continental airports (Sealy 1966: Ch. 2).

Periods when snow is likely to lie are also important, for snow clearance at airports is costly. Prevailing winds affect the alignment of runways and also the relationship of the airport with its surroundings. At Ringway the prevailing winds (Fig. 4.8) are overwhelmingly from south to west. The suburb of Heald Green which lies to the north-east of the runway, normally experiences minimal (but considerable) noise from landing aircraft with engines throttled back. But when the wind is from east to north, aircraft take off over Heald Green at full power and the noise level becomes intolerable.

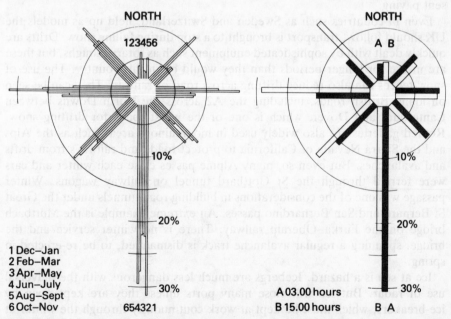

Fig. 4.8 Prevailing winds at Manchester International Airport. (After P. R. Crowe: 18, in C. F. Carter (ed.), *Manchester and its Region*, University Press, Manchester 1962)

Heavy rainfall can cause serious trouble, whether 'normal' or exceptional. Lightly built roads and railways in tropical areas may be regularly breached by 'washouts' each rainy season. In the 1950s the road from Kano to Nguru in Nigeria was abandoned each wet season, each siding on the parallel railway being equipped with a ramp to load road vehicles on railway wagons. If this sort of interruption cannot be tolerated, heavier investments must be made.

Exceptional rain is more difficult to deal with. On 11–12 August 1948, torrential rain after a wet summer caused flooding in south-eastern Scotland, washing out bridges, culverts and embankments. Because the road net was reasonably close-meshed alternative routes could be found, but the whole railway system was brought to a standstill. Seven bridges were destroyed between the adjacent stations of Reston and Grantshouse (8.0 km apart) on the Berwick–Edinburgh main line. The line was closed to all traffic for over two months. Similarly, a series of exceptional thunderstorms over the Home Counties on 5 September 1956 completely disrupted the South Eastern Division of the Southern Region. For several days it had to be operated as a series of isolated sections connected by bus services.

Snow causes even more trouble. While it is falling, visibility may be reduced to zero; drifts block roads and railways; melting snow causes avalanches and floods. In many parts of Great Britain snow is infrequent, but to deal with it a fleet of snow-ploughs must be maintained by the road authorities and by British Rail. This represents a heavy investment in equipment that is only occasionally used. To provide more would be unjustified. When exceptional snowfall causes what is invariably headlined as *traffic chaos* the mass media always ask why this cannot be avoided. It can, but at a price ratepayers and passengers would resent paying.

Even in countries such as Sweden and Switzerland, held up as models the UK should follow, transport is brought to a stop during falling snow. Drifts are quickly dealt with by sophisticated equipment such as rotary ploughs, but these are in use for longer periods than they would be in this country. The use of snow-fences can also reduce drifting across road or railway. They can be seen on many British roads, including the A2 across the North Downs between Canterbury and Dover, which is one of the worst roads for drifting snow. Roofed galleries are also widely used in mountainous areas such as the Alps and the Sierra Nevada of California to protect roads and railways from drifts and avalanches. But even so, many Alpine passes close each winter and cars were ferried through the St Gotthard tunnel on railway wagons. Winter passage was one of the considerations in building road tunnels under the Great St Bernard and San Bernardino passes. An extreme example is the Müttbach bridge on the Furka–Oberalp railway. There is no winter service and the bridge, spanning a regular avalanche track is dismantled, to be re-erected in spring.

Ice at sea is a hazard. Icebergs are much less dangerous with the universal use of radar. But ice will close many ports unless they are kept open by ice-breakers, which must be kept at work continuously through the winter at considerable cost (Couper 1972: 60).

The physical factor is a most important aspect of transport studies. Technological advance may overcome the physical barriers. Mountain ranges can be crossed by high-speed motorways, the Atlantic flown in a few hours and ships enter port in thick fog. But the physical barrier is replaced by an economic one, reflected in increased costs. In Switzerland rail fares were formerly standardised at so much per kilometre. But the published distances were based on the *tariff-km*, which diverges further from the true distance as difficulty of terrain increases and traffic potential decreases. Thus, while the distance between Basle and Zurich is just over 80 km, that between Montreux and Zweisimmen across the Bernese Oberland massif is 40 km. But the tariff-km, on which fares were based, were calculated as 89 in the former case and 166 in the latter. Travel was thus much more costly on the mountain line.

Chapter 5
The economic factor

PT 1

In the preceding chapters the cost factor has received frequent mention. But until recently geographers have tended to ignore the fundamental importance of cost and price as influences. C. A. Fisher (1948) wrote: 'Geographers tend to fight shy of such sordid matters [as cost and price] and cling to the purity of rainfall figures and soil profiles.' They have tended to study the inland port of Manchester largely in terms of locational advantages in its proximity to a large and highly industrialised hinterland. In fact Manchester can remain in business as a port only if by managerial skill its operating costs can be kept lower than those of Liverpool. Port dues, which reflect operating costs, must be maintained at such a level that they will offset the cost of ships spending the extra time and incurring the extra dues ascending and descending the canal to and from Manchester, *less* the cost of road haulage to and from Liverpool. The net result must be that a Manchester exporter can ship through Manchester at a sum less than – or at least equal to – the sum it costs him to ship through Liverpool. If it costs him more, then he will use Liverpool.

Clearly, study of the nature of transport costs and pricing, at least in so far as they affect the spatial patterns of transport phenomena, is basic to transport geography

The structure of transport costs

The total cost of moving a tonne of goods or a passenger between any two points is made up of *fixed costs* (usually called by economists *inescapable costs*) and of *variable costs* (*escapable costs*).

Fixed costs. These are costs which are incurred before any traffic at all passes. They include the costs: (i) of providing the infrastructure (i.e. the roads, the

46

port or the railway line); (ii) of providing, equipping and staffing the terminal facilities (i.e. bus depots, railway stations or airports); (iii) of providing managerial, administrative and maintenance staff and their offices and workshops. These costs are *inescapable* because they cannot be avoided except by abandoning the whole operation. They also do not vary with the level of traffic, but remain independent of it. A railway signal-box of the old fashioned kind, controlling a short stretch of line, must be manned (and thus incur wage costs) whether there is one train or six trains per hour over the line.

Variable costs. These are costs incurred by the actual movement of traffic and therefore vary with the level of the traffic passing. They include the cost of fuel, crew wages and the maintenance of vehicles due to the operation of those vehicles in traffic service, for example the replacement of worn bus tyres or routine inspection of an aircraft after so many hours airborne. They are called *escapable* because they can be avoided or escaped by not running a particular train, suspending a particular flight or a private motorist leaving his or her car in the garage and walking to the shops.

But there is one very important consideration which complicates an otherwise simple concept. In the very short run, to suspend the last bus on Saturday night will probably save only the fuel and tyre wear, for even the driver will have to be paid the guaranteed minimum weekly wage. Over a slightly longer period, all the drivers' duties could be rearranged and perhaps one of them given notice. In the medium run of several years, bus schedules could be redrawn and four new buses ordered as replacements instead of five. In the long run the whole bus service could be closed down and then all the costs previously regarded as fixed would become escapable. We must therefore talk in terms of short-, medium- or long-term escapable costs and must remember that a short-term inescapable cost may become escapable in the medium term.

Because of differences in the basic technology of the various transport modes, the proportion of fixed (inescapable) and variable (escapable) costs in the total costs varies as between those modes. For example, the railway is characterised by having a high proportion of fixed costs in its total costs. It has been calculated (Munby 1968) that 44 per cent of railway costs are fixed and 56 per cent variable. In contrast, road transport is characterised by a much lower proportion of fixed costs in its total costs (which may of course be higher, equal to or lower than rail costs in a given situation). On average 22 per cent of road haulage costs are fixed and 78 per cent variable.

Thus, as traffic increases, *unit costs* (Fig. 5.1) (cost per tonne-km or passenger-km) fall off more rapidly in the case of rail than of road. In other words, as we have seen already, railways potentially show more economy of scale than does road haulage. If traffic is light, unit costs of rail are impossibly high, but if flows are very heavy unit costs are greatly reduced and rail becomes very competitive. Unit costs of road transport vary much less. The reason why road is so competitive with rail in most situations is that most individual traffic flows are generally comparatively light.

All transport operations also give rise to *terminal cost* (Fig. 5.2). These are both fixed and variable. An airport must be built and equipped (fixed costs), it

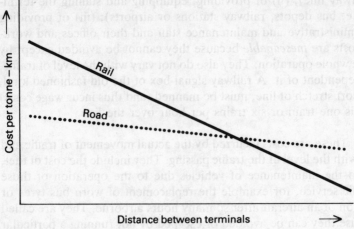

Fig. 5.1 Unit costs in road and rail transport

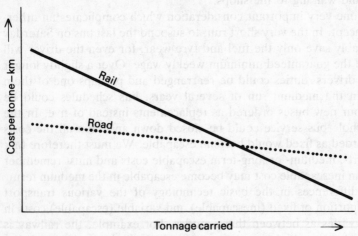

Fig. 5.2 Terminal costs in road and rail transport

must also be manned by flight controllers, porters, customs officers and so on, who will vary in numbers with the level of traffic at a particular time (variable costs). Again, the proportion of terminal costs in the total costs varies between modes. On the one hand, road haulage terminal costs can be negligible. For instance, lorries park in the High Street while unloading goods for shops. On the other hand, to send goods by rail may entail conveying them by lorry from factory to goods depot, loading them into wagons and reversing the process at the other end.

Terminal costs are fixed irrespective of the distance the goods or passengers are conveyed. It costs no more to process a passenger at London Airport and get him seated in his plane whether he is going to Paris or to Hong Kong. The proportion of terminal costs in total costs will therefore fall with the length of journey. In those modes where terminal costs are heavy, advantages accrue over longer distances. Table 5.1 shows some of the estimated costs prepared by

Table 5.1 Relative road–rail costs: pence per capacity ton

	12½ ton rail container	16 ton lorry using motorways
100 miles (trunk distance)		
operating costs	32½	44
fixed costs	14	27½
C & D	72½	70
Total	119	141½
Cost per mile	**1.19**	**1.42**
300 miles (trunk distance)		
operating costs	46	126
fixed costs	41	82½
C & D	72½	70
Total	159½	278½
Cost per mile	**0.53**	**0.91**

Source: British Railways Board evidence to the Geddes Committee on Road Transport Licensing, 1964.
Fixed Costs: include contribution to road and rail track costs.
C & D: Road collection and delivery, operating and fixed costs.
Note: The figures are old, but more recent ones are hard to
come by. They are also open to question, especially the 100-mile
ones, which almost certainly favoured rail. But they illustrate
well certain principles of transport costs.

the British Railways Board as evidence to the 1964 Geddes Committee, which
reveals something of the greater 'taper' possible in rail costs.

Marginal and average costs

Marginal cost. This is the additional cost incurred in order to produce one more
unit of output. What this unit is depends on the immediate circumstances.
Marginal cost may be incurred by carrying an extra passenger on a bus with
seats to spare or another tonne of goods on a half-empty lorry, in which case
the cost will be negligible. It may mean the addition of an extra lorry or of a
wagon on a freight train (or even an extra train), which will be more costly. It
may even mean the resignalling of a suburban railway to allow 22 trains an hour
instead of 20, or the purchase of another jumbo jet which would cost millions.
Marginal costs are therefore time linked, and we can talk about short-run or
long-run marginal costs.

In general, marginal costs do not represent constant addition to costs. If any
traffic at all is accepted, considerable marginal cost is incurred. Up to the
capacity of the *transport unit* (vehicle, vessel, aircraft or train), any further
increase in traffic incurs negligible marginal costs. Then there is a sharp increase at the point when a second unit becomes necessary. Assuming we have a
fleet of 100-seater aircraft and assuming, as on the London – Glasgow *shuttle*

service, a seat is guaranteed to all comers without prior booking, there will be a big jump in marginal costs with the 1st, 101st and 201st passenger carried. But the upward slope of the graph between the jumps is for all practical purposes negligible, as virtually no extra costs are incurred (Fig. 5.3)

Again, marginal costs vary between modes, largely with the capacity of the transport units. When these are small, marginal costs tend to be higher. If we assume a road haulier has a fleet of 20-tonne lorries: to convey a consignment of 100 tonnes will require five lorries and five drivers; to convey one of 110 tonnes (a 10% increase) will need an extra lorry (a 20% increase in lorries, drivers and fuel, therefore in variable costs). We assume there is no malpractice of overloading the original five lorries! With rail, marginal costs tend to be lower, because the traffic unit is bigger. If the 100 tonnes is on a freight train, a 10 per cent increase in the consignment would only entail the addition of another wagon on the train. No extra crew would be needed and only a small increase in fuel. Even the cost of providing an extra train is not great, particularly if viewed against fixed costs.

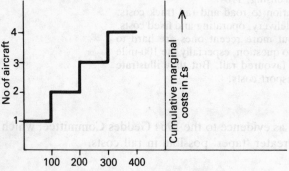

Fig. 5.3 Step function in marginal costs

Average costs. These are obtained simply by dividing the total costs of the operation by the work done, expressed in terms of passenger-km, tonne-km or transport-unit-km. Thus a bus company can express its costs in terms of so much per passenger-km or per seat-km or per bus-km. Average costs will of course vary with output, for the greater the product the more the fixed costs can be spread. The principle can best be illustrated from the cost of running a private car. In 1980 the Automobile Association made the following calculations, assuming a new car with a 1,001–1,500 cc engine. The fixed costs (depreciation, interest, insurance and garage) amounted to £1,240 per year irrespective of mileage. Variable costs (petrol, oil, tyres and maintenance) with petrol at £1.35 per gallon were 7.573p per mile (4.695p per km). If the car did 5,000 miles (8,047 km) in the year the average cost would have been no less than 32.621p per mile (20.225p per km). But if it did 15,000 miles (24,140 km) the average cost would have fallen to 16.073p per mile (9.964p per km).

For the motorist and for the small road haulier, bus operator or ship-owner, average costs are meaningful and make a good basis for fixing rates and fares. But as the systems become more complex, average costs may become misleading. Until recently it has been the practice for large bus companies to calculate average costs and use them as a basis for fixing fare levels which were universal throughout the system. But this may conceal differences in the average costs of say an inter-urban bus route and one connecting three villages with a market town. Because loads and therefore receipts per bus km are better on the former, there is a tendency to assume they are more *profitable*. However, more careful analysis may reveal that costs of the latter operation are lower. In the case of British Rail the assumptions which have to be made when calculating average costs of individual lines and services are heroic to say the least. They depend on arbitrary decisions as to what costs are escapable and what are inescapable.

A final aspect of the concept of cost structure is that of *joint* costs, the costs incurred by producing service B as a consequence of providing service A. If an aircraft is chartered for a flight to Spain, it must incur cost to return home, whether it has a return load or not. Again, if we have a passenger and a freight service over the same railway line, the cost of maintaining the track is a joint cost to be shared (in a purely arbitrary manner) between the two services (British Railways Board 1978).

Quality of service

Finally, we must distinguish between the cost of transport to the operator and to the user. To the latter, the cost of transport as expressed in rates and fares is only a part of total *transit costs*. These are all the costs incurred in transferring goods from the point of production to the point of consumption. They will include the working capital tied up in goods in the transport 'pipeline', the cost of warehousing stocks at the destination, the cost of packing, insurance and so on. For the passenger it is the total cost of getting himself to the place where he wants to be, and may include cost of food consumed on the journey, the time lost at business and so on.

Thus *quality of service* is of equal importance to cost of service, and in many cases users are prepared to pay for quality. As Table 5.2 shows, the attributes of quality vary as between passengers and freight.

Passengers look for reliability above all, the likelihood that the service will fulfil the promise of the timetable. For urban bus passengers the most

Table 5.2 Quality of service – not necessarily in order of importance

Passengers	Freight
Reliability	Reliability
Frequency	Speed
Speed	Freedom from damage
Comfort	and pilferage
Safety	

frustrating experience is to wait 15 minutes for the next bus on a 5-minute service at the end of which time three buses come along together. For short journeys frequency is important, as this reduces waiting time. Speed is important for the businessman and he is prepared to pay higher fares for a faster service. Conversely, for the student money is more important than time and he will be prepared (if he cannot hitch) to go by motor coach, slower but cheaper than rail, at least before the introduction of railcards. Comfort is another quality that passengers are prepared to pay for. To provide first-class accommodation in trains and aircraft is more costly to the operator because fewer passengers can be accommodated in a given space. First-class fares are therefore higher, but some people are prepared to pay these. Obviously, too, passengers demand safety and because of this pay higher fares, though they may not realise that the higher the safety standards the higher the costs.

The freight shipper may be prepared to pay more for better-quality service, as this may allow him to reduce his total transit costs. Although rates for air cargo are higher than by surface routes, it may pay the shipper to use the air, as the extra cost may be outweighed by the reduction in cost of packing and insurance (due to greater freedom from pilferage and breakage) and the reduction of the quantity of goods in transit due to greater speed. If the service is reliable and frequent, warehouse charges can be reduced or eliminated. A Hull manufacturer of heating appliances eliminated a London depot by using the new Freightliner service, which provided reliable overnight delivery direct to the customers in the London area.

Pricing

The price of transport to the user is the other side of the coin from the cost to the producer of providing the service. In the long run, of course, price must be related to cost so that revenue can be related to expenditure, even if the revenue is made up by open or concealed subsidy. But in the short run of the day or the week, or in one direction of a two-way service, or on some branches of a system, this is by no means necessary. In fact, sometimes price is fixed irrespective of cost.

This is because a transport service cannot be stored. Once created, the service is wasted if unused. To run a 50-seater bus 20 km produces 1,000 seat-km. If only 10 passengers travel for 10 km, only 100 seat-km are sold and 900 seat-km are wasted: yet the costs incurred are the same as they would be if the bus were full.

The price of a particular service should (though not invariably) be fixed to cover the cost of the service. If the buses on our hypothetical route cost 25p per km to run (or a total of £5 for the 20-km journey) and the operator could always expect a full load, he could fix the fare at 12p and make a reasonable profit. On the other hand, if he knows that on the average day he will only have 25 passengers he must fix the fare at 24p and hope the extra passengers (who will of course yield a clear profit) on wet days will counterbalance the shortfall of passengers who will cycle on fine days (representing a dead loss).

Airlines are particularly concerned with this, the *load factor*, on which they base their fares. Thus a load factor of 50 per cent on a particular service means the airline can expect to sell half the seat-km produced. Fares are therefore fixed to cover costs on the assumption that half the seats are sold. To increase profitability, every effort must be made to fill the otherwise empty capacity.

It may cost no more to provide a seat on a suburban train at 08.00, 14.00, 17.00 or 22.00 hours. Suppose the cost per seat-km is 2p, the distance 20 km and an 80 per cent load factor is expected, the cost per passenger would be 50p. At 08.00 hours and 17.00 hours large numbers want to travel to and from work. It may be possible to charge them 60p without driving them on to slower buses or to using their cars. On the other hand, shoppers and theatregoers have to be enticed on to the 14.00 hours and 22.00 hours trains (which have to be run anyway) by charging them only 40p. The whole secret of success in this form of fare manipulation is to maximise revenue. There is no point in raising fares beyond the point that loss of passengers more than counteracts increased revenue from those remaining; or to fix them so low that the extra passengers do not compensate for the reduced revenue from each passenger. In practice, too, extra costs may be incurred by providing peak-hour services: this point is dealt with in Chapter 10.

Sometimes a different fare or rate may be charged for a service which costs the same to provide. Thus on almost any train you will find people with ordinary tickets, cheap-day returns, HM Forces concession tickets, season tickets and children with half-fare tickets. All these are in possession of tickets based on different mileage rates, but are occupying seats which cost exactly the same per kilometre to provide. Economists refer to this as *discriminatory charging*. With careful manipulation, discriminatory charging can ensure that revenue is maximised, but care must be taken lest too many people buy tickets below the cost they would otherwise be willing to pay. In the middle 1960s the then British European Airways introduced on their domestic flights very low *standby* fares. In theory these would have led to the selling of a few extra seats above the expected normal load factor, which, as we have seen would represent a clear profit. In practice, too, many regular travellers, well aware of the usual loading of their planes, came for *standby* tickets knowing they would be available. In contrast to charging different rates for a similar service is the practice of charging the same rates for services with widely differing costs. The most obvious example in transport is the Post Office, which charges the same to transport a letter from one part of Bristol to another as it does to take one from that city to a remote shepherd's cottage in the Scottish Highlands.

This latter system leads to *cross-subsidisation*. The best example is the development of the Territorial bus system described on page 17. Many economists are much opposed to cross-subsidisation as they consider prices should reflect cost difference and that if some services, such as country buses, are needed for social reasons there should be unconcealed public subsidy. But some measure of cross-subsidisation is necessary between various journeys on a single route or between routes on a system. For the geographer it is necessary to bear cross-subsidisation in mind as an important factor in shaping the physical layout of networks. Certainly the bus and rail networks of Great Britain in the 1950s would have been very different but for the deliberate policy of cross-subsidisation.

Charging methods

In the case of road haulage it is a relatively simple matter to calculate the cost of conveying a particular consignment and to use this as a basis for charging. It is not so simple for a railway with heavy fixed costs and numerous differing consignments (Sharp 1965: Ch. 3). If, therefore, British Rail are negotiating with Shell or Esso a rate for the carriage of petrol, they can work out the variable costs, but must then add what is in fact a notional figure as a contribution to fixed costs. Rail rates are therefore generally geared to marginal costs, and road rates to average costs.

Now the value of one article or commodity in proportion to its weight (or volume) differs from those of other products. For example, the value of a tonne (cubic metre) of cement is much less than that of a tonne (cubic metre) of electric motors. The *value/weight ratio* is an important concept. Goods with a high value/weight ratio can withstand the addition of heavier transport costs without distorting their cost to the consumer. They can therefore be transported over longer distances and/or more costly transport modes. For example: if the distance between A and B is 100 km and the transport rate is 5p per tonne-km, then all goods produced at A will cost £5 more at B. If a tonne of cement costs £5 at A, its price at B would be increased by 100 per cent and consumers would look for a substitute, building with local bricks perhaps. But a tonne of machinery cost £500 at A would cost only 1 per cent more at B, which would be neither here nor there. However, in practice high value/weight goods are more costly to transport since they are normally bulkier. A tonne of steel sheet will occupy less space than when it has been stamped out into motorcar bodies. But, since these goods are often more fragile, they require more costly loading methods.

Rate-making can therefore be approached in two ways. We can have a tariff by which high value/weight ratio goods are charged more for the same distance than low ratio goods, irrespective of real cost differentials. This practice is known as *charging what the traffic will bear*. On the other hand, rates can be based on the actual costs, whether these are average costs or variable costs.

At this point we must note that time may mean money for the shipper of perishable goods such as spring flowers from the Scilly Isles. There is no point in selecting a lower-priced but slower means of transport if as a result the best prices on the market are lost. Newspapers and mail are also perishable in the sense that the information quickly becomes out of date: today's *Times* can be sold for 20p, yesterday's is only suitable for wrapping fish and chips. Time is also money to the businessman after a contract. In certain circumstances shippers and passengers are prepared to select a higher-priced but faster mode.

So far we have thought only in terms of single journeys by transport units, which must eventually return from B to A, even if it is via D and E. The round trip is the total cost of a lorry despatched with a load of export goods from Birmingham to Southampton. If the lorry returns empty the whole cost must be debitable to the shipper. If the operator can obtain a return load of fruit from Southampton, the cost per tonne-km of the two loads is reduced and, if necessary, the price of the outward load can be lowered. Sometimes a *backload* is obtained by offering a cut price. Road haulage is a very competitive industry, and any revenue is better than none if the outward shipper has been charged less than the cost of the round trip. But note that the advantages of conveying loads in bulk (p. 145) may outweigh the chance of backloads and the numbers of specialised lorries, which have to return empty, are rapidly increasing on our roads.

In conclusion, we can select from Nigeria an example of the importance of cost and price. In 1963 the rate for groundnuts for the 1,120 km from Kano to the port of Apapa was £7.50 per long ton. But besides the all-rail route, produce could be railed to Baro (730 km) on the Niger and shipped thence to the Delta ports. But the rail rate from Kano to Baro was kept disproportionately high at £5.43 per long ton. Obviously, the overall cost of this route could not exceed that of the all-rail one, so the river operators could not charge more than £2.07 per long ton. While they would accept some traffic, they refused to invest more capital to increase capacity. So in 1963/64 only 75,000 long tons of groundnuts were despatched by the river route as against 10 times that amount by the all-rail route. Geographers must be prepared to seek explanation for the spatial patterns of transport phenomena in terms of cost and price.

Chapter 6
The political and social factors

In the previous chapter we have considered the extent to which economic factors affect the spatial patterns of transport. But some transport operations are not being provided on an economic basis. Many people drive to work, even though it may cost less to go by bus. Some national airlines are run more as prestige symbols than as profitable investments. In many cities suburban railways are operated for social reasons, even though costs exceed revenue. In many countries, Switzerland and Ghana among them, it is deliberate policy to prevent development of road services parallel to railway routes. In the United States, because of labour agreements, freight trains have a crew of five when two would suffice. Transport patterns are influenced by political and social factors, and these affect cost and price structures, methods of operation and division of traffic between modes, as well as the shape of the transport patterns themselves.

Political motives for the provision of transport facilities

So far we have been concerned mainly with the economic demand for transport, but in many cases lines of transport have been built more for political than for economic reasons. The principal factor in the development of the Roman road network was to enable an imperial postal system to be set up for the speedy conveyance of despatches. A number of very important railway lines were built to provide political cohesion in large continental areas with no alternative forms of transport. The Trans-Siberian Railway was built to extend and consolidate Russian rule over the land-mass of Siberia (Tupper 1965). Here the main line of movement for the post, armed forces, civilian administrators and settlers was from west to east, but the rivers mostly ran northward to the icebound Arctic Ocean. When the Dominion of Canada was being created as a union of previously separate colonies, British Columbia felt itself isolated from the rest of Canada, being separated from it by the mountain barrier of the Western Cordillera and the sheer distance across the prairies. A condition of British Columbia's entry into the Dominion was a rail link. The Canadian Pacific Railway (completed in 1886) (p. 34) was built to link the East and West coasts with the aid of government grants (Innes 1972).

In recent years roads have also been built for political reasons. A well-known example is the Pan-American highway. This was a scheme started in the 1930s to provide continuous road communication from the USA through Central and South America. It took the form of links, sometimes very long ones, between and within the various national road networks. Its provision has done little to stimulate trade, as the line of the highway runs athwart the main lines of economic movement. The Trans-Amazonia highway is being built by the Federal Government of Brazil through the vast rain-forests of the Amazon Basin. It will run for 5,300 km from the existing road net of the eastern plateau of Brazil. The route lies about 500 km south of the Amazon through the tiny trading posts of Otaituba and Manicoré to the Peruvian frontier near Cruzeiro do Sul, an extremely sparsely peopled area: as E. P. Leahy (1973) says, 'the economic value of the Trans-Amazonia highway is questionable'.

Governments as a source of capital for transport

The provision of a transport infrastructure, especially when there are only scanty economic returns in view, must often be left to governments in default of action by private enterprise. Government, either central or local, is the traditional provider of the road network. For other modes, the capital may be provided directly by the Government, or special measures introduced to encourage private enterprise.

Although most road networks have been built to supply economic demands, governments have also been concerned with providing national networks for politico-strategic purposes. It was for these more than for economic motives which led Louis XIV in the eighteenth century to plan the French *Route Nationale* system. In the 1930s the German *Autobahn* network was planned for military purposes as much as economic, though extensions to the system made after 1945 were for purely economic reasons.

Elsewhere governments have created transport facilities to tap resources of wealth. The railways of Peru were built and operated by private firms, but under favourable concessions from a Government which was anxious to exploit the mineral resources of the Altiplano. In Australia each state provided its own independent railway system to open up its own particular part of the continent. Conversely, in Great Britain a dense population and considerable industrial and economic development provided an economic basis for railway-building and capital was readily forthcoming. But in the western USA private invest-ment in railways only became available when the Government offered a guarantee of some immediate return.

The first trans-continental railway in North America (opened in 1869), the Union Pacific–Central Pacific line from Omaha to San Francisco, was built under a direct subsidy for each mile (1.6 km) built (Griswold 1963). But the network was extended by indirect subsidy. Under the system of land apportionment in the USA, the land was divided into sections, each of 1 sq. mile (2.6 sq. km). Under the special terms of the Homestead Act of 1864 settlers were given the title to a quarter-section. In addition railway companies were granted alternate sections up to 10 miles (16 km) on either side of their lines, which they could lease or sell as they pleased. For example, the Illinois Central Railroad were granted 2.5 m. acres (606,900 ha) for building 705 miles (1,128 km) of line in six years.

At a slightly later date, 1885–1915, a very close network of railways was built to open up the Pampas of Argentina. J. C. Crossley (1971) points out that a cart-haul of more than 16 km to a railway station made wheat production unprofitable. So the area had to be *saturated* with rail lines. The railway companies would buy up estates, sub-divide them and sell the smaller lots to settlers, who paid by instalments.

So far we have only mentioned roads and railways. But governments have also provided ports and harbours for non-economic motives. The massive harbour works at Dover, Portland and Holyhead were to provide harbours of refuge for the naval fleet. The naval ports of Portsmouth and Sheerness were also provided for strategic reasons. In recent years airports have also been built for military purposes. Many such wartime airfields had been adapted for civilian purposes, Manchester's Ringway among them. Many airports have been built by municipalities and more for prestige than with any economic justification. The city of Coventry maintains an airport only a few kilometres from Elmdon Airport, which is owned by Birmingham, and which is located between Birmingham and Coventry.

Government intervention and initiative in the transport industry

So far we have considered the political factor mainly in terms of the provision of infrastructure for non-economic reasons. But government intervention and initiative in all aspects of the transport industry has a very long history. These have grown with the growing complexity of transport systems, and, very recently, as a result of increased public awareness of the fundamental importance of transport in the economy and the environment.

Motives for intervention partly spring from the peculiar nature of the transport industry. There is, for instance, a need to ensure uniformity in the infrastructure: a railway system should be of uniform gauge; the weight of lorries permitted on a road is the weight which can be supported by the weakest bridge. There is also a need to ensure minimum standards of service. It would be undesirable if a bus company operated its services only at peak hours.

The aspects which have attracted most attention, even from the more *laissez-faire* governments of the nineteenth century, include the following.

1. The provision of the infrastructure

We have already seen some examples of this. In Britain a national trunk system developed in Roman times. Throughout the Middle Ages the network was mainly based on local tracks connecting villages with market towns. But by the Highways Act of 1555, the provision and maintenance of the system was made the responsibility of the parishes. With the great increase in traffic after 1700 (the consequence of the Industrial Revolution), the inadequacy of such control was exposed. Improvement was left to private enterprise, which provided the capital for the turnpikes (Albert 1972). But this network was piecemeal and local, 1,100 turnpike trusts controlling 33,600 km of road.

With the decay of the turnpike trusts in the Railway Age, responsibility perforce shifted to local government. The present division of responsibility for the secondary road systems by local authorities emerged as the powers of those bodies were codified during the second half of the nineteenth century (Savage 1966: Ch. 4).

But the coming of the motor vehicle revived long-distance traffic and with it the need for national control of the trunk system. In 1909 a Road Board was set up to administer funds for road works raised by petrol and vehicle taxes. But after 1926 motor and fuel taxation went into the general Treasury pool. The Trunk Road Act of 1926 designated which were trunk roads and gave control of them to Central Government. The Special Roads Act of 1949 defined the motorway, breaching the principle of the *Queen's Highway* which was open freely to all, but not reintroducing the concept of tolls. The Act also provided powers for motorway construction and led to the development of the first nationally planned highway network since Roman times.

As a contrast, we shall summarise the position in an underdeveloped area, namely West Africa. Funds for building and maintenance of trunk roads are the responsibility of central governments, normally from their own taxation resources, though occasionally foreign aid funds are specifically earmarked. The secondary system is the responsibility of provincial and local authorities. Produce marketing boards have provided funds for feeder roads to aid agricultural development, while roads have been built by timber and mining companies to aid their operations. Individual villages also provide themselves with a link to the nearest main road on a self-help basis (White and Gleave 1971: Ch. 9).

2. The control of monopoly

Because of the heavy investment in infrastructure, it is seldom economic to duplicate railway and canal lines and systems. In the nineteenth century, also, there were no efficient alternative modes of inland transport. Legislation, therefore, aimed at controlling monopoly. Amalgamations of railway companies required enabling Acts and frequently the Bills were thrown out to prevent emergence of regional monopolies. Only the North Eastern, and to a lesser extent the Great Western, ever achieved a virtual regional monopoly.

In addition there were extensive controls over rates and fares. Measures included the 1854 Railway and Canal Traffic Act, which included the *undue preference* concept, which was abandoned only in 1953. If a special rate were granted to a shipper, it had to be published and available to anyone else. In 1873 an Act set up the Railway Commissioners to administer the law on preferential rates (Parris 1965; Savage 1966: Ch. 3).

3. The control of competition

In contrast with the railways, road transport is inclined to competitive situations. The infrastructure is provided by Government and relatively limited capital is needed for entry to the industry. *Undue* competition can lead to: (i) a decline in quality of service; (ii) a decline in standards of safety and maintenance; (iii) inroads into the carryings on government-owned railways.

Legislation to control road transport usually aims at the control of new entrants to the industry. The 1930 Road Traffic Act set up Area Traffic Commissioners with powers to control entry into the bus industry, with the important geographical consequences we have examined (p. 17). The 1933 Road and Rail Traffic Act gave the Commissioners similar licensing powers over road haulage. But because of the diffuse and fragmented structure of the industry there were fewer geographical consequences (Hibbs 1971).

4. Safety

Much legislation has been aimed at ensuring safety standards. The *block* signalling system and continuous automatic brakes on passenger trains were made compulsory by the 1889 Regulations of Railways Act. But most progress in rail/safety was made as a result of the 1840 Act setting up the Railway Inspectorate, which ever since has held an enquiry on every movement accident and issued a report making recommendations. Judicial enquiries are also made on shipping accidents in territorial waters or anywhere else for ships flying the national flag. A similar procedure is also followed for aircraft accidents. Safety on roads is achieved by a complex code of law administered by the police and law courts. The setting of safety standards obviously has economic consequences for any transport mode. A single example will suffice: the 1967 Road Safety Act severely limited drivers' hours for both buses and lorries, thereby increasing transport costs.

5. Working conditions

Government control over wages and conditions began with the sea. Throughout the world British seamen are called *limeys* because of the Act of 1849 which enforced a daily issue of lime juice to crews of British ships to combat scurvy. Such intervention can have important geographical consequences. It was the US Government's legislation, imposing very high standards of wages and conditions to ships flying the American flag, that led to American capital investment in ships flying *flags of convenience* such as Liberia and Panama. So great has been this trend that, in 1971, Liberia ranked as the world's largest merchant fleet. It also explains why US ship-owners were so eager to introduce containerisation in the later 1960s (Ch. 12).

6. Transport co-ordination

This is a comparatively recent aim of government intervention, but it is of growing importance and has the most wide-reaching geographical consequences. Two things are meant by this term: (i) the integration of services by the provision of connections between modes and of through rates and fares; (ii) the correct allocation of capital resources between the various modes making up a national transport system in order to maximise total output with minimum overall costs in terms of both capital investment and operating expenses. These two aspects are both important. Though separate, they in fact are thoroughly confused, not only in the popular mind but often in the minds of legislators. The ordinary traveller may be forgiven for thinking of co-ordination as the hourly bus arriving at the station 5 minutes *before* the departure of the hourly train instead of either 5 minutes *after* or at the bus station 10 minutes' walk away.

The 1933 Act setting up the London Passenger Transport Board partially aimed at the first aspect, and London Transport has made sporadic efforts at achieving this end, especially in recent years. Many bus routes have been focused on important Underground stations, such as Uxbridge, Edgware and Finsbury Park, while other stations, such as Tottenham Hale have been developed as multimodal interchanges between Underground, British Rail, buses and cars. The second aspect is even more important and more recent. The need for action stems from increasing investment and increasing competition, not only between road and rail, but between the 'public' and 'private' sectors, represented by rail, bus and road haulage operators on the one hand and private cars and 'own-account' commercial vehicle operators on the other (Ponsonby 1969).

Government intervention in the UK since 1945

In 1947 the Labour Government passed the Transport Act, which effected partial nationalisation and aimed at achieving co-ordination in both senses of the word. 'The British Transport Commission' (BTC) was set up to provide 'an efficient, adequate, economical and properly integrated system of public inland transport *and road facilities*' (author's italics). The method of carrying out these intentions was co-ordination by integration. The BTC was to control all nationalised transport, which included:
(a) the railways;
(b) the railway-owned docks;
(c) the railways' financial interest in bus companies;
(d) London Transport;
(e) long-distance (over 40 km) public road haulage.
This it did through executives, each with rather limited powers of decision-making (Gwilliam & Mackie 1975).

During the post-war recovery period investment in roads and railways received lower priority than housing, social services and industry. It was cynically said there were 'no votes in roads', but at the same time, to boost exports, the motor vehicle industry was allowed vast expansion. On the Continent, Marshall Aid funds were used to modernise the war-shattered railways. In the UK the railways were certainly in a run-down condition, but they could carry on.

The 1951 Conservative Government also sought co-ordination, but through competition and decentralisation, and thus passed the 1953 Transport Act. It is only fair to say they were no more successful than their predecessors. Under this Act the BTC were relieved of their duty to co-ordinate transport, now its only obligation was to cover its costs. Road haulage was to be denationalised (in the event not all the British Road Services fleet could be sold). The railways were relieved of most of their restrictions on charging and were to be con-trolled by regional boards instead of the Railway Executive.

Roads and railways remained starved of capital. The former were becoming ever more congested as private cars proliferated and most of the increased freight traffic became road-borne. After 1955 the financial position of the railways deteriorated. By then leeway in public investment, especially in housing, had been made up and in that year the Government accepted the BTC's Railway Modernisation Plan. But this was a technical plan, with such measures as the substitution of diesel traction for steam. There was no clear economic policy, no thought on the role of a railway system which was virtually unchanged in shape since 1939.

Then in 1962 came yet another Transport Act, continuing the policy of decentralisation and competition. The BTC was abolished and independent boards created for:

(a) British Railways;
(b) British Docks and Harbours;
(c) London Transport;
(d) Inland Waterways.

All other assets, especially British Road Services and bus investment, came under the Transport Holding Company, which worked through subsidiary companies. All these bodies were now regarded as commercial undertakings and almost all social obligations were abolished.

In 1963 the British Railways Board published its plan to achieve full commercialisation, the well-known Beeching Report (British Railways Board 1963a). Implementation brought about the radical change in the railway system dealt with elsewhere (p. 78). To do this there was both a positive and a negative side, and unfortunately public attention ever since has remained focused on the latter rather than the former.

The geographer must approach the Beeching Report with reservations (White 1963): some of the data on which it was based was inadequate and suspect; but the main criticism is its geographical inflexibility. A declared assumption, made at a time of rapid change, was that the distribution of population and industry would remain static.

The negative side of the Beeching Report was the withdrawal of service from the carriage of short-distance and low-volume passenger and freight traf-fic for the reason already outlined (p. 48). This entailed the total closure of about half the 32,800 km system and the closing of the smaller freight and passenger stations on the lines remaining. In 1963, it must be remembered, 33 per cent of the system carried only 1 per cent of the traffic and 33 per cent carried over 80 per cent.

The positive aspects included the development of profitable freight traffic, the movement of bulk commodities by the train-load and of general goods by Freightliner, p. 152. On the passenger side there was to be the development of a fast, frequent and comfortable long-distance Inter-City network. Unfortunately the implementation, especially on the freight side, has tended to be delayed by government reluctance to invest and by trade union opposition.

The 1964 Labour Government embodied its revised theories on transport in a series of White Papers (White Papers 1966, 1967). These showed a willingness to learn from past mistakes, together with, perhaps for the first time, a realisation by Government of the social and environmental implications of transport. Though far from a return to 1947, it aimed at co-ordination between the various nationalised bodies concerned with transport.

The full proposals were not, however, implemented fully in the 1968 Transport Act. But its geographical consequences were very far-reaching. The Act recognised that some passenger services were socially necessary, and the Minister was given power to subsidise any rail services so considered. In 1969 the grant-aided services were announced (Allen 1968a, b). As for the network of inter-urban and rural bus services, all *Territorial* bus companies were brought under the control of the National Bus Company in England and Wales and the Scottish Bus Group. Local authorities were given powers to subsidise those services they considered socially necessary, and if they did, the Minister was obliged to make an equal contribution.

Secondly, an entirely new principle was introduced, that planning of public transport, road improvements and land use in large cities must all be co-ordinated. Passenger transport executives (PTEs) were set up to plan investment, operate buses and control suburban rail services. The Government could make grants towards replacing bus fleets and to improve or build new rail lines.

Under the 1972 Local Government Act, the Metropolitan counties became the passenger transport authorities, with the PTEs responsible to them. London was dealt with separately under the 1969 London (Transport) Act, which abolished the London Transport Board and transferred control to the Greater London Council. The 1972 Act also increased the duties and powers of the *Shire* counties in transport planning. After 1974 the individual grants were replaced by a single block grant. The counties must prepare annually for submission to the Department of Transport a Transport Policy and Programme statement (TPP), giving details of expenditure on roads and public transport. The money comes to the county through the Transport Supplementary Grant and also through the General Rate Support Grant.

On the freight side, the 1968 Act radically overhauled the road haulage licensing system, essentially unchanged since 1933. In the first place, the distinction between transport *on own account* and *for hire and reward* was abolished. In the second, entry into the latter branch, the professional hauliers, was relieved of most restrictions. There was a change from *quantitative* licensing to *qualitative*. At the time of writing there is less government control over road haulage than in any other EEC country. As for organisation of the nationalised sector, the *National Freight Corporation* was established to take over: (a) British Road Services and BRS (Parcels) (now *Roadline*); (b) the British Rail *Sundries* (less than wagon-load) service, the railway's biggest loss-maker and which was now to be operated as *National Carriers Ltd*; (c) a controlling interest in *Freightliners Ltd*, owned jointly by NFC and BR and operating the railway Freightliner service, though control was returned to BR under the 1978 Transport Act.

Finally, the Act provided for a *Freight Integration Council* with a membership including all nationalised bodies concerned with freight transport. The idea was to ensure as much long-distance and bulk freight as possible went by rail. In the event this was never implemented.

Just as the TPPs replaced funding of individual schemes, the 1974 Railways Act replaced grant aid to individual passenger services by a single block grant to support a rail network of agreed size, the Public Service Obligation (PSO) Grant. Increasing recognition of the role of Central and Local Government in transport planning, and of the social and environmental implications, were revealed in the 1977 White Paper and the consequent 1978 Transport Act.

We have examined in detail some of the consequences of government intervention in inland transport in Great Britain. Examples can be multiplied and include the widespread consequences of intervention by the various governments of the Common Market countries (Bayliss 1965). The forging of a common transport policy is also an important task of the Community as a whole (Hibbs 1967). Government control over the development of air transport is even more wide-reaching at both national and international levels (Wheatcroft 1956, 1964; Corbett, 1965).

Labour as a factor

Transport is a very important employer of labour in any country (Christensen 1966). Those engaged in public transport in the UK accounted for 6 per cent of the working population in 1966, an average level for an economically advanced country. But to this figure we must add the large numbers employed by virtue of the use of private cars, i.e. roadmen, petrol-pump attendants, garage staff and traffic police.

Labour costs invariably account for the major part of total transport costs and there is continual search for higher productivity in order to reduce unit costs. For example, if, during his day's work, a lorry-driver drives a fully laden 10-tonne lorry for 150 km, he will have produced 1,500 tonne-km. But if he can cover 200 km with a laden 20-tonner, he will have produced 4,000 tonne-km, a 166 per cent increase of output at no increase in labour costs. Larger traffic units partly account for increased productivity. A 300-seater jumbo jet requires no bigger flight crew than a 150-seater aircraft. The fully automated 484,000 dwt super-tanker *Globtick Tokyo* needs a crew of only 38, while we

have already seen something of the scope for automation in railway operation (p. 24).

But full attainment of labour economies requires the co-operation of the
workers. Restrictive practices by the American Teamsters' Union (truck-
drivers) was one of the reasons behind the growth of *trailer-on-flat-car* (TOFC)
or *piggy-back*, the practice of conveying road-trailers by train over long
distances. In this country, while agreement was reached on the single manning
of electric and diesel locomotives, there was for years considerable resistance
by the locomotive men to guards riding in the locomotives of freight trains to
save haulage of 25 tonnes of dead-weight in the brake vans. In Nigeria, even in
1967, the conditions of service of locomotive drivers were based on those of
European drivers many years before, 160 km for express trains and a lesser
distance for freight trains was a day's work and this obviously raised costs.

The social factor

The social consequences of transport development are widespread and of
fundamental importance. Some of them are referred to in other parts of the
book, but the principle must be mentioned here. From the beginning of the
Railway Age to the present proliferation of car ownership, the use of transport
has become greater and more universal and in many ways the real cost has
fallen. This has led to a number of social consequences, such as increasing
length of journey to work, the separation of work and residence and the
availability of holidays for all. The first two will be referred to again in Chapter
10; the latter can be briefly dealt with here.

Excursions were run by the railways from their opening and allowed mass
movement to the seaside and for special occasions. On Easter Monday 1844 an
excursion train arrived at Brighton from London with 6 engines and 54
third-class carriages (White 1969: 18). The Great Exhibition of 1851 attracted
excursionists in their tens of thousands. By 1914 nearly the whole population
would visit the seaside at least once a year, and by 1939 a majority were taking
a period holiday. The development of air transport, especially in the form of
package tours after 1960, led to foreign holidays becoming ever more widely
available. In 1978 Sir Freddie Laker introduced his *Skytrain* between the UK
and the USA revolutionising the fare structure in favour of the tourist
(Fig. 6.1).

But the principal social consequences have stemmed from the spread of car
ownership (Fig. 6.2). In 1938 there were 1.9 m. cars registered in Great
Britain, one vehicle to 20 persons. By 1960 the number had grown to 5.5 m.,
one to 9 persons. By 1970 they had reached 11.5 m., one to 4.7 persons. At
present, car ownership per head is highest in the rural areas. The 1971 Census
revealed that there was one car to 3.5 persons in Montgomeryshire and one car
to 3.3 persons in neighbouring Radnorshire. It is in these areas that perhaps the
greatest changes have taken place in the quality of life. However remote their
dwellings, most people are now able to make regular visits to towns for
shopping and leisure, while longer journeys to work can be made, increasing

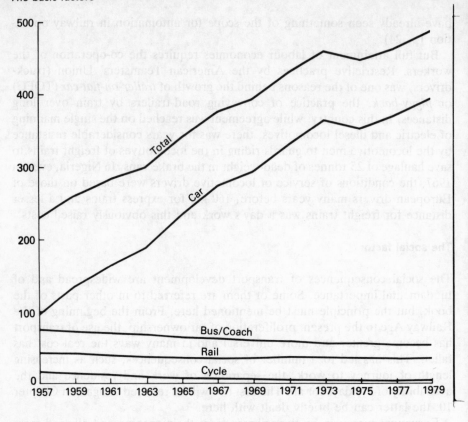

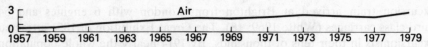

Fig. 6.1 Trends in passenger transport in Great Britain. Share of various modes of passenger-km. (*Source: Transport Statistics*, HMSO, *passim*)

the variety of employment available. A detailed example of rural change brought by transport will suffice. During the 1920s dairy farmers had to finish the morning milking by 06.00 hours so that churns could be taken to the railway station for despatch by early trains. Now the milk is collected from the farm (often by tankers) and milking often does not start until 09.00 hours. The life of the countryman is being brought closer to that of the townsman.

Levels of car ownership in the inner areas of large cities are lower than in the remoter countryside. In 1971 Bootle County Borough, in the inner area of Merseyside, had only one car to 9.8 persons, while Salford County Borough, occupying a similar position in Greater Manchester, had one to 10.0 persons, while in Bootle 68.9 per cent of the households had no car. In contrast, however, Hale Urban District, a commuter suburb of Manchester, had one car to 2.9 persons and only 28.7 per cent of the households were without a car. But in cities, too, vast changes have taken place, particularly in the journey to work. People have a much wider range of choice as to where they can live in

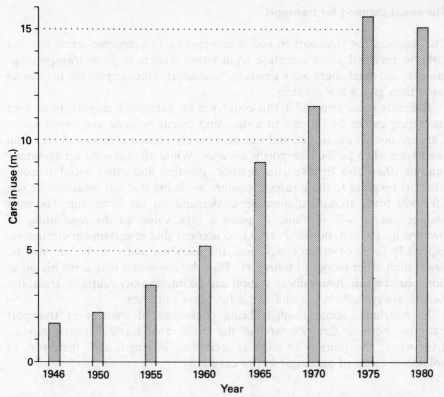

Fig. 6.2 Private cars registered in Great Britain. (*Source*: British Road Federation, *passim*)

relation to their work, or alternatively where they can find work without moving house. At the same time shopping habits are changing. Car ownership means wider choice of shopping centres, and there is a movement away from large town centres where parking is difficult, and from corner shops where choice is limited. Daily shopping is also giving way to twice-weekly visits. In addition, many more leisure journeys are being taken.

There are a number of social problems and costs which must be offset against the undoubted benefits of near-universal car ownership. The phenomenon of congestion in towns is well known and is dealt with in Chapter 12. But this is also now becoming serious at peak holiday times in rural areas such as the Lakes, the Peak District and other national parks. So many people visit the open space of Cannock Chase, on the edge of the West Midlands, that considerable vegetation changes are taking place, while great efforts must be made to prevent spoliation of the whole coastline (Patmore 1971). Atmospheric pollution from motor-vehicle exhausts has become a major problem in Californian cities and must increase in all large cities. Intrusion into their environment of the necessary roadways and noise pollution are also becoming problems. The social costs of road accidents are considerable. In 1971 for Great Britain they were quantified at £375 m.

The social demand for transport

The demand for transport in social as opposed to economic terms has not hitherto received much attention from either writers or from transport operators, and much more work needs to be done. It is thus impossible here to do more than give a few pointers.

The main social demand in this country is for personal transport, to an ever increasing extent by car and to a declining extent by cycle and motor cycle. Cars are not always owned and run on a purely economic basis and are often used even when public transport is cheaper. While often bought for economic reasons, they also involve convenience, prestige and other social reasons. There is no point in the transport planner assuming that any measures he can take will bring about a diminution of demand for car ownership. He must assume people will continue to place a high value on the *total utility* of ownership. He can, however, take into account that in certain circumstances, especially those of urban congestion, the *marginal utility* of the car may be lower than other modes of transport. Thus the commuter may leave his car at home or at a suburban railway station and go into the city centre by train, but he will always have a car and use it for other purposes.

To conclude, social changes bring consequential changes in transport patterns, both in direction and in the division of traffic between modes. Everywhere the journey to work is increasing in length and, therefore, in volume in terms of passenger-km or car-km.

Chapter 7
The morphology of transport modes

No observant student can travel far without becoming aware of how transport fits into the landscape; railway embankments across valleys and cuttings through high ground, the Humber and Forth bridges carrying roads across major estuaries, the canal meandering along the contour of a hillside, the ship-dotted Channel as seen from Dover cliffs. Where the landscape is a crowded urban one, transport becomes yet another competitor for scarce resources of land. Thus London Airport competes with housing, industry, agriculture and leisure activities for land on the overcrowded Thames terraces; 'spaghetti junction', the motorway interchange, occupies a large slice of inner Birmingham; and multi-storey car parks obtrude into town centres.

They will also become aware that the shape and form of the various transport modes differ in many ways. Roads are wider than railway lines, while the latter are characterised by passenger and freight stations located at intervals, where road and rail come into contact for purposes of interchange. Again, while ships and aircraft do not need continuous tracks, they do require extensive terminal facilities in the form of seaports and airports, which involve a large consumption of land.

The form or morphology of one transport mode differs from that of another because of the technological differences between them. The most obvious example is the basic difference in morphology between those modes which require a continuous infrastructure – roads, railways and canals – and those which require only discontinuous infrastructure at terminals – shipping and airways. Again, road freight haulage does not usually require terminal facilities, as most transits begin and end at factories, warehouses or shops, while railways, unless they lead straight into factory or mine, require elaborate terminal facilities for interchange between rail and road.

Within the modes themselves morphology also differs with the differing functions they are expected to perform in different geographical situations. Lightly trafficked rural lanes meandering between tall hedges are quite different in form from trunk motorways with separate carriageways, grade-separated crossings with other roads and limited access points. The form of the Southern Region railway at Clapham Junction, concentrating on the mass movement of suburban passengers and with multi-tracks and numerous junctions, is quite different from that of the single-track Miferma iron-ore railway across the Sahara Desert in Mauritania.

Form and function are thus closely linked in transport geography. As we have just seen, the morphology of a line of transport differs according to its function. The same is also true of a transport node. The form of a grass landing strip in the Australian outback differs from that of Kennedy Airport, New York, in aspects other than simple scale. It will lack the terminal buildings, maintenance hangars and navigation aids. It is also true of networks. The network of narrow roads with passing-places, which hitherto has served the needs of north-western Scotland, has a fundamentally different morphology than that of the motorway network of the English Midlands. The morphology of the London Underground railway system differs from that of the narrow-gauge system of Corsica.

Conversely, the function that a line, node or network is expected to perform must to a great extent depend on its morphology. Any significant change in function must therefore be accompanied by morphological change. The network of 'arterial' roads which grew up between the wars in Great Britain was adequate to perform the functions required of it during the 1930s, but with the rapid expansion of car and heavy lorry traffic after 1950 fundamental changes in the morphology of trunk roads had to be made. Single-carriageway, three-lane roads became death-traps and had to be converted to dual-carriageway roads, with the number of junctions reduced and the remaining ones modified. A good example of such a conversion is the A1, the main trunk road between London and Edinburgh. Similarly, the growth of containerisation of ships' cargoes has led to fundamental changes in the morphology of seaports (p. 150). The major British ports are now characterised by closed and derelict docks along the upper parts of the estuaries on which they stand and by new and busy container berths lower down.

The morphological approach to transport studies is thus a fundamental one. The morphology of a line, node or network has important consequences, not only on its function but on the amount of land consumed for a given level of traffic and on the environment generally. This in turn has implications for the cost of providing the level of service to match demand.

The study of transport morphology is therefore of importance, not only to the geographer but also to the economist, planner and engineer. For the geographer it is of special importance as it forms the link between the technology of the particular mode and the level of traffic on the one hand, and the relationship between the line or network and the terrain on the other. Those wishing to pursue the matter further are referred to the pioneer work in the field by J. H. Appleton (1965). But while this approach is immediately acceptable to geographers by virtue of their training, its significance has been to a great extent overlooked by economic planners and unrecognised as such by physical planners.

In recent years, however, there has been increased interest in the consequences of transport, among other activities, on the environment. It is becoming more widely recognised how land is being consumed by the effects of motorisation, motorways, multi-level junctions and parking areas. Yet the supply of urban land is one of the resources which must be regarded as fixed, and in most towns the supply of land in relation to demand is very limited. Nor are problems confined to urban areas. In recent years problems are arising from increasing pressure on the National Parks and Areas of Outstanding Natural Beauty. The dilemma is how to increase the capacity of the road network without altering its character and thus causing intrusion into the landscape. It is becoming increasingly clear that morphological as well as economic studies of transport must be used as a basis for planning decisions.

The morphology of transport modes

1. Roads

As we have just seen, there is a clear distinction between modes which require a continuous infrastructure and those which do not. Roads are in the former category. They take the form of a narrow and continuous corridor across land used for a variety of other purposes, though of course the uses to which that land is put will to a great extent depend on the possibility of access to a road.

The continuity of that corridor is all important, in the sense that right of passage along the corridor must be guaranteed. Permanent or temporary interruption at any one point renders the whole road useless for through traffic. In fact this is done deliberately on some urban roads. In Chester the Cross, where the four main city streets meet, was closed to cars, thus freeing the city centre from through traffic. Again, though the surface and light gradients of a motorway would make it ideal for cyclists, it is useless to them as access is prevented by law. Since 1945 the ability of the Russians and East Germans to delay autobahn traffic between West Germany and Berlin has been of great political nuisance value. The decay of the Roman road network in Britain was due as much to the breakdown of law and order as to lack of maintenance. On the other hand, with increasing size and sophistication of wheeled vehicles, the infrastructure itself must have no physical interruption. Pedestrians, cyclists and pack animals may negotiate a broken bridge, but not motor vehicles.

Road networks represent an adjustment to the physiography. The rural road network of the South Lincolnshire Fens takes the form of straight, parallel and fairly wide roads, which contrasts with that of the Midlands where it tends to consist of narrow, winding and hedge-bound lanes. But the relationship is not always a direct one. There is a clear contrast between the network in Central Wales and the Scottish Highlands on the one hand, where roads follow the valleys, and those of the High Weald of Kent and Sussex on the other, where they tend to follow the parallel ridges (Fig. 7.1). This is because in both cases

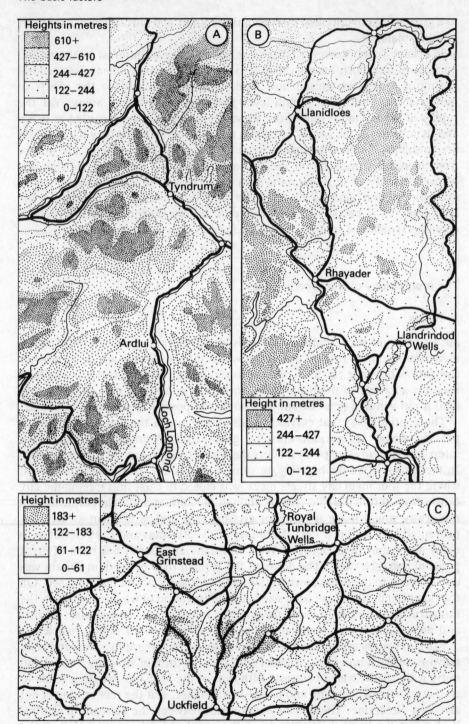

Fig. 7.1 Road patterns in upland areas: (a) The West Highlands; (b) Mid-Wales; (c) the High Weald (Kent and East Sussex)

the network evolved to serve the settlements. It is these which are controlled by the physiography, being in the valley bottoms in the first two areas and on the ridge tops in the Weald.

The density of the road net will depend on two main factors, the density of the settlement and the level of economic development. In a developed country such as the United Kingdom the network is 'universal'. Virtually every house, farm and industrial plant has access to it. There will therefore be a close relationship between the density of the network and the density of population. But we must distinguish between urban and rural areas. A rural road net will have a much greater length per 100 dwellings than will a suburban one. If the majority of rural dwellings are nucleated into villages a lower road mileage is required than if the same number of dwellings are widely scattered over the countryside, as they are over much of Northern Ireland.

In developing countries the network is by no means universal. Many villages and large areas of farmland are without access to roads of any kind. But again the density of the network is related to population distribution and level of development. In Nigeria the network is closest in the cocoa belt of the South-West where, comparatively, population is dense and the economy evolved. It is most open in the Middle Belt, where population is sparse and development very limited. But the network is only moderately closely meshed in the densely settled area of Hausaland in Northern Nigeria, where the economy is not highly developed.

The quality, as opposed to the density, of the network is also important. Quality in a road consists of width, curvature, gradient, visibility and surface. On the quality depends average speed, capacity, vehicle life and maximum size and weight of lorries. Two roads may be of the same width, but if one is straight and without fencing and the other with continuous curves and high hedges, average speeds and possibilities of overtaking will be greater on the former and in consequence its capacity will be greater. Unsurfaced roads increase maintenance costs and reduce vehicle life. Road widths and strength of bridges control size and weight of vehicles. It is the narrowest stretch and the weakest bridge which control size and weight over the whole length of road.

The British road network consists of some 336,000 km of public roads or 1 km to 155 persons. In 1978 there were 15.9 m. vehicles or 48 for each kilometre of road. But traffic densities vary very greatly, not only according to time of day but from road to road. Thirty per cent of the network carried only 2 per cent of the traffic, while 30 per cent carried over 80 per cent.

Terminal facilities are represented by every house with a garage, every industrial premise and every farm. They are also to some extent represented by the kerbside, for buses to pick up and set down, for lorries delivering to shops and for parking. But with the spread of car ownership, increasing attention must be paid to terminal facilities. Parking must be provided in town centres, at factories and railway stations, at entertainment centres such as football grounds and at rural beauty spots.

Motorways are characterised by traffic flows, fully segregated by direction, only the possibility of switching lanes remains. This is also achieved by dual carriageways, limited number of access points and grade separation from other roads. Because of this and because gradients, which may have a negligible effect on cars but will drastically reduce the speeds of heavy lorries, must be kept below 1 in 30, while to maintain high speeds curves must be of wide radius, these roads will require earthworks, viaducts and bridges on a scale at least equal to those found on a main line railway in similar country.

In open and level country a motorway with three lanes in each carriageway will need a continuous strip of land 39.62 m wide. The strip will be wider if on embankment or in cutting. Thus at least 39,000 sq m of land will be required per kilometre of route. For an ordinary intersection in the form of a grade-separated roundabout 8.3 ha are needed, while a full clover-leaf intersection between two motorways requires at least 24.2 ha.

The map (Fig. 7.2) shows the extent of the British motorway network on 30 June 1978. The planned extent is about 3,040 km, of which 1,630 km were then open and 320 km under construction. The main mileage is accounted for by the basic network of the M1, M4, M5 and M6. The Trans-Pennine M62 also forms an important trunk route. The rest consist of isolated sections through particularly congested areas, such as the M2 through North Kent, with a mainly holiday traffic flow, and the M8 through the Central Lowlands of Scotland. For the most part the motorways follow well-established corridors of movement between the principal cities and industrial areas. Beaver (Stamp & Beaver 1971: 709) has pointed to the resemblance between the maps of the motorway network in 1969 and that of the railway system in 1844.

Trunk roads vary greatly in quality. The A1 has been improved along almost its whole length, with virtually continuous dual carriageways, bypasses round major towns at motorway standard, and reduced access by minor side roads. The A74, which continues the M6 northward from the Border to Glasgow has been similarly improved. But on many trunk roads there are only short and discontinuous lengths of dual carriageway, there is no grade separation at intersections and there is usually access from all intersecting minor roads. In addition there is usually unlimited access from adjoining property. But more and more settlements are being bypassed. No particular effort is made to reduce gradients other than by the alignment of the road and therefore only moderate earthworks and minor engineering works are required.

Urban roads are dealt with more fully on page 122. Sufficient to mention here that the network is close meshed and intersections very numerous. The roads are generally continuously lined with buildings and access is virtually uncontrolled. However, planning measures over the last 20 years have resulted not only in the construction of urban motorways, but the limitation of access to other main roads. The width of the roads vary greatly, but unfortunately not necessarily in proportion to traffic densities. Many main roads are heavily congested, but widening is slow and costly, while in some suburbs lightly trafficked streets are often wide.

The network of secondary and minor rural roads has a much more open mesh. Though the roads are mostly narrow and winding, traffic densities are very low.

In the countries of Tropical Africa the morphology of the road network differs. The networks are more open and, as has been said, are by no means

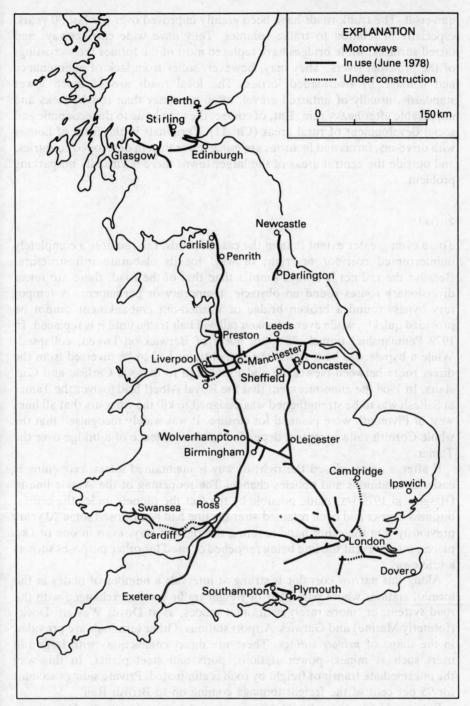

Fig. 7.2 The motorway network in Great Britain

universal. The trunk roads have been greatly improved over the last 30 years, especially in relation to traffic volumes. They have wide carriageways and tarred surfaces, while bridges have replaced most of the former ferry crossings of the principal rivers. They may, however, suffer from lack of maintenance and damage by overloaded lorries. The local roads are of much lower standards, usually of untarred gravel, often no better than rough tracks and impassable after heavy rain. But, of course, they are basic to the economic and social development of rural areas (Ch. 11). Terminals in the form of houses with drive-ins, farms and factories are much fewer than in developed countries, and outside the central areas of the larger towns there is virtually no parking problem.

2. Rail

To an even greater extent than in the case of roads, rail requires a completely uninterrupted corridor or 'right of way' for its elaborate infrastructure. Because the rail net is always simpler than that of the road, there are fewer diversionary routes round an obstacle, temporary or permanent. A temporary bypass round a broken bridge or washed-out embankment cannot be provided quickly, while even a broken rail will halt traffic until it is replaced. In 1979 Penmanshiel tunnel, 28.5 km north of Berwick-on-Tweed, collapsed. While a bypass was built round the tunnel trains had to be diverted from the direct route between Newcastle and Edinburgh to that via Carlisle and Carstairs. In 1968 the announcement that the Royal Albert bridge over the Tamar at Saltash was to be strengthened was designed to kill the rumours that all lines west of Plymouth were planned for closure. It was widely recognised that the whole Cornish railway system depended on the existence of a bridge over the Tamar.

If after a line is closed the right of way is maintained intact, reopening is easier if conditions and policies change. The reopening of the Argyle line in Glasgow in 1979 was made possible by the fact the tunnels under the central business district had been retained after the line had been closed some 20 years previously. On the other hand severing the right of way, even in one or two places, may prevent the line being reopened or used for other purposes such as a bridleway.

Along this narrow corridor is strung at intervals a number of nodes in the form of stations where passenger or freight traffic can be exchanged with the road system, or, more rarely with other modes, as at Dover Western Docks (formerly Marine) and Gatwick Airport stations. Other terminals are provided in the shape of *private sidings*. These are direct connections with large rail users such as mines, power stations, ports and steel plants. In this way the intermediate transit of freight by road is eliminated. Private sidings account for 95 per cent of the freight tonnage coming on to British Rail.

But in addition these nodes often carry out service functions. Depots are needed to maintain and service the locomotive and passenger coach fleets and marshalling yards needed to transfer wagons between freight trains. Freight terminals are tending to become more specialised with elaborate equipment for handling in bulk such commodities as cement, aggregates, petroleum products and coal.

The nodes may be very small. A wayside station may consist of no more than a loop to allow trains to pass on a single-track line, with a simple building to house the signalling equipment and houses for the staff, though to an increasing extent operation is carried out remotely from control centres many miles away. Stations such as this are to be found throughout the world, in Australia, Africa, South America, large areas of North America and parts of Europe. On the other hand the railway installations forming the central node of a large city or of a major junction such as Crewe will consume much land, though usually still in corridor form. To cite an example, the London Midland Region's terminal facilities on the West Coast main line into London extend discontinuously along the railway line for 13.0 km from the southern end of Euston station to the northern entrance to Willesden yard at Wembley Central station. Facilities include the passenger and parcels station at Euston, 7.2 ha, and the complex at Willesden which covers 83.3 ha. The latter includes marshalling yards, carriage sidings, motive power depot, the Freightliner terminal and specialised depots dealing with chemicals and with steel scrap.

Because of the need to reduce gradients and curvature, earthworks are heavy, especially if the terrain is at all irregular. The influence of physiography on route selection is dealt with in Chapter 4. But its influence on morphology can be illustrated by the 82 km line from London (Victoria) to Brighton. The route crosses the grain of the Weald, involving crossing a series of cuestas and intervening vales with a degree of relief of about 200 m. The North Downs cuesta is crossed by a long and deep cutting through the chalk leading to Merstham tunnel (1,674 m), while the Vale of Holmesdale is crossed on a long embankment leading to the short Redhill tunnel through the Lower Greensand Cuesta. The Weald Clay is traversed by a low but wide embankment carrying four tracks. The first ridge of the High Weald is pierced by the 1,042 m Balcombe tunnel, followed by the spectacular viaduct over the Ouse valley. Finally, the crossing of the South Downs is achieved by the Clayton tunnel (2,065 m) and the deep cutting to the south. Brighton station itself is built on an artificial terrace on the valley side, with the goods station below. The crossing of major estuaries has involved the building of bridges which have become monuments of Victorian engineering such as those across the Firths of Forth and Tay.

In urban areas the corridors of railway installations can cause barriers to movement, funnelling road routes on to relatively infrequent bridges. If the lines are on the same level, level-crossings lead to long delays, and costly replacement bridges have to be provided as at the Anlaby Road crossing in Hull. In many towns railway lines have come to act as boundaries of social areas; 'the wrong side of the tracks' is a well-known expression from North America. But in suburban and rural areas intrusion into the environment, both visual and aural, is normally less than with motorways or trunk roads.

A railway, in capacity terms, is also a lesser consumer of land than a road. A four-track railway requires 28,625 sq. m per km, 60 per cent less than that of a motorway. Such a line has a theoretical throughput capacity of 335,000 tonnes per 24 hours against that of 150,000 tonnes for the motorway. This represents a capacity tonne-km per square metre per day of 11.6 for the railway and 3.9 tonne-km per day for the motorway (Wilson 1967). A railway is also a smaller consumer of land in terms of passenger terminal facilities. When we compare the amount of land needed for a station with that needed for parking the cars of an equal number of persons to those using the station, we realise this is a very important consideration in cities.

In Great Britain, far more than in other countries, there has been a fundamental change in the morphology of the railway system since 1965 (Appleton 1967). Because of the withdrawal of rail transport from serving rural areas, the rail net has become much more simplified, with very few branches still left and even many secondary through routes closed. On the main lines, wayside stations have been closed for passengers and freight and the platforms and buildings demolished, signal-boxes have disappeared and sidings torn up (Figs 7.3, 7.4). On the West Coast main line between Bletchley and Carlisle, 403.3 km, only 15 stations remained open for passengers by 1980, while freight depots are equally few and far between. On the 118 km between Carlisle and Carstairs (junction for Edinburgh) only Lockerbie remained open. Correspondingly, on the East Coast main line the 377.6 km section between Hitchin and Newcastle had only 13 passenger stations. In contrast, the 1975 Swiss time-tables showed that the 121 km section of the Simplon main line in the Rhone Valley between Montreux and Brig had 29 intermediate passenger stations, 23 of them with freight facilities. In addition 5 had adjoining narrow-gauge branch terminals.

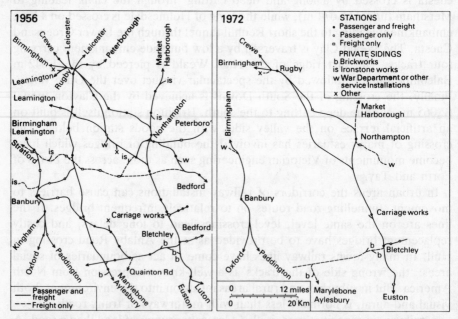

Fig. 7.3 Change in the rail network in a rural area (the South Midlands). Note: (i) virtual elimination of branch lines; (ii) almost total closure of passenger and freight stations on the main lines

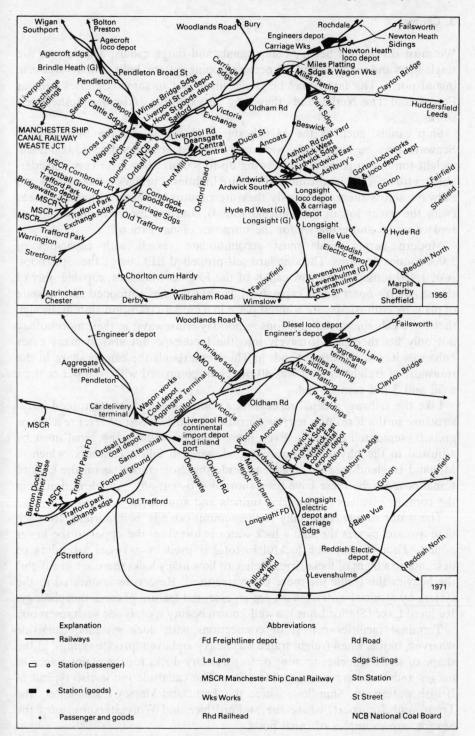

Fig. 7.4 Change in the rail net of an urban area (Central Manchester). Note: (i) some simplification through closure; (ii) retention of passenger stations; (iii) extensive closure of freight depots

3. Canals

We must distinguish between ship canals and barge canals. The former are single lines and really part of the ocean shipping system, built to allow access to inland ports. The latter may be single lines, but in some countries such as France and The Netherlands they may be extensive and close-meshed networks.

Ship canals, such as the Manchester Ship Canal and the St Lawrence Seaway, may be sufficiently wide and deep to accommodate 15,000-deadweight ton ocean-going ships drawing up to 8.0 m. They form very considerable features in the landscape and require high-level bridges to take roads and railways across them. Obviously they are only to be found in lowland areas (with the exception of the Panama Canal), and are used to supplement or replace rivers and estuaries for the purposes of navigation.

Modern barge canals must accommodate vessels with capacities of 1,000 tonnes or more. The standard self-propelled EEC barge the 'Spitzboot' is of 1,450 tons. The narrow canals of the English Midlands, capable only of taking *narrow boats* with a capacity of 25–30 tons, are outmoded and, in spite of plans by enthusiasts, are without place in a modern transport system, though they have valuable social functions as holiday cruiseways, as their morphology not only fits them unobtrusively into the landscape but also in many cases enhances it. On the other hand, in The Netherlands the canal's share in the transport of freight in 1977 was 40 per cent, compared with 56.0 per cent by road and 3 per cent by rail.

Like the railway, a canal represents a continuous and uninterrupted infrastructure in the form of a narrow corridor. It must consist of level reaches or *pounds*, separated by locks. Even more than the railway the canal must be adjusted to the physical features. Canals tend to follow contours, which in Midland England means constant meandering. Sometimes, as on the Oxford Canal near Rugby these have been shortened by cut-offs. Any deviation from the contour involves earthworks, tunnels and aqueducts.

The water supply, especially to the summit pounds, is important, for each time a vessel passes through a lock water is lost from the upper to the lower pound. Though only one lockful in total is used by a vessel ascending or descending a flight of locks, irrespective of how many locks there are in a flight, the heavier the traffic the more the water used. Reservoirs connected to the system by artificial watercourses are an essential feature of canal morphology. Rudyard Lake (Staffordshire), a well-known beauty spot, is one such reservoir.

Terminal facilities consist of connections with dock systems, canalside wharves, basins when freight traffic was heavy and even 'private sidings' in the shape of short branches to mine or factory. Dry-docks for the maintenance of barges and boats are occasional features. The canalside inn is also typical of British waterways. Shardlow, where the Trent and Mersey Canal enters the Trent, and Stourport, where the Staffordshire and Worcestershire joins the Severn, are examples of canal ports.

Inland waterways are of natural origin, rivers and lakes. Sometimes these can be converted into systems by the deepening of shallows and the provision of locks or by lengths of canal connecting one river basin to another. The Great Lakes system of North America, in which the lakes are interconnected by short canals and with the sea by the St Lawrence Seaway is the best-known example. This not only enables internal movement of bulk traffic such as iron ore and grain to be made by lakes vessels, but allows ocean shipping up to Chicago and other Great Lakes ports. In South Sweden there is a network of natural waterways connected by short lengths of canal.

4. Pipelines and power lines

Pipelines for the conveyance of water, petroleum, gas or slurry[1] can be buried and the land above used for agricultural and other purposes. They can also be laid along the continuous right of way occupied by a road or railway. Therefore they do not compete for land nor do they intrude into the environment. On the other hand, electricity must be transferred by overhead line on cost grounds. To lay high-tension cables underground is prohibitively costly. But while an overhead line is not particularly demanding of land, it represents a considerable intrusion into any landscape, urban or rural.

5. Seaports

Ocean shipping obviously has no continuous infrastructure, with the exception of short lengths of canal connecting oceans and seas, such as the Suez Canal, or with inland ports, such as the IJmuiden Canal connecting the North Sea with Amsterdam. Ships do, however, require elaborate terminal facilities in the form of seaports (Bird 1971).

The morphology of a seaport can clearly be divided into three aspects, the features pertaining to:
(a) seaward approaches;
(b) landward approaches;
(c) the quays where they meet.

The seaward approaches to the port may be up an estuary or river, which may be improved in some way, or even along a canal. If the port is on an open stretch of coast there will be a need for harbour works to protect the ships in port. The port of Dover can be operated intensively throughout the year only because the exposed waters of Dover Bay have been enclosed by the three massive moles of the Admiralty Harbour, completed in 1909. These shelter 243 ha of water, allowing ferries to tie up beside the Western Docks station or at the six roll-on-roll-off berths in the Eastern Docks, train ferries to enter the special dock, cargo vessels to enter the commercial docks and hovercraft to leave the water on to the terminal apron. Where the tidal range is great, as in the Thames and the Bristol Channel where it exceeds 7.5 m, the ships must be berthed in enclosed wet-docks entered through very large locks. This is to provide sufficient depth of water to float the ships whatever the stage of the tide outside.

The landward approaches include the roads, including the motorways, and the railways which connect the port with its hinterland. The port may also be the terminus of a canal system, as are Dunkirk and Antwerp. The roads and railways must be provided with terminal facilities in the form of parking space and marshalling yards.

The equipment on the quays depends on their purpose. If they are for general cargo, transit sheds and quayside cranes are needed. A container berth (pp. 149 *et seq*) needs one or two very large cranes (portainers) and a stacking area for the containers which should have an area equal to the length of the berth by three times that length. Thus a 200 m berth will need a stacking area of 120,000 sq. m. There must also be a Freightliner-type terminal with travelling portainers to load and unload lorries and trains. A roll-on-roll-off berth needs a ramp to allow vehicles to be driven on and off the ship. Specialised equipment is needed at berths where cargoes such as grain, ores and petroleum are handled in bulk.

Many ports serve as foci of industries depending on imported raw materials. Such activities as oil-refining, steel production, flour-milling and sugar-refining are frequently associated with ports. The port and the shipping using it are also employers of labour, quite apart from associated industries such as ship-repairing and victualling, and most ports are associated with towns. Exceptions, such as Immingham, which depends on labour from Grimsby, are few.

6. Airports

Like ocean shipping, air transport needs terminal facilities in the shape of airports. In a few cases the landing-strip may be a natural feature, such as the beach at Barra in the Hebrides. In others it may be no more than a strip of earth or grass. But if the traffic is heavy and the aircraft large, long runways and extensive taxiways are needed. These must be of thick layers of concrete and tarmac to support the weights of loaded aircraft. The runway at Manchester (Ringway) with about 4 m. passengers in 1980, was 2,805 m. At the time of writing this was being extended to 3,048 m across the valley of the River Bollin, incised into the Cheshire Plain.

The capacity of a runway is 32 movements (landing and/or taking off) per hour. If this is to be exceeded a second parallel runway is needed at least 400 m away. London (Heathrow) occupies 777 ha.

An airport needs a large area of flat land on the suburban fringe of a city which is already subject to pressures from competitive land uses. As with seaports the approaches from the hinterland must be adequate. A good road or motorway access must be provided, or if the traffic is very heavy a railway line, such as at Amsterdam, Zurich and Heathrow. There must also be adequate parking, both short-term for people meeting passengers and long-term for those travelling. There must be ranges of terminal buildings for passengers and for cargo. Accommodation for air traffic control, for telecommunications and for meteorological services, together with large hangars for maintaining the aircraft are also needed. An airport is also a large creator of jobs. Employment at Heathrow is of the order of 54,000 and at Ringway 5,000.

Because of the morphological characteristics of an airport, its location must be a matter of compromise. There can be no ideal location (Sealy 1966). From the operating viewpoint there must be a considerable area of level, low-cost land free from buildings and other physical obstructions and from fog and smoke. In addition there is a requirement for a *public safety zone* beyond the airport perimeter and under the *glidepath*. Within this buildings must be low and preferably warehouses with low employment characteristics rather than factories, while houses and schools should not be allowed. An airport is also a source of noise pollution. In other words the most suitable site is as far away from the city centre as possible. On the other hand, from the commercial viewpoint the nearer the city centre the better, in order to reduce as far as possible the time spent in getting to and from the airport.

With the development of hovercraft services a new type of terminal is needed. One such has been built at Pegwell Bay in East Kent. Here is a wide, open bay with some measure of protection from the worst Channel waves, but which virtually dries out at low tide. The terminal itself consists of a concrete apron, which can be approached by the hovercraft at all stages of the tide, together with the usual appurtenances of a small airport: range of terminal buildings, car-parking area and approach road.

Note

1. A solid, such as coal, reduced to powder and suspended in water.

Part II

Locational studies

Chapter 8
Transport and the location of economic activity

The study of location by using the concept of the spatial variable is a particular contribution of geography to the analysis and further understanding of socio-economic activities (Chisholm 1970). Hence, while in the first part of this book we started by considering what was the basic function of transport and what was the nature of the demand for the fundamental service industry, these are now brought together in a series of case studies. These will take the form of examining the connection between transport and the location of various human activities.

Economic activity includes:
(a) manufacturing industry;
(b) primary activities such as agriculture and mining;
(c) the provision of services.

The connection between economic activity and the transport facilities available is a two-way one: on the one hand the existence of economic activities will generate a demand for transport; on the other hand the provision of transport facilities will affect the level and nature of economic activity.

The existence of economic activity will create a demand for transport, which will result in the establishment of transport facilities and in the improvement of existing ones. Thus the two centres of population and of commercial and industrial activity, London and Birmingham, created a demand for transport to close the 179 km gap between them. By 1805 there was direct canal connection in addition to a turnpike road, and in 1838 a trunk railway was opened between them. In 1961 the M1 was opened, the first long stretch of motorway in the country, and in 1967 the railway was electrified.

In the same way the demand for transport between the industrial areas of South Lancashire and West Yorkshire have led to transport developments across the intervening Pennines. The first stage was represented by the three canals (no longer in commercial use), the Leeds and Liverpool, the Rochdale and the Huddersfield. In the second stage two railways were built along the same routes as the two last-named, together with two lines further south connecting Manchester and Sheffield. Three of these railways still function as through routes. The fourth, via Woodhead, was electrified in 1954, but closed in 1981 as coal traffic declined. In the third stage the seven road crossings have been greatly improved since 1930 in a piecemeal fashion, but not enough to keep pace with the increasing numbers of lorries which have been using them since 1955. This led to the fourth stage, the building of the M62, opened in 1971.

Demand from coalfields has led to the development of railway systems to service them, varying in complexity with the size of the field and the number of collieries. One such example is the railway system in the area between Nottingham and Doncaster, where many of the lines were built in response to the development of the *concealed* coalfield after 1900 (Appleton, 1956). Another example is the system in South Wales, built to meet the demand from the coal and the iron industry. It showed a particularly close adjustment to the physical structure of the deeply incised valleys. In some cases two and even three competing lines were forced to use the same narrow valley. But the system has contracted considerably with the decline in the number of collieries and ironworks. As an agricultural example we can cite the closely meshed railway systems of the Canadian prairies and of north-western Victoria in Australia, both created in the early 1900s largely to transport the wheat crop.

The vigorous suburban development of Greater London after 1920 created a demand for mass suburban transport into Central London. South of the Thames a railway system already existed and was electrified by the Southern Railway. North of the river the infrastructure was inadequate and the demand was met by new construction, extending the Underground system (as it is still popularly known, in spite of most of the extensions being on the surface!). Tourism in the Swiss Alps led to the building of a mixed transport system of roads, railways, funiculars and cable lines in a very mountainous area.

As an example of the way in which existing lines of transport will affect the siting of new industrial plants (and new service industries) the *super power stations* built in the North Midlands since 1965 are considered (Fig. 8.1). Apart from the availability of suitable land, there are three constraints on their location. The first is the need to minimise transmission costs, viewed in terms of the total cost of transferring power in the form of coal and of electricity. It costs less to transmit electricity by power line than coal by rail. So the stations were located as near as possible to the collieries. Secondly, there is the need for vast quantities of cooling water, so stations were sited along the River Trent. The third is the existence of a railway connecting the river with the collieries and capable of transporting some 5 m. tonnes of coal per year to each station. The stations were therefore located along the Trent where there are railway crossings, at Rugeley, Drakelow (Burton-on-Trent), Ratcliffe-on-Soar, Cottam and West Burton (White 1979b).

It must be remembered that the facilities offered by a line of communication are not static. Advances in technology lead to cost changes and therefore to changes in location. It is not usual for an existing plant to be moved in response to this (it is always easier to stay put), though the Dowlais steel plant on the coast at Cardiff, 35 km from the inland town of that name, reminds us this can

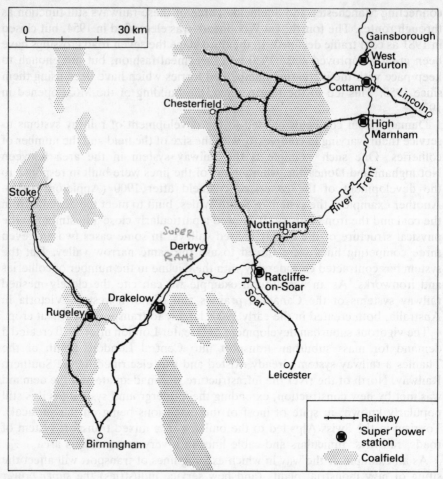

Fig. 8.1 The site of 'super power stations' in the Trent Valley

happen. Rather, new plants are built in different locations and the old ones eventually phased out. With the reduction in unit cost made possible by bulk carriers, ore can be imported at lower cost to Western Europe than it can be provided from local fields. Thus the bulk of the South Wales steel-making capacity is concentrated on the two plants at Port Talbot and Llanwern, whereas a century before the plants were located at the heads of the valleys. In turn the siting of one major plant at Port Talbot led to the improvement of that port to accommodate larger ore ships. Steel-making is also being concentrated at Scunthorpe (Humberside), where ore can be imported through nearby Immingham (p. 148).

Transport and theories of location

The pattern of economic activity is an uneven one. We find that manufacturing industry is highly concentrated in some areas, while in other areas it is poorly represented or completely absent. In some areas agriculture is intensive and specialises in the production of high-value fruit and vegetable crops, while in others it is extensive, specialising in grain crops. In other parts pastoral activities dominate. Service activities such as wholesaling and banking are often highly concentrated.

The factors underlying these variations in the distribution of economic activity are of course numerous. Among them transport is important, but it is by no means the only factor, or even the dominant one. There can be no mining industry if there are no minerals present. But on the other hand mineral deposits have remained unworked in the absence of adequate transport facilities. Again, the physical factors of climate, soils and slope will limit the range of crops and livestock available to the farmers of a particular area. But the level of the transport facilities connecting that area with the market may further restrict the choice open to the farmers. The existence of manufacturing industry in a particular place may depend on the availability of capital and of labour skills. But it also depends on the availability of transport for the assembly of raw materials and the distribution of the finished products.

As we have already seen in Chapter 5, the availability and the level of transport facilities can usually be measured in terms of cost and price. In all economic activity the total cost of all the transport operations involved in assembling raw materials (and energy) and distributing finished products (or of making services available) in relation to the final price paid by the consumer for the goods (or services) will have a very important effect on the location of the particular activity. It might be said that *other factors being equal*, the activity will locate at the point where transport costs are minimal.

In trying to formulate theories to explain patterns of location, workers have had to take into account transport as a factor. In 1826 von Thünen published his *Isolated State*. His theories are well known to geographers and have been fully discussed elsewhere (Chisholm 1962; Tarrant 1974). His land-use model (which is therefore also one of agricultural activity) was one of concentric rings of land use around the central, isolated city (Fig. 8.2). They resulted from increasing distance, and therefore increasing transport costs. For von Thünen postulates a flat plain with uniform soil conditions, and all produce being transported by horse-drawn carts along radial roads into the city. Thus any points equidistant from the city will have equal production costs, lower than places further out and higher than places further in. But any improvement in transport facilities along any radial, for example a navigable river, will reduce transport costs from any point on the radial below those of any other point a similar distance along any other radial. This will tend to elongate the land-use zones, along the line of improved (and therefore lower-cost) transport.

A. Weber, writing in 1909, argued that industrial location was largely a matter of transport costs and that the best location is one which minimises transport costs, and therefore total costs. Weber has been criticised as emphasising the importance of transport costs at the expense of other costs making up total costs. Hoover (1948) developed Weber's arguments and suggested that total transfer costs, of which transport costs are a major element, are basic to location theory. However many recent writers, Chisholm

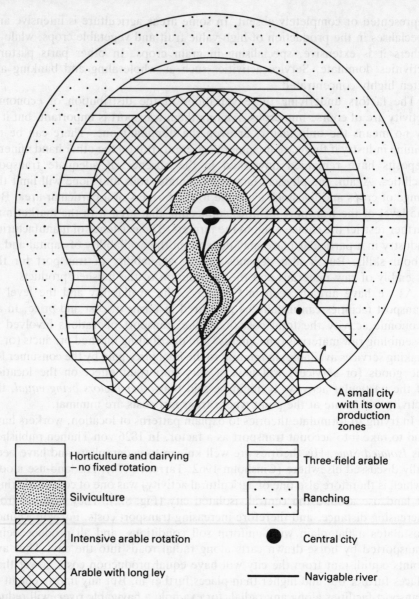

Horticulture and dairying
– no fixed rotation

Silviculture

Intensive arable rotation

Arable with long ley

Three-field arable

Ranching

Central city

Navigable river

A small city
with its own
production
zones

Fig. 8.2 Von Thünen's model of an 'isolated state'

(1970) among them, point out that other factors are often of greater importance. In any case the concept of optimum location may be of academic interest only. For example, in pursuit of their regional policy, government pressure applied to the expanding motor manufacturing industry in the 1950s enforced the building of new plants remote from existing ones instead of extensions to existing ones, increasing rather than decreasing transport costs. Again the underlying balance of causative factors may change during the life of a plant without bringing about any location change.

In the final costs of the products of various industries, in many cases the transport element is less than 5 per cent of total costs. Even if relocation reduced transport costs by 20 per cent, a very large amount, there would be no more than a 1 per cent change in total costs. On the other hand, in certain other industries transport costs loom large and in these transport costs are an important locational factor.

The functions of transport in manufacturing industry

But, while transport costs may frequently be an unimportant factor in relation to the specific location of a particular industry or other economic activity, nevertheless the transport industry almost invariably looms large in the day-to-day management of the activity.

The functions of transport in its service to manufacturing industry may be regarded as threefold:
(a) the assembly of raw materials;
(b) the transfer of semi-finished products between plants when all the manu- facturing operations are not concentrated in a single plant;
(c) the distribution of the finished products.

The motor-vehicle industry of the West Midlands can be used as an example of all three functions. The large assembly plants located in Birmingham and Coventry depend on component plants scattered throughout the region. These in turn depend for their supplies of semi-finished materials such as nuts, bolts and tubes on numerous small metal-working plants. There is now no longer a primary steel plant in the West Midlands and raw materials, steel sheet in coil, steel bars and non-ferrous metals are concentrated on the region by numer- ous lorries and block-trains arriving from all parts of the country (Fig. 8.3). Before the block-trains were started in 1965 individual wagon-loads of steel were delivered to 150 stations and sidings for onward road delivery, a slow and costly process which was losing traffic to road hauliers. The number of terminals has been reduced to 5, steel being delivered to them by about 14 trains a day.

Transfer between plants is normally by lorry. These movements are very numerous and require careful planning. Capital and plant are saved by reducing or eliminating stocks at the receiving factory, so regular and punctual deliveries are needed to create a steady flow of small quantities. Here the flexibility of road haulage is exploited to its best advantage. Origins and destinations are very numerous, and speed, frequency and punctuality are all vital. Many firms operate their own lorry fleets in order to keep full control over the scheduling. Others use – in addition or instead – either British Road Services or private hauliers under contract. If the flow is sufficiently heavy to be moved by the train-load and if the originating and receiving plants both are rail connected, rail can be used even for very short distances. Steel bars are conveyed by the trainload over the 16 km between Round Oak Steelworks and Tube Investments' new tube mill.

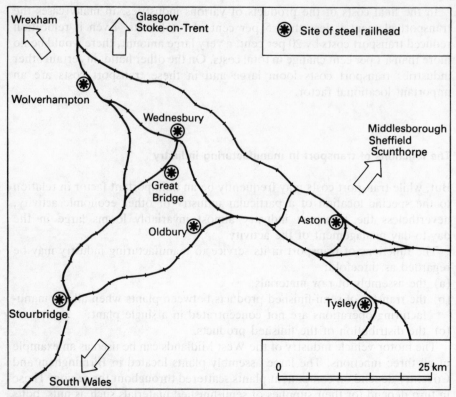

Fig. 8.3 Steel railheads in the West Midlands – 1971

The finished vehicles are distributed on their own wheels, by road transporter and by rail. In general, the means used depends on the distance to the delivery point and the volume of traffic. It was only from the middle 1960s that a significant proportion of cars were distributed by rail, following the establishment of specialised terminals in the Birmingham area at King's Norton and Dorridge. These are also used to import vehicles into the area.

Transport and heavy industry

1. Petroleum refining in the UK

In 1938 imports of petroleum products amounted to 18 m. tonnes. Refinery capacity was very limited (1.9 m. tonnes) and the country was almost wholly dependent on the import of refined products. After the war priority was given to investment in the refining industry and the associated petrochemical industries. Until the oil crisis of 1974 demand for petroleum products constantly expanded and therefore existing plants were enlarged and new ones brought on stream. By 1972 there were 16 large plants established with a combined capacity of 123 m. tonnes a year (Fig. 8.4). In that year 105.6 m. tonnes of

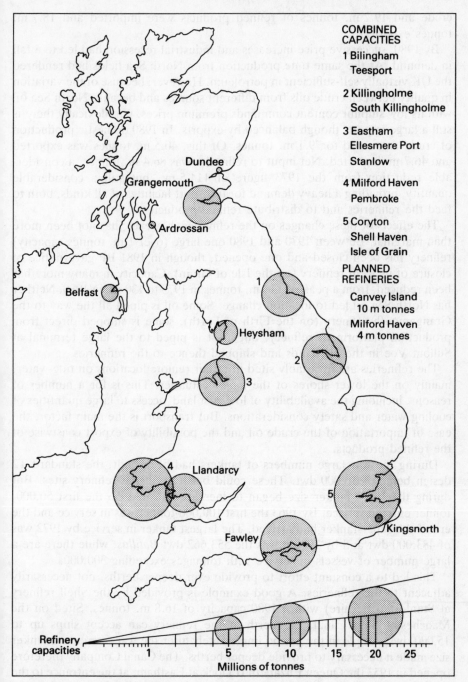

COMBINED CAPACITIES

1 Bilingham
  Teesport

2 Killingholme
  South Killingholme

3 Eastham
  Ellesmere Port
  Stanlow

4 Milford Haven
  Pembroke

5 Coryton
  Shell Haven
  Isle of Grain

PLANNED REFINERIES

Canvey Island
10 m tonnes

Milford Haven
4 m tonnes

Fig. 8.4 Petroleum refineries in the UK, 1976. (Source: Petroleum Information Bureau statistics)

crude and 19.2 m. tonnes of refined products were imported and 18.7 m. tonnes exported.

By 1980, successive price increases and industrial recession had led to a fall in demand. At the same time production from North Sea fields had rendered the UK virtually self-sufficient in petroleum. However, because of the variation in quality between crude oils from different sources and because North Sea oil with its low sulphur content commands premium prices, paradoxically there is still a large import, though balanced by exports. In 1980 domestic production of crude amounted to 79.1 m. tonnes. Of this, 40.5 m. tonnes was exported and 46.7 m. imported. Net input to refineries was 86.4 m. tonnes, a considerable reduction from the 1973 figure of 114.5 m., but still a considerable quantity, providing a heavy demand for transport facilities of all kinds, both to feed the refineries and to distribute refined products.

The effects of these changes on the refineries, however, has not been more than marginal. Between 1970 and 1980 one large (over 1 m. tonnes capacity) refinery has been closed and one opened, though in 1981 BP gave notice of closure of its Kent refinery (on the Isle of Grain). Capacity in many more has been reduced, from a peak of 148 m. tonnes in 1975 to 130 m. in 1980. Neither has North Sea oil led to location change. Some oil is piped all the way to the Grangemouth refinery (on the Firth of Forth), some is shipped direct from production platform to refinery, but most is piped to the large terminal at Sullom Voe in the Shetlands and shipped thence to the refineries.

The refineries are invariably sited in rather remote locations on tide-water, mainly on the lower shores of the major estuaries. This is for a number of reasons, including the availability of low-cost land, access to large quantities of cooling water and safety considerations. But transport is the main factor, the ease of importation of the crude oil and the possibility of export coastwise of the refined products.

During the war large numbers of tankers had been built, the standard T2 design being of 16,000 dwt. These could berth at all the refinery sites. But during the 1950s tanker size began to increase and in 1956 the first 50,000-tonner entered service. By 1963 the first 100,000-tonner was in service and the era of the super-tanker had arrived. The largest tanker in service by 1972 was of 483,000 dwt and by 1980 it was the 553,662 dwt *Batillus*, while there are a large number of vessels in service with tonnages exceeding 300,000.

This led to a constant effort to provide ever deeper berths, not necessarily adjacent to the refineries. A good example is provided by the Shell refinery at Stanlow (Cheshire) with a 1980 capacity of 16.8 m. tonnes. Sited on the Manchester Ship Canal, the berth at the refinery can accept ships up to 15,000 dwt. Ample in the period immediately after the war, increasing tanker size made it necessary to provide deeper berths. The Canal Company therefore opened in 1953 the Queen Elizabeth II Dock at Eastham, at the entrance to the canal, in order to take vessels up to 50,000 dwt. But even as it was opened it was really too small. Shell therefore opened a terminal at Tranmere (Birkenhead) in 1960 to accommodate 80,000-tonners. In 1970 this was enlarged to take a 100,000-tonner. But larger vessels of up to 250,000 dwt had to discharge some of their cargo into smaller vessels out in Liverpool Bay before they could enter the Mersey. A terminal was therefore opened in 1978 at Amlwch (Anglesey) to accommodate ships up to 500,000 dwt. In essence this consists of a single-buoy mooring in over 37 m of water and connected by pipeline first with a tank-farm and thence to Stanlow refinery. Thus the point of unloading has been moved 123 km downstream from the refinery.

In 1967 the only ports in the country capable of accepting 150,000 dwt tankers were Finnart, on the Clyde Estuary, and Milford Haven. Finnart can now (1980) accept ships of 326,000 dwt, while a dredging programme at Milford Haven was completed in 1970 and 270,000-tonners can now enter. Vessels of 150,000 dwt can be accepted at Fawley on Southampton Water and at Grain and Thameshaven on the Thames. It is therefore necessary in many cases to follow the practice described for Tranmere, i.e. partially to unload very large tankers into smaller ones to allow them to berth and discharge the remainder of their cargo.

Nowadays refineries in the UK are sited more for reasons of availability of low-cost land and considerations of safety and pollution than for estuarine locations for ease of import. In addition, expansion of existing sites is less costly than the building of new plants on new sites.

The refined products include both petrol and diesel fuel (DERV). These are conveyed in bulk to regional depots, from whence they are distributed by road tankers to filling stations and to the private pumps of large fleet owners such as bus companies. They also include feedstocks for petrochemical plants. If these are not immediately adjacent to the refineries (as they often are), the feedstocks must be transported in bulk. Finally, there are the residual fuel oils which must be transported in bulk to power stations and industrial plants or to regional depots for delivery as heating oil to houses, schools and factories. Bitumen is also delivered for application to roads. The finished products of the chemical plants must also be delivered. For the most part these form raw materials for further processing. Sometimes they can be distributed in bulk, but mostly this is in smaller consignments by the lorry load.

The distribution patterns of petroleum products are therefore very complex. There are numerous points of origin, even more intermediate depots, while final destinations are numbered in tens of thousands. The tendency, however, is to transport in bulk whenever possible, either to final destination or to intermediate depot. One example of the latter is the Shell-BP terminal at Haydock, Lancashire, opened in 1969. This had a throughput of 2.0 m. tonnes a year. The lighter products were received by a 41.6 km pipeline from Stanlow refinery, the heavy oils by rail in three trains from Heysham and two from Stanlow daily. Distribution was by road tanker within an area bounded by the Mersey to the south, the Pennines to the east and a line from Fleetwood to Skipton in the north. For this purpose the position of the depot at the junction of the M6 and the East Lancs Road is excellent.

Over the country as a whole a wide variety of modes is employed for the distribution of petroleum products. Local delivery from refinery or depot is by road tanker and these fleets are now very large. They are often owned and operated by hauliers on contract to the oil companies, though painted in the latter's liveries. But road does not provide sufficient economies of scale for trunk movement, which is by other modes. Up to the 1960s the main method was by coastal tanker, which still remains very important. For example in 1968, of the three refineries at Milford Haven, Texaco shipped 100 per cent of its production, Esso shipped 95 per cent and railed 5 per cent, and Gulf shipped 75 per cent and railed 25 per cent (Watts 1970).

The refineries ship the products for eventual retail sale to depots located as far inland as possible. These may be located in ports with a general traffic, but many are small and otherwise unimportant. They include Shoreham (Sussex), Faversham (Kent), Felixstowe (Suffolk), King's Lynn (Norfolk) and Preston (Lancs). Coastal power stations such as those at Plymouth and at Ballylumford in Northern Ireland are also served in this way. Tankers of 500 tons are also used to convey products from Killingholme refinery on the Humber up the Aire and Calder Canal to a depot at Leeds.

Transport by pipeline has, however, expanded considerably in recent years. Crude oil pipelines connect deep-water terminals with refineries. The first was from Finnart on the Clyde Estuary to Grangemouth, opened in 1951 (Foster 1969). Others connect Milford Haven with Llandarcy refinery and Tranmere with Stanlow and Heysham. Chemical feedstocks are conveyed in this way from Fawley refinery to the ICI complex on Severnside, and between refineries and chemical plants along a line from Billingham-on-Tees to Stanlow (see Fig. 3.2). Product pipelines are also in use to connect refineries and distribution depots. The main trunk connects Thames-side refineries with those on the Mersey, with branches to depots at Northampton, Birmingham and Uttoxeter.

In recent years, too, rail has increased its carryings from 4.8 m. tonnes (13.1% of consumption) in 1963 to 15.0 m. (18.8% of consumption) in 1968. In 1979 16 m. tonnes were carried, 10 per cent of total BR freight carryings. The reason is twofold. Technological advance in tank-wagon design has achieved a very high payload/tare ratio, while operating methods through the use of block-trains with short turn-rounds lead to intensive utilisation of equipment. The second is that the heavier products, fuel oils and bitumen, which account for about 47 per cent of consumption, cannot be pumped through a pipeline, but must be carried in steam-heated wagons to remain sufficiently viscous to be off-loaded. Rail is therefore used to transport the heavier products and to supply all products to depots, power stations, gas-works and factories where flows are insufficient to justify a pipeline.

The products from chemical plants are mostly transported by lorry to other factories. Often the products may be in liquid, powder or pellet form and can be carried in tankers. The Partington plant of Shell Chemicals receives its naphtha feedstock by pipeline from Stanlow. Propylene comes by rail from Baglan Bay (Port Talbot). By-products include ethylene and other high-grade spirits, which are returned to Stanlow by tanker down the Manchester Ship Canal. The other products, such as polystyrenes, are delivered to plastics factories by lorry. If flows are of sufficient volume, rail transport becomes economic. Ammonia produced from oil is railed in trains of 500 tonnes payload from Billingham-on-Tees, Ince (Cheshire), Severnside and Thameshaven to fertiliser and man-made fibre plants. About 750,000 tonnes of bagged fertiliser is produced at the Shellstar plant at Ince (adjacent to Stanlow). This is distributed to 24 depots, located throughout the country from Stirling in the north to Horsham in the south. Six of these are served by road from Ince, the other 18 are rail connected and are served by block-trains.

2. The UK cement industry

Cement is a bulky commodity of low value in proportion to its weight. Its raw materials, pure limestone and clay, are comparatively restricted in occurrence and considerable quantities of fuel are needed during manufacture. On the other hand it is a vital material with a nation-wide market in the building, civil engineering and road-making industries. Transport and transport costs loom large in its manufacture and distribution.

In 1966 16.5 m. tonnes were produced from 47 plants in the UK. Most of these plants were located close to the sources of raw materials. The only exceptions were the plants at Rugby and Southam which were supplied by a 91.2 km slurry pipeline from chalk quarries near Dunstable, the adjoining quarries in the Jurassic limestone having become exhausted. Between 70 and 80 per cent of the production was distributed directly from the plants to the customers. The rest was transported in bulk to about 47 depots and distributed from there. Final distribution from plant or depot to customer was by lorry, of which about 3,000 were employed. Since 65 per cent was delivered in bulk to silos at pre-cast concrete plants, building sites, motorways and so on, the majority of the vehicles were pressure-discharge tankers. The other 35 per cent was delivered in bags.

Some 27 of the 47 plants were located on or near chalk outcrops, so much of the movement from plants to depots is from Thames-side, where there is a surplus, to depots in the Midlands and North. Otherwise the movement is from plant to large cities. In 1968 (Grimshaw 1972) two depots were wholly and one partly supplied by road from works between 32 and 48 km away. Depots at Leith and in the Isle of Wight were supplied by seaborne transport from Thames-side. The majority of the depots were supplied by rail, which expanded its carryings from 1.99 m. long tons in 1963 to 3.35 m. in 1967. Cement was now carried in a variety of specialised bulk-wagons with payloads of up to 78.5 tonnes. The longest regular run was from Cliffe (Kent) to Uddingston (Strathclyde).

The position in 1971, mapped by P. N. Grimshaw (Fig. 8.5) shows little change in the three years since 1968, except that the regular long-distance flows from Cliffe to Uddingston had been superseded with the development of the Dunbar plant, though occasional specials are still run. Bulk carrying methods have meant that rail can now successfully compete with coastal shipping on long hauls and with road on short hauls. The Northenden (Manchester) depot is now rail-fed from Hope (Derbyshire), a 36.4 km haul.

As in other heavy industries, economies of scale can be obtained from large plants. This has implications for transport. In 1970 a new cement-manufacturing plant was inaugurated at Northfleet (Kent). This has a capacity of 4.0 m. tonnes a year and replaces the other A.P.C.M plants in North Kent.

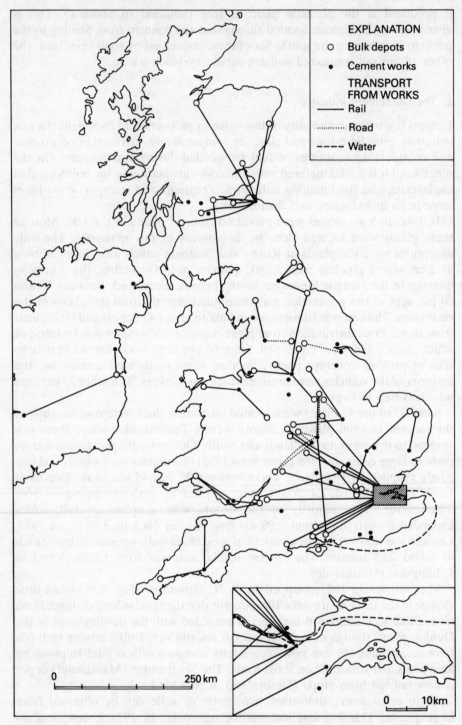

Fig. 8.5 Bulk cement movement in the British Isles, 1971. (Mapped by P. N. Grimshaw)

Clay is brought by an 11.2 km pipeline under the Thames from Ockenden in South Essex to Swanscombe on the Kent bank, mixed with chalk and pumped a further 4.8 km to Northfleet. About 1.0 m. tonnes of coal is brought in by 28 block-trains a week from East Midland collieries. Each train has a payload of 1,264 tonnes. Some 240,000 tonnes of gypsum comes in 9 trains a week (each with a 660-tonne payload) from the Mountfield gypsum mine near Hastings. In the outward direction up to 1.4 m. tonnes of cement is railed annually in 60 trains a week to distribution depots. The other 2.6 m. tonnes is for local distribution by bulk-lorry.

It will be seen that when the plant is in full production 97 loaded trains weekly are needed. Since these are of specialised wagons a balancing number of empty trains are needed. Thus 194 freight trains a week to and from the plant must be run on a line which already has an intense passenger service with an off-peak frequency of 6 trains an hour and a heavy freight service to and from industrial plants and freight depots. In addition about 400 loaded lorries will be despatched daily, coming on to the already very overcrowded roads of North Kent.

To bring the story up to date. Cement production in 1980 was nearly 15 m. tonnes, the decline being due to a major recession in the building industry. But this has not led to any major changes as far as transport is concerned. No major plants have been closed, but a number of rail-fed depots have been opened and others enlarged, subsidised under Section 8 of the 1974 Transport Act, under which assistance towards the cost of private sidings is given. Depots have been established at Middlesbrough, Gateshead, Carlisle and Bangor, while an existing depot at Coatbridge has been enlarged.

The proportion of the output conveyed by rail as far as the trunk haul is concerned remains constant. In 1979, 0.75 m. tonnes of cement was railed from the Dunbar plant, 75 per cent of the output. Daily trains were run to six distribution depots throughout Scotland, at Inverness, Aberdeen, Dundee, Grangemouth, Uddingston and Irvine. Local distribution to Edinburgh and south-eastern Scotland is by road.

Transport and light industry

One of the main features of British industry over the last 50 years has been the growth of light industry (Estall & Buchanan 1966). These industries are characterised by smaller inputs of raw materials and energy in relation to the output of finished goods, whether measured in terms of value or volume. The demand for transport by each individual plant is less than that by plants of heavy industry. They tend to be smaller, while the volume of raw materials and finished products are less. Power is normally supplied by electricity and gas from the mains. But light industry is now such an important sector of British industry, it is so widespread and plants are so numerous that the total demand is large. Again, transport costs tend to be a much smaller proportion of the costs of the finished product to the consumer than they are in the total costs of products from heavy industries. Location in relation to supply of raw materials and to markets is therefore of much less importance. Light industries are said to be *footloose*.

It is no coincidence that the period since 1920 which has seen the growth of light industry has also seen the establishment and growth of road haulage. Because of its inherent flexibility and its economic characteristics (p. 47) it is ideal for the handling of complex but small-scale traffic flows from a multitude of origins to an even greater multitude of destinations. Between 1953 and 1968 carryings by road haulage rose from 875 m. tonnes (31,320 m. tonne-km) to 1,550 m. tonnes (72,200 m. tonne-km). In 1965 £2,450 m. was spent on transporting goods by road, £284 m. on goods by rail and £60 m. by other forms of land transport (mainly pipelines).

Few geographical studies of road transport exist apart from the work of Chisholm and O'Sullivan (1973). The patterns are so complex and the data needed to construct those patterns so difficult to obtain, that geographical analysis is much more difficult than it is for transport for heavy industry. Particularly lacking are details of origins and destinations. It is of little use knowing how many lorries per day pass a check point without knowing where they come from, where they are going to and what they are carrying.

Many firms use their own vehicles for delivery from their industrial plants to other plants, the ports, distribution depots or to shops. Professional hauliers who perform the same function for the most part work on a small scale. In 1965 47.3 per cent of lorries were in fleets of 10 or less and only 20.8 per cent in fleets of 50 or above (Edwards & Bayliss 1971). Most haulage is short-distance and with a limited number of origins and destinations. Obviously most of the traffic is in and around the large conurbations and cities.

Some industrial firms have numerous plants and nation-wide operations. Unilever owns a subsidiary company called Speedy and Prompt Deliveries to operate its road-haulage operations. Lorries from SPD can be seen unloading goods in any high street. Other firms use public hauliers or rail for trunk movement between factory and distribution depots and their own vehicles for local distribution.

A random 1981 example of distribution methods, which vary greatly from firm to firm, is provided by a Merseyside firm producing cakes for a nation-wide market. Those cakes sold in Canterbury (Kent) are trunked by lorry to the Regional Distribution Centre at Southampton, conveyed thence to the Transit Depot at Swanley (Kent), from which cakes are distributed direct to retailers throughout Kent.

Transport and agricultural activities

The influence of transport on the distribution of agricultural activities and therefore on rural land use can be considerable. Before the advent of modern low-cost transport, farming was largely on a subsistence basis, for there were few opportunities for importing food or marketing surplus crops or animals. Dr Johnson's famous definition of oats as food for horses in England and men in Scotland reflects this point. The climate prevented wheat being grown over a large part of Scotland and the lack of low-cost transport prevented the importation of wheat from England.

With the provision of adequate road transport in even the remotest parts of the country, hill farmers could engage in the activities best suited to the restrictions imposed by the environment, the rearing of grass-fed livestock. In addition, after the mid-1930s, the Milk Marketing Board undertook milk collection from all farms able to produce it. This meant hill farmers now had a regular cash income in the shape of the monthly milk cheque. Food for the farmers and their families and any feeding-stuffs for stock could be bought in. Thus the upland areas of western Britain can specialise in the crop best suited to the environment, grass, and over large areas no other crop is now grown.

In the same way the development of road transport has had important consequences on the location of intensive crops such as high-value fruit and vegetables. When transport to market depended on rail or horse-drawn carts, intensive crops were mainly grown near large towns, such as in North-west Kent, or within reach of railway freight depots such as Wisbech (Cambs.) and Evesham (Worcs.) from which fast services to markets were organised. Dudley Stamp (1943) showed how market gardening spread over the fertile Thanet Sands east of Canterbury after 1920. The area was unserved by rail and too far from London for the produce to be carted. But it was well suited to market-garden crops, which could now be despatched to London by lorry. Best and Gasson (1966) considered that with the universal availability of road transport and the falling proportion of transport costs in the final cost of intensive crops, these crops are now grown on the land best suited to them instead of in areas with adequate transport facilities. In other words, the physical environment had once more become the dominant geographical factor instead of availability of transport.

Conclusion

The relationship between transport development and economic activity is of central importance in transport geography. Economic activity without transport may be possible on a subsistence or local exchange basis. But any economic progress will depend on the provision of transport facilities adequate for the level of economic development.

But in spite of this, transport has direct consequences on the actual location of economic activity in comparatively few cases. The provision of transport facilities does not automatically bring about optimum location from the transport viewpoint. This does not always occur, even in heavy industry in which transport costs are a high proportion of finished costs. On the other hand many major steel plants and oil refineries have been located in order to minimise transport costs, while the choice of crops made by many farmers has been influenced by transport factors. But in many cases the nature of economic activity and its location are due to factors other than those of transport.

But the lack of direct importance as a factor in location theory should not allow us to minimise the importance of the connection between transport and economic activity.

Chapter 9
The location of transport nodes

Any passenger journey or any shipment of freight involves a start and a finish to the transit. It also frequently involves a change from one mode of transport to another. In total these transits are very numerous. In a city of 500,000 inhabitants the number of transits involved in the journey to work will correspond with the number of people employed. The origins will be all the houses in which employed persons live and the destinations, the factories, offices, shops and all other places of work. Obviously analysis of traffic flows cannot include details of all individual origins, destinations and inter-modal transfers.

These must be grouped to produce meaningful generalisations and the size of these groups will be related to the scale of the study. If the last is one of journey to work in our hypothetical city, origins of journeys can be grouped into wards, census enumeration districts or similar small areas sometimes specially-defined sectors designed to suit transport-planning needs. On the other hand, if the study is of the hinterland of a major port, the individual export consignments must be grouped into larger areas, perhaps each town.

In some cases the transport operator is directly concerned with the origins and destinations of the transits. These would include owner-drivers and many road-hauliers. For other operators the transit will be regarded as starting from bus-stop, railway station or airport (or perhaps from the airline's town terminal). These terminals will not of course necessarily be terminals of the particular transport service. If a transatlantic flight is non-stop between London and New York the terminal points of all the passengers will naturally be those of the service. But for a stopping train from Victoria (London) to Brighton the former will be the originating point and Brighton the terminal point for some of the passengers. But each of the 22 intermediate stations at which the train calls may be both the originating and the terminating point of individual journeys.

Where two or more modes of transport meet, that is at all seaports, airports and at every railway passenger and goods station, exchange takes place. All these are therefore *transport nodes*, however simple. In addition nodes also exist where two or more lines of the same transport mode meet, railway junctions, bus stations and also seaports and airports. Many nodes belong to both these classes. Crewe passenger station is a junction where six rail passenger-carrying routes meet and many passengers change from one train to another, but many more will arrive at and leave from the station by car or bus or even on foot.

Thus, although we are inclined to think first of all of *lines* of transport, we cannot have even a single line without at least two *nodes*. Most single *lines*, a bus route or a rapid-transit railway line will have a number of nodes, for each intermediate bus-stop or railway station will be a node. Even the simplest *network* will have a large number. The study of transport nodes, their morphology and their location must be basic to the geography of transport.

The simplest example is a completely self-contained suburban or rapid-transit rail line with no branches. A suburban electric line connects Manchester (Victoria) with Bury (15.6 km), its trains shuttling between the terminals. The Glasgow Underground is a 10.4 km circle with trains following each other round the inner and outer lines. But even on such simple layouts there are as many nodes as there are stations, 10 on the Manchester line and 15 on the Glasgow one. Some of the nodes may have limited catchment areas, passengers walking to and from the station, as at Besses-o'-th'-Barn (Manchester) and Kinning Park (Glasgow). Others may be important purpose-built interchanges. The station at Bury is integrated with a large bus station and that at Partick (Glasgow) with the resited British Rail station.

At the other extreme is the complete transport system of a large city. On the national scale the city itself is a nodal point on the country's road, rail and air networks. But the node of the city itself will have a very large number of sub-nodes. These may include two or more railway passenger termini, together with a dozen or more suburban stations; several railway goods stations and a large number of road freight depots: a coach station and a central city bus station, together with a large number of junction points on that bus system and several hundred or even thousand bus-stops. Finally, the airport will be another transport node.

Having examined briefly the morphology of transport modes in Chapter 7, we will now examine the locational aspects of various types of nodes.

1. Seaports

The distinction between *harbour* and *port* functions was drawn on page 26, but in recent years *port terminals* have become of increasing importance. Whereas a port exists for interchange of traffic between land and sea transport, a port terminal is where seaborne traffic arrives for processing or consumption by industries situated at the port (Bird 1971). Milford Haven provides an excellent example. In terms of shipping tonnage entering the port, Milford Haven now ranks second only to London among British ports. But in 1978 over 99 per cent of the imports consisted of crude petroleum, which was processed at the three refineries on the shores of the Haven or piped 96 km to the Llandarcy refinery near Swansea. Similarly, over 99 per cent of outward cargoes were of refined petroleum products from the Haven refineries.

As we have seen, if there are few possibilities for trade, however good the harbour, port functions will remain unimportant. Milford Haven is one of the best natural harbours in the British Isles. But it is remote from any industrial area and, in spite of repeated efforts to develop it during the nineteenth century, it remained a very minor port. But because it could even then accept large tankers, it was selected as a port terminal for the Esso refinery which came on stream in 1960 and since then it has been greatly expanded.

On the other hand, even if there is no natural shelter available, a port will grow up if there is a potential for trade. If that trade develops people will be prepared to invest heavily to provide artificial protection. Dover is only 35 km from the French coast and therefore always had great commercial and strategic importance as a ferry terminal and a naval base. Its history as a port dates back to Roman times. Its precise location is the only possible one, where the valley of the Dour forms a gap in the line of the cliffs, giving access to the interior. But the Dour Estuary, even in Roman times, could accommodate only small vessels and in the Middle Ages it silted up altogether. As trade increased after 1815 there has been constant investment in both harbour and port facilities. Wet-docks were provided, but by 1833 the entrance to them had silted up. Between 1847 and 1871 shelter from the south-west was provided by the building of the Admiralty Pier, which also shut off the drift of shingle. Then, between 1895 and 1909 the Admiralty Harbour was built to enclose the whole of Dover Bay within three long moles.

Inside, the Marine Station on the Admiralty Pier was completed by 1915 and the Train-ferry Dock and Terminal in 1936. The growing accompanied tourist car traffic led to the opening of the Car-ferry Terminal in 1953. Continued increase, coupled with the growth of lorry traffic after 1965, led to subsequent enlargement to eight roll-on-roll-off (Ro-Ro) berths by 1981 (see p. 154), two of them for freight vehicles only. A Ro-Ro berth was also provided on the Admiralty Pier. In 1968 a Hovercraft Terminal was established and in 1978 this was relocated and enlarged.

The location of ports must therefore be studied in relation to the availability of shelter, actual and potential traffic flows and the relationship of the port with its hinterland. This latter depends on:

(a) the production for export within the area of the hinterland and the demand for imports;
(b) the physical capacity of the transport links between port and hinterland and the cost of using them;
(c) the location of neighbouring and competitive ports and the nature of their links with their hinterlands.

The concept of *hinterland* as the land area served by and tributary to the port is a useful one. But the reality is complex. It is even more complex than the parcelling-out of the area behind neighbouring ports, with zones of overlap where they compete. Each port will have a different hinterland for each commodity in which it trades. Traditionally, London had a nation-wide hinterland for its imports of meat, wool and tobacco. But imports of semi finished steel and coal would have been for local distribution only. The industrial areas of East Lancashire and the West Riding will be most likely to receive imports of raw wool through London, raw cotton through Liverpool and vegetable oils through Hull.

In the same way the area of the hinterland will be influenced by the *foreland* of the port, the area overseas with which the port trades. Ports in the same country often have trading links with different countries. Thus Manchester specialises in links with the ports of the north-eastern seaboard of North America and with the Great Lakes via the St Lawrence Seaway. On the other hand the general-cargo links of Southampton are mainly with South America and southern Africa.

Thus the West Midlands will lie in the hinterland of most British ports, the particular port varying according to the commodity exported or imported or the foreign port to which the exports are consigned or from which the imports originate. On the other hand, most British exports originate within 80 km of the port of export. In addition, not all ports are in competition. Harwich and Felixstowe are very near neighbours, but the former is a North Sea ferry port and the latter principally a deep-water container port, though it does have some ferry services.

The situation in Great Britain, however, is too complex for generalisations to be made easily. In the case of West Africa we can devise a *model* of port development.

West Africa – a case study

The coast of West Africa extends for 3,840 km from Cape Verde to Mount Cameroon (Fig. 9.1). There are only two natural harbours, Dakar Roads and

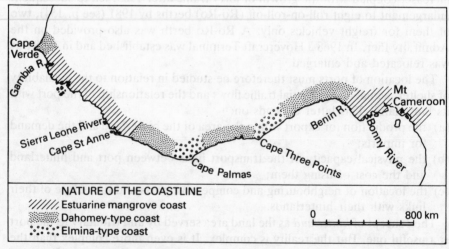

NATURE OF THE COASTLINE
///// Estuarine mangrove coast
⣿ Dahomey-type coast
∴∴∴ Elmina-type coast

0   800 km

Fig. 9.1 The West African coast

the Sierra Leone River. For the rest the coast is more a barrier than a zone of contact. It is continuously beaten by a heavy surf which may reach 2.5 m in height. Unless protection is given, ships cannot tie up to a quay. They must lie offshore and transfer cargo to and from small surf-boats of $1\frac{1}{2}$ tons capacity and with a skilled crew of 11 (White 1970).

The surf breaks at an angle to the beach, creating an eastward drift which will transport sand past a fixed point at the rate of 1 to 1.5 m. tonnes a year. This creates almost continuous dunes or offshore bars across, even wide bays and estuaries which latter are often lined with mangrove swamps which can be penetrated neither by vessels nor by vehicles.

There are, however, two counterbalancing advantages. Bad storms are almost unknown, so ships can work cargoes offshore in safety. There is also a very limited tidal range, at Lagos it is only 0.9 m. Vessels can thus enter port at any time and wet-docks are unnecessary.

The coast is divisible into three sections, as follows.

1. *Cape Verde to Cape St Anne (1,040 km).* This is a ria coast. Though the estuaries are impressive on the map, their utility is reduced by the offshore bars and fringing mangrove swamps.
2. *Cape St Anne to the Benin River (2,160 km).* This is a stretch of smooth, featureless and surf-beaten coast. There are two contrasting types of coastline. The first is the dune and lagoon coast one of the authors has named the *Dahomey type* (White 1970), though perhaps Bénin would now be a more appropriate name with the renaming of the country. The second has been named the *Elmina type*. While the estuaries are also closed by dunes, these latter are interrupted by low bluffs which protect the beaches to the leeward or eastern side from the surf.
3. *The Benin River to Mt Cameroon (640 km).* This is principally the delta of the Niger and the Cross rivers. The surf breaks more gently, but the bars are shallow. That of the Escravos River, the approach to three delta ports, was only 4.3 m before recent dredging.

As far as the landward communications are concerned there are two considerations. The first is the nature of landward communications. Before 1900 these were very primitive and costly. The second is that the coast was (and is) divided between 11 political units. There is little trade between each country and each has planned their own port development. Thus Freetown on the magnificient harbour of the Sierra Leone River is limited as a port because its hinterland is limited to Sierra Leone.

The pattern of port development

In response to the rudimentary landward communications and the ease with which the very simply equipped ports could be established, trade was carried on in numerous small ports with very restricted hinterlands. During the late nineteenth century some 150 would have been in operation. These little ports were of two types, surf and estuarine.

Certain of the ports began to gain at the expense of their neighbours by extensions to their hinterlands, first by the use of one of the rare navigable rivers or, in the case of Cape Coast, by the construction of a trail or road, but chiefly from 1900 onwards by the building of railways into the interior. These ports increased their trade and in turn attracted more investment in facilities. They thus became foci of the local road systems which grew up during the interwar years.

Investment in these favoured ports reduced working costs and above all reduced the time spent in loading and unloading cargo. To shorten journey times, ship-owners preferred to concentrate their operations on the improved ports. This in turn was an encouragement to concentrate investment on a small number of ports to produce the greatest results.

On the Elmina type of coast the natural shelter of the bluffs could be supplemented by a breakwater. This was done at Accra and Sekondi, the two ports in Ghana that were also railway termini. The main limiting factor of the surf-ports was the small size of the boats. At a number of ports on both the Elmina and the Dahomey types of coast, piers were built out through the surf. This allowed the use of high-capacity barges towed out to the ships by tugs. The provision of two such piers at Sekondi allowed six neighbouring ports to be closed between 1919 and 1921. Similar piers at Lomé and Contonou led to the abandonment of all other ports in Togo and Dahomey (now Bénin) respectively.

Further growth of traffic led to the replacement of Sekondi by the artificial harbour and port at Takoradi nearby, which opened in 1928. This led to the elimination of still more ports. Meanwhile the greatly improved trunk road system developed after 1950 was again focused on the larger ports and by 1955 there were only five working ports. Subsequently, a second 'Takoradi-type' port went into service in 1962 at Tema near Accra and all other Ghanaian ports closed except Takoradi. There are now seven 'Takoradi-type' ports (see Fig. 9.2) superseding dozens of the original surf ports.

The same trend of concentration is observable among the estuarine ports, where the *successful* ports are those with good communications with wide areas of the interior and in which large investments have been made. Dakar, with natural protection from the tombolo of Cape Verde, good road and rail links and adequate cargo-handling equipment has led to the decline of all other Senegalese ports. Lagos and Abidjan were improved by the provision of better access to the deep lagoons and again they superseded all neighbouring ports. The once numerous *Oil Rivers* ports of the Niger and Cross deltas have also been greatly reduced.

A theoretical model based on the area of this case study has been devised (Taaffe, Morell & Gould 1963), but it must not be taken to be of universal application.

Anyport

Unlike West Africa, Western Europe abounds in estuarine sites for ports and a similar situation pertains in many other parts of the world. J. H. Bird (1971) has developed a model of port growth based on the evolution of port installations. *Anyport* is an important aid in location studies as it provides a

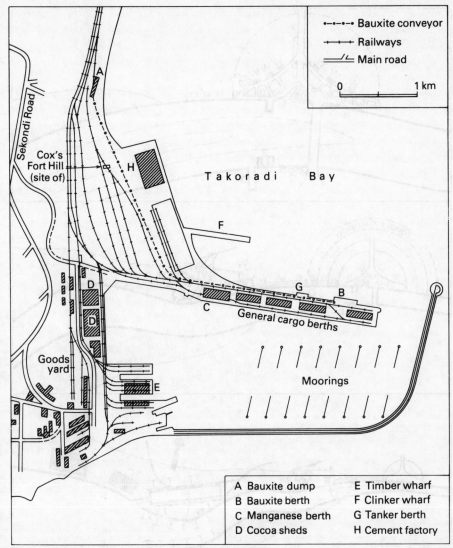

Fig. 9.2 Takoradi port and harbour (Ghana). (After Hilling: 135 in Hoyle & Hilling 1970)

base with which to compare the development of actual ports. There are six stages postulated in the development of *Anyport* (Fig. 9.3).

1. *The primitive port.* This is located on the estuary shore where an easier place for a harbour can be found and where there is dry ground to establish the town.
2. *Marginal quay extension.* This begins when the port extends along the town waterfront until eventually the quays begin to outstrip the areal growth of the town.
3. *Marginal quay elaboration.* Extension cannot go on indefinitely as customs surveillance will become difficult. So additional quayage was sought without

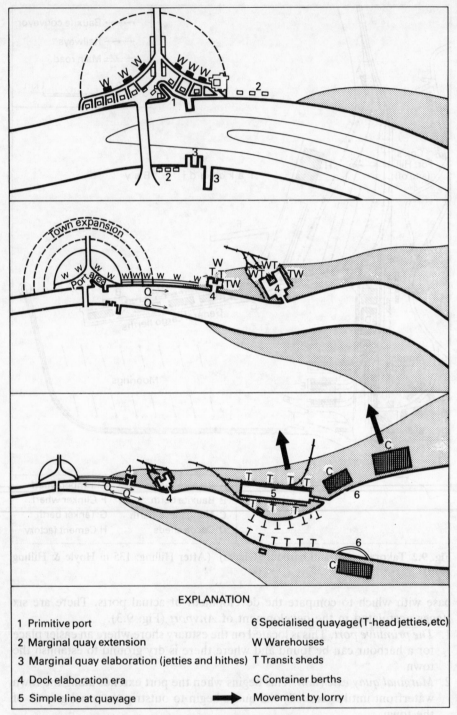

Fig. 9.3 The evolution of 'Anyport'. (After Bird 1963)

EXPLANATION

1 Primitive port
2 Marginal quay extension
3 Marginal quay elaboration (jetties and hithes)
4 Dock elaboration era
5 Simple line at quayage

6 Specialised quayage (T-head jetties, etc)
W Warehouses
T Transit sheds
C Container berths
➡ Movement by lorry

increasing the port area by the building of short jetties and the cutting of *hithes* (small docks) into the banks.

4. *Dock elaboration*. Increasing traffic and size of vessels leads to the building of wet-docks. These are gradually built further downstream with road and rail connections.
5. *Simple lineal quayage*. Eventually it becomes difficult to expand docks for larger vessels. The outlines of dock quays must be simplified and extended.
6. *Specialised quayage*. The growth of bulk cargoes and later of container and Ro-Ro traffic leads to the provision of specialised berths.

2. Airports (Sealy 1976)

The approach to location studies of airports can be similar to that for seaports as the nature and functions of both are basically similar. Like the seaport the airport provides the interchange point between surface transport and aircraft of passengers and cargo with maximum convenience and minimum costs – *the port function*. Secondly, it is a place of refuge from the elements and a place where maintenance and refuelling can be carried out – *the harbour function*.

The location of an airport will depend on:
(a) physical factors;
(b) the relationship of the airport with its *catchment area or hinterland*;
(c) the location of neighbouring airports and the level of services they offer.

Physical factors

These will include the prevailing and exceptional conditions of wind, fog and snow. The proportion of the time the wind will blow from various directions will affect the direction of the runways and therefore the shape of the airport and its demand for land in relation to competing land uses in the surrounding area. In addition the number of days on which high and gusty winds which might delay take-off are significant, as is the number of days in a year on which fog and falling snow might be expected to close the airport. Even if there are wind-landing aids and other devices for reducing the effects of climate, the more adverse the climate the greater the cost of installing and operating these aids, which will increase the operating cost of the airport (p. 43).

Relations with the hinterland

Obviously the airport must be located at a point which is convenient to the hinterland. Since the hinterlands of most airports are conurbations or other large centres of population, the nearer to the city centre the centre of their hinterland the better. On the other hand, aircraft operations require large land areas, possibility for expansion and freedom from obstructions surrounding the airport. To meet these needs locations which are as far as possible from centres of population are preferable.

It will thus be seen that there cannot be an ideal location for a large airport. It must be a compromise between the technical requirements which demand a peripheral location and the commercial requirements which demand a central one. To this conflict of interest must be added that of planning objectives. An airport is a source of noise pollution and it intensifies already strongly conflicting demands for scarce land.

The main volume of traffic arriving at an airport will be making for the city centre. The proportion will vary, but it will include not only those people whose journey will terminate there, but those wishing to continue their journey by surface routes to suburbs in other sectors of the city or to neighbouring towns. The location of the airport will affect that proportion. In the case of Manchester Airport, a very large proportion of the higher-income-group suburbs, which provide most of the potential traffic, are located on the same side of the city centre and within 8 km of the airport. In contrast, Speke Airport is south of Liverpool and its immediate area is one of working-class estates from the city. On the other hand, many of the residential areas of the kind in which business travellers by air live are in other sectors of the city, notably northward to Southport and across the Mersey in Wirral. On the face of it, given similar traffic volumes, connections with the city centre are more important for Liverpool.

The nature of the links depend on distance, the time spent on the journey and the volume of traffic. The distance/time is of greater importance for short hauls. Of the 150 minutes it takes from Central London to Central Manchester, more than 85 per cent of the time is spent on the ground. To Amsterdam the ground time is 65 per cent on average, but to New York it is only 22 per cent.

Time and convenience in reaching the city centre have not kept pace with increasing aircraft speeds. While air traffic is increasing, roads are becoming more congested. Even motorways, such as the M4 which serves London Airport (Heathrow), are heavily overloaded at certain times of day. Large airports can no longer depend on cars and buses, especially as aircraft capacity is increasing so fast. A 40-seater aircraft is matched in capacity by that of the connecting bus. But a 300-seat jumbo jet must be matched by a train.

For these reasons planners are now favouring rail links from large airports. Gatwick, by chance, lies alongside the main London-Brighton Road and also the railway, which has a very frequent service. At Gatwick the terminal buildings include a railway station, and a large proportion of air travellers reach Gatwick by rail. A rail link to Heathrow Central, a 5.6 km extension of the Piccadilly line from Hounslow West, was opened in 1978 with a 4-minute peak-hour service. In 1979 some 8 m. passengers used the new line. The £22 m. cost was shared by London Transport (50%), the Greater London Council (25%) and the Government (25%).

Neighbouring airports

To establish the need for an airport the population density of the potential hinterland must be taken into account, together with the structure of industrial and commercial activity. Also to be considered is distance from neighbouring airports together with the range and frequency of their services. Unfortunately, prestige has also been a factor: every go-ahead large town hankers after a costly airport.

The range and frequency of services from London means that for many purposes the whole of the UK is in its hinterland. For provincial airports distance from London is important. Those within about 80 km must specialise to survive. Luton is concerned with charter flights and Southend has developed a large cargo traffic as well as being the terminal of a cross-Channel car-ferry. Airports within a 80–240 km range of London have special difficulties. Domestic flights to London provide one of the heaviest potential flows, but they are too near to take advantage: thus traffic from Birmingham's Elmdon is small in relation to the size of the West Midland conurbation. Manchester is just clear of the London attraction and has a sufficiently populous hinterland to sustain international flights. For these last it in turn overshadows Liverpool and Leeds/Bradford, which must depend on domestic traffic and summer package-tour charters. It is the volume of London traffic which supports Glasgow (Abbotsinch) and Belfast (Aldergrove). The White Paper of 1978 setting out a government policy on location of airports has had to take these facts into account.

The protracted search for a site to develop a third major airport for London as an alternative to the overcrowded Heathrow and Gatwick illustrates the difficulties of establishing a new site. In 1963, after two years' deliberation a Parliamentary Committee pronounced the small airport of Stansted (Essex) as suitable. Opposition to this proposal became so strong that by 1968 the Roskill Commission was set up to evaluate a number of alternative sites. In 1971, after a massive cost–benefit exercise, Cublington was chosen as the *best* site (Roskill Report, 1971), but the Government of the time put a higher value on environmental effects and chose Maplin despite its greater monetary development costs. By 1974, public expenditure problems combined with a growing realisation that a third London airport was not as urgently needed as previously thought, led to the cancellation of the Maplin project. However, by 1979 that sense of urgency had been revived, with Stansted once more a likely candidate for London's third airport. After 18 years and considerable cost the project has come full circle (Buchanan 1981).

3. The location of railway passenger and freight stations

The location of railway passenger stations has received little attention, theoretical or practical. Yet this study is very important, for on these locations depends the volume of rail traffic in general and the contribution of the rail system to relieving road congestion in urban areas in particular. An inconveniently sited station will lead to travellers seeking alternative transport, especially if they are on short journeys: thus Temple Meads Station is peripheral to the Bristol Central Business District. It is for this reason that the level of rail commuting is low for a city of this size and even greatly improved suburban services introduced in the 1950s failed to attract custom. On the other hand, Oxford Road Station in Manchester is relatively convenient for the Central Business District and thus has a very large suburban traffic (16,893 commuters daily in 1980).

Planners have sometimes shown little appreciation of station location. In the interwar years the London County Council had schemes to close the well-sited Charing Cross Station and cut the railway back to the south bank of the Thames, while a plan for Edinburgh, commissioned soon after the war, envisaged the removal of the centrally situated Waverley Station to a remote southern suburb. Almost incredibly, the London County Council refused British Rail permission to develop office accommodation over the rebuilt Euston Station as it would increase street congestion (when most of the workers would arrive and leave by main-line or Underground trains without coming on to the streets at all), while granting permission for office blocks along Euston Road remote from any station. Two office blocks have since been built in front of the station, though the flat roof remains wasted city centre space.

In the past at least, British Rail has also been reluctant to provide new stations to accommodate new traffic resulting from land-use change. For 20 years before 1971 rail travellers were swept past the centres of Stevenage and Basildon New Towns. It was only in that year agreement was reached to resite Stevenage station alongside the town centre and to provide Basildon with a new station in its centre. It was also their policy for operating and commercial reasons not to provide a station at Milton Keynes. However, the New Town Corporation eventually persuaded BR to alter its mind and provided the finance for a combined station and office block. Work started in 1979, BR now emphasising that the new station posed no closure threat to the nearby stations at Bletchley and Wolverton and opened in 1982.

The position is therefore changing, and planners have become more concerned with the proper siting and design of railway stations (White, 1976). Thus in 1976 the main-line station, Birmingham International, was opened to serve the National Exhibition Centre. Two years later, University Station was opened on behalf of the West Midlands PTE immediately adjacent to Birmingham University and a large hospital complex.

The siting of railway freight depots has not yet received the attention it deserves. The migration of industry and warehousing from central areas of large cities left the older goods stations inconveniently located as well as obsolete in layout. The new Freightliner terminals, where containers in very large numbers are exchanged between road and rail, generate a very heavy lorry traffic on their approach roads and their siting is important. But hitherto these have been sited without much consideration other than that land became available in the shape of redundant sidings and locomotive depots. Bad siting may increase rather than reduce road congestion, and by increasing distances and slowing average speeds may also increase the cost of collection and delivery of containers.

The first Freightliner terminal in Manchester was opened on the site of a disused station at Longsight. This was in a densely populated residential area and a stream of heavy lorries approached the depot through narrow residential streets. The Trafford Park Terminal, on the site of a former engine-shed, is in the middle of the Trafford Park Industrial Estate, and this is a better site. But a much better one could have been in South Manchester where the electrified line from Manchester to Crewe passes under the M63 near Gatley. This motorway acts as an outer ring-road and provides connections with most of the industrial areas of the conurbation.

In 1974 a railhead for Continental fruit and vegetable traffic using the Dunkirk–Dover train ferry was opened at Paddock Wood (Kent) on the main line from Dover to London. Large-scale transfer to road vehicles takes place for distribution throughout the South-East. But Paddock Wood is served only by a B road leading to the M20, 15 km to the north, though 10 km to the west the railway is crossed by the A21 (M). The selection of the Paddock Wood site was influenced by the availability of railway-owned land more than by the nature of the local transport system.

4. Bus stations

For obvious reasons bus routes converge on town centres. Terminals may take the form of a number of 'stands', each used by a single route or a group of routes, with or without shelters, scattered at various points, more or less convenient as far as other vehicular traffic is concerned. Alternatively, the stands may be grouped into one place as a bus station.

These stations may be owned by a single operator for its exclusive use or by the local authority and used by a number of operators. Like railway stations, they are often inconveniently located. Sites were selected less for the convenience of passengers than for other reasons. These may include historical accident, pressure from local authorities to reduce town centre congestion and to 'tidy up', the availability of low-cost land or the proximity of the bus operator's garage.

This is not always the case. The bus station of Cardiff City Transport is located in the forecourt of the main railway station, and in Manchester the Piccadilly bus station is very centrally located. But the Leeds station is remote from both the centre of the Central Business District and the railway station.

Planners are becoming more concerned with the location of bus stations. In Birmingham the main bus station is alongside New Street railway station and both are integrated into the Bull Ring development. In Manchester the Arndale bus station, opened in 1979, is also located in the basement of a major shopping precinct. More attention is also being paid to layout and design.

5. Multi-modal interchanges

Planners have also come to realise that the best use of railways with their fixed tracks is integration with other transport modes. If the railway is the most efficient mover of large volumes of commuter traffic between suburbs and city centre along main corridors of movement (Ch. 10), to develop its potential to the full, interchange facilities with suburban feeder bus routes and with the private car must be provided. These suburban rail – bus – car interchanges must not only be well designed but must be properly sited in relation to the catchment area of the interchange and to the road network serving it. An unnecessary walk of a few yards from the car park or poor co-ordination between bus and train times will reduce potential users out of all proportion.

One of the first specially designed and deliberately located interchanges was at Wandsbek Markt, 5 km from the centre of Hamburg. The *U-bahn* (metro) station is located under the bus station. A bus despatcher, with full information on train arrivals can co-ordinate bus departures with them or call up extra buses. In Stockholm, stations serving new suburbs are not only integrated with bus terminals but with shopping centres and cinemas.

In North America from the start interchanges were designed and located with the car in mind. In 1969 the Englewood interchange was opened in the southern suburbs of Chicago. The rapid-transit rail line was extended 2 km to a location better placed in relation to the road net. Below the elevated railway station is a covered bus station and a car park for 250 cars. At Finch, the suburban terminus of the Yonge Street subway in Toronto opened in 1974, 1,564 parking places are provided together with a 'kiss and ride carousel', purpose built to provide maximum flow for cars meeting arriving passengers. There are also two integral bus stations, one for Transit Commission short-distance buses, the other for the buses of outer-suburban operators. Wilson, the terminus of the newer Spadina Line, has a similar layout and is located at the end of a slip road to two freeways. Many of the Toronto interchanges are carefully designed to facilitate their purpose. At St Clair West, trams and buses are brought down from street level to platforms immediately above the subway platforms and directly connected by escalator. Nor are there any ticket barriers for passengers changing modes. In the city centre many of the subway stations provide direct connection between shopping precincts and office blocks.

In outer London, British Rail and London Transport are following these examples. Thirty-four thousand car park spaces are already provided at such places as Colchester (500 spaces), Bletchley (400), Sevenoaks (330) and Newbury Park (410). On the Victoria Line, opened in 1969, Underground – main line railway – bus – car interchanges have been built at Walthamstow Central and at Tottenham Hale.

Greater Manchester Transport opened a bus – rail – car interchange at Altrincham in 1976. The railway station at the terminus of an electrified suburban line 13.6 km from Central Manchester is very conveniently sited for the centre of a town which is rapidly expanding as a retail centre. Greater Manchester Transport provided a bus station in the forecourt and co-ordinated the bus services with the train times. The local authority provided a large car park in the former goods yard. In 1980 a similar interchange was inaugurated at Bury, north of Manchester, though here the railway was diverted to a more convenient site than the old station.

British Rail have also begun to cater for long-distance travellers arriving by car without having to drive into the city centre to catch trains. The first such out-of-town interchange was at New Pudsey between Bradford and Leeds. In 1972 Bristol Parkway was opened at the junction of the lines from Bristol and South Wales to London. It is on the northern outskirts of the city, accessible from the Almondsbury intersection of the M4 and M5. Alfreton and Mansfield Parkway (Notts.), located at an access point to the M1, was opened in 1973.

The catchment areas of stations can be analysed along the same lines, though on a smaller scale, as has been outlined in connection with airports. It should be noted, however, that outer suburban stations tend to be eccentric to their catchment area, on the city side of the centre. There is an objection by commuters to drive or to travel by bus *away* from their general direction of travel (Fig. 9.4)

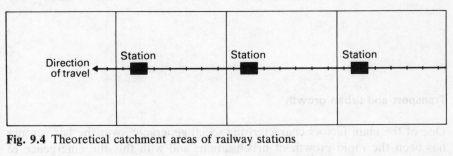

Fig. 9.4 Theoretical catchment areas of railway stations

Conclusion

Transport nodes, whether they are large or small, a world port or a bus-stop, are very important components of the transport system. Their location in relation to their catchment areas is therefore very important. Unfortunately, however, locational studies of transport nodes are deficient. Studies of port location have been carried out over a long period and have been published in large numbers. There have also been some important studies of airport location. But location studies of railway and bus stations are of equal importance and yet it is a field which has been grossly neglected.

Chapter 10
Transport in the urban scene

Transport and urban growth

One of the main factors characterising social geography over the last century has been the rapid growth of urbanisation, and with this the emergence of *million plus* cities. The number of these is constantly increasing and is by no means confined to Europe and North America. Transport developments were one of the major factors in this growth. They allowed first the concentration of raw materials and fuel required by the industries which formed one of the principal economic bases for urban growth; secondly the distribution of the finished products; and thirdly the provisioning of the urban population.

But it was not just a simple growth of population. Urban growth was accompanied by three important changes in the structure of the cities.

1. The separation of work and residence

This began with the most wealthy, but by 1914 was common in Britain among the middle classes. Since then the gathering momentum of slum clearance and the introduction of land-use zoning in connection with town planning has made this separation almost universal in Great Britain and increasingly common elsewhere.

2. The drain of resident population from the Central Business District

The commercial centre of large cities, and in this country even of comparatively small ones, no longer has a resident population of any size. The City of London had in 1971 a daytime employment of about 450,000, but its night resident population numbered only 4,245. There is a saying attributed to Lady

Simon that in the old days the merchants of Manchester lived over their businesses in Piccadilly, but nowadays live over their incomes at Alderley Edge (a well-known commuter suburb).

3. Areal expansion

In consequence of lower housing densities, which accompany rising living standards, areal expansion has been much greater than that of population. In 1841 the 1.94 m. Londoners lived on about 47 sq. km (an equivalent area to that of present-day Brighton and Hove with a 1971 population of 234,437). By 1971 the population had increased just over four-fold. But the built-up area had expanded to 1,870 sq. km, a 35-fold increase. This has resulted in constantly increasing distances in journeys to work, school and shop.

These three trends have been made possible by developments in transport (Barker & Robbins 1963/74). But since these took place in the following well-marked stages, it is possible to trace their consequences in the structure of the existing urban sub-regions.

The walk to work

Separation of work and residence began in London from about the mid-eighteenth century. The wealthier merchants were moving into the West End and south of the River Thames. The senior clerks were moving out to Islington or following their employers across the river. But these areas were within walking distance – up to 3 km. This phenomenon was also increasing in provincial cities and even in the smaller towns (Vance 1966; Warnes 1970).

The steam railway

The railway system rapidly developed after 1840 and made possible further separation of work and residence. From about 1860 residential growth took place in relatively tight nuclei within walking distance of stations which might or might not have been close to the villages they were built to serve. The houses were either large villas standing in large gardens, such as are to be found in the Beckenham and Sydenham areas of South London or at Altrincham (south-west of Manchester), or small terrace houses occupied by clerks or skilled artisans, as in Tottenham or Hornsey in North-east London or Stretford in Manchester.

The electric tram

These became common between 1900 and 1914, in many cases replacing horse-trams. Tramways created ribbon development along the main roads outward from the city centres, joining up the nodes created by the steam railways. Where, as in Manchester, the central area was connected to surrounding towns by tramlines (it was possible in the early 1920s to travel from Liverpool to Leeds by tram, except for a short walk across the Pennine watershed) these ribbons joined the main city with its satellites and the conurbation had been created.

The motor-bus/electric railway

To some extent before, but generally after the First World War, the motor bus, with its greater flexibility and the consequent ease of creating networks, led to the infilling of the sectors of open countryside which remained between the long and narrow ribbons of development along the tram routes.

Where, as in Greater London, the built-up area is too big to depend entirely on buses, the electric railway, often bus-fed, created an urban sprawl which, in the case of London extended far out on to the clay plains of Middlesex and South Essex as well as southward into Kent and Surrey (White 1971). Typical 1930s suburbs were vast areas of semi-detached, three-bedroomed brick houses built at comparatively low densities (Jackson 1973). The complement to these speculative private-enterprise suburbs were the large local authority housing areas such as Dagenham and St Helier, built by London County Council, and Wythenshawe, built by Manchester Corporation.

The post-war suburb

The car has freed people from dependence on public transport for the journey to work. Suburbia since 1950 is spreading discontinuously into the countryside. Urban sprawl of this kind is generally uncontrolled in the USA and under some control in Great Britain only because of the more rigid planning procedures. As a result, the Home Counties around London and also wide areas around the other conurbations can no longer be called *rural*, though building is not continuous. The 'adventitious'[1] population everywhere exceeds that sector of the population which depends on the land or on servicing this sector of population.

Two points emerge from this. The first is that the underlying factors in urban growth lead to both the extension of the urban transport system and the intensification of the traffic flows through those systems. Even in 1939 when commuting by car was on a very small scale, a whole complex of problems in urban transport had been created; but it is the spread of car ownership after 1960 which is making these problems so much more pressing. The Motor Age is changing the way of life of larger numbers each year (Rivers 1972; Schaeffer & Sclar 1975). The growing numbers of cars is changing the nature of suburban development and must inevitably change the nature and functions of our city centres. But the adjustment to near-universal car ownership in towns has been both painful and costly.

The second point is that there is a direct connection between the type of urban land use and the nature of the circulation patterns it creates. The various sub-regions of the city, themselves created by technological developments in transport, create different circulation patterns.

The central business district (CBD)

The circulation pattern of this sub-region is dominated by the two great diurnal traffic peaks as commuters pour into the CBD between 08.00 and 10.00 hours and leave again between 16.30 and 18.30. In turn this is the single most important traffic flow in the conurbation as a whole. Between the two peaks, circulation within the CBD is intense, but after the evening peak the area becomes dead, except in those streets which have entertainment functions. These peak periods vary according to the particular part of the world. The times just quoted are those common to the UK. In Continental Europe longer lunch breaks are common and consequently the evening peak is often later. Indeed, in Spain and in parts of Latin America there is a 4-hour midday break and this creates four peaks a day.

Industrial areas

Areas of industrial concentration, such as Trafford Park in Manchester with some 50,000 jobs or the Acton–Wembley area of North-west London, have similar diurnal traffic peaks, though on a smaller scale. But they are also centres of attraction for a heavy lorry traffic, which is constant for some 16 hours of the day.

The inner suburbs

These are of either uncleared Victorian working-class housing with pockets of decayed former middle-class houses or new local authority slum clearance housing. These days the level of car ownership is significantly high. But cars are used for the journey to work almost solely by male wage-earners. Working women and the children are dependent on public transport. These areas are reasonably well provided with bus services, at least along the main roads converging on the CBD. But these latter are intolerably crowded with traffic which debases the environment and tends to divide the suburbs into small isolated areas. To a great extent these areas are included in that part of the urban area now known as the 'Inner City'.

Medium-density outer suburbs

Medium-density outer suburbs grew up mainly between 1920 and 1939. They cover very extensive areas around all large towns and cities. A few random examples have been selected, Sidcup, Sutton and South Harrow–Ruislip in Greater London, Sutton Coldfield in Birmingham and Timperley in Greater Manchester. These generate similar journey-to-work patterns, though car ownership is higher and journeys longer. There is also an intense local circulation by car and to a lesser extent by public transport for shopping and recreational journeys. While public transport is much used for the journey to work, especially to the city centre, off-peak carryings are declining.

Low-density outer suburbs

Examples of low-density outer-suburbs are Chislehurst, Pinner and Amersham in the London area. We can also cite Balsall Common in the West Midlands and Alderley Edge in Greater Manchester. These generate a very intensive local circulation dominated by the car. Commuting to the city centre may, if the city is large, be by train, but all other journeys are mainly by car. Many households have more than one car and each household may generate 9–12 trips a day by car. Thus the provision of local bus services is becoming more and more uneconomic.

With the dispersal of industry from central areas and the growth of suburban shopping and commercial centres, peripheral journeys to work and for other purposes are becoming very important in the outer suburbs as well as the radial journeys to the city centre. This trend is particularly marked in North America, but is rapidly becoming a problem in Europe. It creates severe local traffic congestion on roads often quite unsuitable. It is difficult to relieve congestion by providing public transport. The patterns of traffic flow are complex and the volume of each flow is low. Some are large enough for buses, but buses suffer from car-induced congestion. Few flows are large enough for fixed-track systems.

Urban road systems

Urban transport is therefore dominated by:

(a) the journey to work, of which that to the CBD is the largest single flow;
(b) the rapidly diversifying and intensifying circulation patterns created by journeys to school, for shopping and for recreation;
(c) the spread of car ownership and the increasing proportion of trips made by car.

To cope with the growing number of cars in cities, especially those used for the journey to work, transport planning has been aimed at the provision of more road space, adequate for the movement of the increasing car traffic. From 1950 onwards in the USA and from 1960 in Western Europe there has been a vast and increasing investment in urban roads. These have included:

(a) traffic management schemes such as one-way systems;
(b) local improvements such as street widening and underpasses;
(c) most important of all, the building of urban motorways.

The key question, however, hinges on a definition of *adequate road space*. There is no doubt that at first the aim was to provide road space for a majority of commuters wishing to use their cars. But it proved impossible to create a wholly motorised city, even in Los Angeles where planning was directed to this end. In addition, the provision of urban motorways brought in its wake as many problems as it solved. In the first place the private car is a prodigious user of space, and space is in very short supply in the city centres everywhere and, at least in Great Britain, in the suburbs as well. In Chicago a four-lane motorway with a capacity of 10,000 commuters per hour (assuming 1.7 persons per car), requires a strip of land 36 m wide as a minimum and an interchange will occupy at least 4.0 ha (10 acres) and 16.2 ha (40 acres) if two motorways are involved. On the other hand, an electric railway can handle up to 28,000 persons per hour per track. A double-track right of way will need a strip only 11.3 m wide.

In addition, the terminal requirements in the city centre for car commuters are enormous. Nearly half the space of the Los Angeles CBD is occupied by car parks and we must add road space to this. In a survey of Manchester car traffic made in 1962 it was found that of 341,000 vehicles per day passing the ring of census points, only 9 per cent represented through traffic which would be taken away by a ring-road. On the other hand, 48 per cent of the vehicles were making for the central area and would be needing parking space there.

No matter how lavish the provision of road space, peak period congestion is rife and this congestion is costly. G. Roth (Roth 1967: 29) calculated that costs in pence per mile due to one additional vehicle-mile rose from 2p (1967 prices) when the traffic is moving at 20 mph (32 kph) to 30p when congestion causes speed to fall to 8 mph (12.8 kph).

But congestion is not the only cost incurred. The Buchanan Report of 1963 (Buchanan 1963) drew attention to the deterioration in the urban environment which was due to the motor car generally and urban motorways in particular. This deterioration is the result of atmospheric pollution, constant high noise levels, loss of amenity to properties bordering main roads and motorways and the sterilisation of large areas of valuable space for roads, interchanges and parking.

Providing for a high level of motorisation will also have a fundamental effect on the nature of the city centre. With too much space submerged under roads and car parks it loses its attraction and this leads to decentralisation. It can be argued this might be a beneficial trend, though the argument loses force when the city centre is a historic one. But if excessive decentralisation does take place, much investment is lost. On the other hand, not to accommodate cars in the city centre may also lead to decentralisation. The authors do not suggest a simple answer to this dilemma, but it is one of which all inhabitants of large cities must be aware.

The Buchanan Report also drew attention to the fact that no town and especially no large city can possibly be fully motorised. A proportion of the population will always be without cars, while there will always be insufficient road space to allow all commuters to enter the central area by car.

The place of public transport

It is becoming apparent, even in the USA, that the city must still partially depend on public transport, especially for the journey to work in the central area. J. S. Gallagher gave four reasons for this:

1. mass transport is essential to medium- and high-density urban areas;
2. highways cannot satisfactorily deal with peak-period traffic;
3. a decentralised city is weak economically and socially and the costs of public services are increased;
4. urban motorways reduce CBD land values.

In addition, the ability of road improvements to generate entirely new traffic has consistently been underestimated. Improvements aimed at relieving congestion when traffic has reached a certain level have resulted in traffic increasing until congestion is as bad as ever. This coupled with the consumption of scarce land and the residual demand for public transport all means there is a continuing place for public transport in all large towns and cities, especially along corridors of movement where traffic flows are heavy.

Buses are most economic for dealing with traffic flows of up to 5,000 passengers per hour (80-passenger vehicles at 1-minute intervals). Though economies of scale are limited, capital investment is comparatively small. But they are affected by congested roads. Schedules are impossible to maintain and passengers are lost. Buses operate best on segregated tracks, *busways*, though little is known of their real costs. There is only one such system operating in the UK, at Runcorn New Town. Busways can be made even narrower, and thus built more cheaply, if the buses can be guided by a projection from the bus engaging in a slot, rather like a working-model road system. As an interim measure which is becoming much more popular, bus-only lanes can be created where streets are sufficiently wide. These may be in the same direction as the main traffic flow or may be counter-flow in one-way systems.

For peak flows up to about 12,000 an hour, a *light rapid-transit* system is best (assuming 200-passenger units at 1 minute intervals). This is a segregated tramway, employing fast cars coupled into trains. For flows over that figure the *heavy rapid transit system*, or electric railway with sophisticated signalling, is the most suitable mode. These have a capacity of up to 28,000 passengers per hour per line of rail (assuming 40×700-passenger trains).

Old-fashioned tramways are being converted into light rapid-transit systems in many European cities, the lines being laid on segregated track in the suburbs and in tunnels under the city centre. Brussels and Antwerp, Cologne and the Ruhr conurbation, Vienna and Göteborg (Sweden) are all examples. In Great Britain a similar system is being provided for Newcastle upon Tyne, using the right of way of the British Rail lines to Whitley Bay linked to new tunnels under the city centre. Heavy rapid-transit systems are characteristic of very large cities. The London Underground system has 406 route-km, extending out to Ongar in rural Essex, to Amersham and to West Ruislip. Paris also has an extensive system, which has been greatly extended in recent years to serve commuter suburbs. Many other cities are acquiring new systems or extending existing small ones; in Europe Stockholm provides the best example, the system being provided since 1945, but Rome, Madrid, Rotterdam and Lisbon provide other examples. In North America, New York, San Francisco, Philadelphia, Boston, Cleveland, Toronto and Montreal are all actively engaged in rehabilitating and extending existing systems or providing new ones. The Institute for Rapid Transit in 1966 estimated 36 North American cities should be planning rapid-transit systems.

Unfortunately, increasing car ownership has had serious consequences on the financial viability of public transport. This is mainly due to the erosion of off-peak traffic, which has reached alarming proportions. G. G. Harding said that when he became General Manager of Wallasey Transport in the early 1960s the number of late evening passengers aboard the buses in service at any one time was exceeded by that of the bus crews! On the other hand, peak-hour traffic shows little decline. Thus peak costs become even higher as productive work for the fixed equipment and the vehicles decline in off-peak periods. In 1965 London Transport calculated that a nine-car electric train incurred depreciation and capital charges of £10,000 a year before it left the siding. Yet some trains would make no more than one or two revenue-earning round trips five days a week.

Because of this, investment in public transport in the UK and USA has declined. In the USA the systems have, until some recent revivals, badly decayed and in the UK they have stagnated. The cause has been that, unlike many countries of Western Europe, different investment criteria have been applied to road improvements and to public transport. Urban motorways have been provided to cope with peak-hour flows, irrespective of the fact that mass public transport can do the job at lower unit costs. On the other hand, economic criteria have hitherto been applied to public transport, which precludes investment to cope with peaks. In addition, public transport has been financed by interest-bearing *loans* and road improvements by interest-free *grants*.

However, the tide of opinion on the limitations of the car and the continuing need for public transport began to turn in the USA with the 1964 Mass Transportation Act, which allocated federal grants, hitherto available only for urban motorways, to improve public transport. The highway plans of cities submitted for federal approval must now be linked with plans to improve mass transport. In many large metropolitan areas transportation authorities have been set up to plan and operate the extension or the provision of rapid-transit and bus systems. A notable example is the Bay Area Rapid Transit District (BART) which has built a 132 km system to serve the San Francisco–Oakland conurbation. The first section was opened in 1972. The cost was to be partly met by the sale of interest-bearing bonds guaranteed by a property tax, and partly from increased tolls on the San Francisco–Oakland road bridge. Money for the rolling-stock would be met from revenue. Chicago has provided rapid-transit lines along the median strips of the urban motorways. New York, Philadelphia and Boston all have metropolitan transit authorities.

Toronto provides a Canadian example of public transport planning and finance (Allen 1969). In 1954 the Toronto Transit Commission opened the 9.2 km Yonge Street Subway. It proved successful in terms of passengers carried and also sparked off a property boom, residential and commercial development taking place round the stations, some of which were in decaying areas. In 1959 the Metropolitan Toronto Council approved a new Bloor–Danforth Subway. The Provincial Government of Ontario paid one-third of the tunnel and track costs and the Council the remainder. The Transit Commission was to meet the cost of the trains. In addition, the Ontario Government provided funds to rehabilitate a 83 km railway line belonging to Canadian National Railways in order to reduce long-distance car commuting (the GO trains). These schemes have proved successful and led to a reduction in the motorway programme.

In Western Europe, especially in Federal Germany, Holland and Sweden, public transport has never been so seriously starved of investment. Transport and land-use planning have been linked for a long period. The *T-Bana*, as the

Stockholm rapid-transit system is called, was started soon after the Second World War. From the first, new suburbs such as Välingby have been planned with the transit line as their axis and the station as the centre of each settlement. High-density housing is provided near the station, to provide a base-load traffic, and low-density housing further out. The suburban expansion of Copenhagen has also been planned along the routes of the State Railways' suburban system (the *S-Bane*).

In Great Britain the real turning point did not come until the 1968 Transport Act. As outlined on page 72 transport planning in urban areas was to be co-ordinated to a greater extent and government *grants* could be given for public transport improvements as well as for roads. Since 1971, when the first of the infrastructure grants was announced, a number of public transport projects have been completed or were under construction in 1979. Those completed include the Victoria–Brixton section of London's Victoria line (Victoria–Walthamstow had been financed by interest-bearing loans in spite of its contribution to surface congestion and therefore the cost of road improvements); the Jubilee Line from Baker Street to Charing Cross, the electrification of the BR suburban services from Moorgate and King's Cross and the 'loop and link' connections extending suburban lines under the Liverpool CBD. Work is proceeding on the electrification of the Moorgate–St Pancras–Bedford suburban services, the Tyne and Wear Metro and rehabilitation and extensions to the Glasgow rail system.

Greater awareness of the consequences of urban transport on the environment led to the 1973 Land Compensation Act which allowed compensation for environmental intrusion from urban motorways as well as for property actually demolished. This has increased costs of urban motorways, which at the same time are increasingly unpopular (Thompson 1970). The programme has therefore been considerably curtailed.

On the other hand, increasing awareness of the need for energy conservation has not as yet had any real impact on urban transport planning.

Public transport in London

To conclude the chapter, a brief case study of the problems of London's passenger transport has been included. The overriding problem is the volume of commuter traffic to and from the CBD. There are, of course, many cross-currents, some of them of considerable volume, such as the movement of workers to the industrial areas of Middlesex, or the circulation patterns associated with important local shopping and commercial centres such as Croydon, Kingston and Brent Cross.

The central area. As defined by London Transport this covers 16.8 sq. km and has a residential population of only some 90,000. In 1977 between 07.00 and 10.00 hours some 1,052,000 commuters were poured into the area – to leave again between 16.30 and 19.30. This figure declined marginally through the 1970s (1969 – 1,178,000) due partly to the Government's decentralisation policy for offices and to the greater decline in small-scale manufacturing industry.

Of these commuters: 170,000 (16.2%) came by car;
22,000 (2.1%) came by pedal and motor cycle;
139,000 (13.2%) came by bus;
720,000 (68.7%) came by rail;
(400,000 by BR and 320,000 by LT).

Car traffic increased slowly from 125,000 in 1961 to a maximum of 174,000 in 1973 when the petrol crisis of 1974 provided a slight check to growth, but in spite of the congestion caused, accounts for only a minority of the journeys. Bus traffic has fallen constantly, though at a much slower rate in the 1970s compared with the 1960s (1961–69, 26.4%, 1970–78, 8.5%). This is largely due to unreliability owing to road congestion and staff difficulties. The proportion of rail travellers has remained relatively constant.

There are two serious consequences, serious for the whole community as well as for commuters and operators (White 1964).

1. Saturation of facilities in the peak periods.   Table 10.1 and Fig. 10.1 shows the 'peak period index' and 'peak hour index' for 1978 of the Southern Region termini. These indices represent the proportion of daily departing passengers leaving the station between 16.00 and 19.59 hours and between 17.00 and 17.59 hours respectively. In the case of Cannon Street, for example, whereas a daily total of 34,262 passengers were on trains leaving between 05.25 and 22.07 hours, 31,690 (92%) of them left in the peak period and 19,516 (57%) of them in the peak hour.

Table 10.1 Passengers at Southern Region Central London stations – 1978. Weekday averages (figures in thousands)

Station	Arrivals			Departures			Total 24 hours	Peak hour index	Peak period index
	Peak hour	Peak period	Total 24 hours	Peak hour	Peak period	Total 24 hours			
Charing Cross	24	40	56	21	40	57	113	40	71
Waterloo (SE)	6	10	15	4	9	15	30	33	63
London Bridge	24	44	58	22	41	53	111	41	77
Cannon Street	24	39	42	20	32	34	76	58	93
Holborn, etc.*	12	20	23	10	18	21	44	50	93
Victoria	33	55	89	27	59	91	180	33	63
Waterloo	41	64	94	31	65	94	188	38	69
Vauxhall	2	3	4	1	3	4	8	38	75
Grand Total	166	275	380	136	267	369	750	42	72

Based on censuses carried out by Southern Region in October/November 1978.
Peak hour is the actual busiest hour at the station.
Peak period: 07.00–09.59; 16.00–19.59.
Peak hour index: The two peak hours as a percentage of total passengers.
Peak period index: The two peak periods as a percentage of total passengers.
* Holborn Viaduct, Blackfriars, Elephant and Castle.

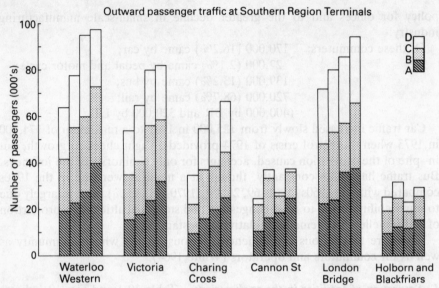

Fig. 10.1 Peak period problems in London. For each station the columns represent (left to right) the figures for 1930, 1939, 1948, 1960. In each column A–D represents 24 hours, A–C 16.00–20.000 hours and A–B the busiest hour. (After White, 1971)

In 1960 29 electric trains left Liverpool Street for the Romford line between 17.00 and 17.59 (one every 2 minutes) (see Fig. 10.2). On the census day they carried 30,630 people, an average of 1,056 per train, each of which would have had either 528 or 726 seats. In the off-peak period similar trains would have had less than 100 passengers each.

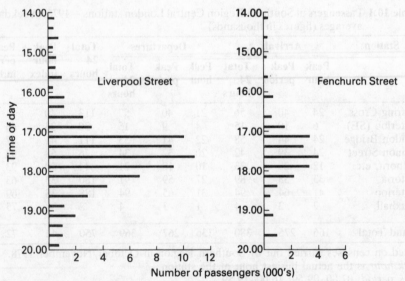

Fig. 10.2 Peak period problems in London. Note the concentration of traffic into the period 17.00–18.15 hours. (Source: British Rail, Census, 1960.) In this and Fig. 10.1 the data are old, but the phenomenon is unchanged

Any capital investment to improve peak-period capacity is thus surplus for most of the day, and is the reason for peak costs. On the other hand, as we have seen, there is no alternative form of transport for the peak. The question is whether these costs should fall wholly on the commuters or partly on the community as well. Whatever the answer to this question the need for similar investment criteria to be applied to both roads and mass transit is obvious.

2. Falling off-peak traffic. Peak costs are also increased by falling off-peak traffic, due to the spread of car ownership. Public transport may be vital for the journey to work, but recreational journeys, especially evening and week-end ones, are increasingly by car. By 1965 London bus traffic was only 75 per cent that of 1960. On the other hand, bus miles had fallen only by 8 per cent, thus leading to a worsening ratio between receipts and expenditure.

There is thus a dilemma facing both operators and the urban community in all cities. In the first place declining traffic leads to reduced services, which in turn lead to further declines, a vicious circle which is extremely difficult to avoid. On the other hand, in the foreseeable future car ownership will not be universal and may even decline. For an area to lose its off-peak services will lead, as it has already done in the USA, to deprivation and isolation of a minority of the population.

Conclusion

Study of transport in the urban scene leads to the asking of a number of very important questions which are fundamental to the whole urban structure and which underline the basic importance of transport as a human activity.

1. Is there an intimate connection between urban land use and transport both private and public? Is there a need to relate the planning policies affecting these three aspects of urban life?
2. Is there a need for the application of common investment criteria (whatever those criteria might happen to be) to both road improvements and mass transport? Will the pricing of road space have to be introduced?
3. Motorway building will have far-reaching consequences on the structure of the city, especially of the central area. Should the latter be allowed to decay or should its dominance be preserved? The answer is by no means clear, but the whole community must be aware of the choice and of its consequences.
4. Everybody must also be aware of the consequences to both the central area and to the suburbs of allowing public transport to lose its attractiveness to both peak and off-peak travellers.

Note

1. L. Dudley Stamp divided the resident economically-active population of rural areas into three:

Primary: those whose work is tied to the area, e.g. farmers and farm workers.
Secondary: those whose employment services the primary population, e.g. shopkeepers.
Adventitious: these include what would now be called commuters and workers in service activities, expanded because of the presence of the commuters.

This is a very useful classification and it would be good to revive its use.

Chapter 11
Transport in the Third World

'Fundamentally transport in an under-developed country is the same as transport anywhere else but there are special problems which may arise . . .' (Sharp 1965: Ch. 9). This assertion will be the theme of this chapter. Obviously, the various factors we examined in the first part of the book – economic, technological and so on – apply with more or less equal force everywhere. On the other hand, in developing countries the nature of the demand for transport and the means of supplying transport services to meet the demand require special study. In addition, the study of transport in developing countries is of particular interest to geographers as the connection between changes in the patterns of transport and those of other human activities is often more direct than in a more highly developed area.

It thus came to be accepted that the provision of transport infrastructure would automatically lead to consequent economic and social development (White 1980). In 1957 Lord Hailey wrote: 'there seems to be no other type of development which can effect so speedy a change in the economic and social conditions of a backward country' (Hailey 1957). But in recent years geographers and economists have tended to the view that transport has a permissive rather than a more deterministic role. Investment in other projects may be more cost effective and over-investment in transport may be wasteful. The line of transport may fail to fulfil its development function because it is inadequate; the area through which it passes may be incapable of development; the cost of using it may be too high; equipment may be over-sophisticated (as often is the case with available aircraft); and managerial skills may be lacking. Special care should therefore be applied to transport investment to ensure that it is kept in step with investment in other sectors. But having said that we may conclude by quoting Gauthier (1970): 'If there is a relationship between capital formation and economic growth, there must be a relationship between important components of that capital formation and growth. Undoubtedly transportation is an important component of capital formation.'

Transport has therefore loomed large in economic development plans formulated by Third World governments. Priority of government investment was given to the improvement of existing trunk roads and the building of new ones, to increasing the capacity of seaports and to the provision of airports for international and internal traffic. There was also investment in increasing the capacity of rail lines by dieselisation, new wagons and laying in new passing loops on the single lines. For the most part it was left to private enterprise to invest in lorries and buses, encouraged by such measures as keeping the duty on motor fuel as low as possible. Occasionally, however, governments would invest in road fleets. The Government of Ghana built up a network of long-distance bus services, while the erstwhile Government of the Northern Region of Nigeria built up a lorry fleet in fierce competition with the Federal Government's railway.

International agencies provide capital for specific projects, particularly seaports and new railways. The World Bank financed the 640 km Bornu railway extension in north-eastern Nigeria. Individual countries have also directly funded projects. West Germany financed the new port of Lomé (République du Togo, West Africa), while France has funded numerous transport projects in her ex-colonies. Direct investment in specific road projects has been less common, though France has provided aid for road schemes in Francophone Africa.

Aid is often tied to equipment, such as railway rolling-stock, produced in the aid-giving country. Sometimes aid for transport projects was the direct result of foreign policy. Funding for the TanZam railway, giving Zambia an alternative sea outlet at Dar es Salaam, was refused by the World Bank on economic grounds. It was considered not to be adequately cost effective, particularly in view of capacity on the route via Rhodesia (now Zimbabwe) Railways. The Chinese, wishing to expand their political influence in Africa, then stepped in. But completion coincided with a change of policy. The Chinese withdrew their technicians and since then the line has been used well below capacity due to deficiencies in management. Nor was aid always beneficial. Costs of operating the Iluyshin airliners given by the USSR to Ghana were so heavy that they became a major contribution to that country's financial difficulties.

Transport development in Third World countries can be measured in a number of ways. The provision of road networks can be measured in terms of either length of road or density of network per unit area. Thus comparisons can be made over time and space, as has been done by Taaffe, Morrill and Gould (1963) for Ghana. They can also be measured in terms of population served. Another approach is to measure the quality of the transport links. Small-scale maps can be deceiving as they do not indicate whether roads are tarred or the axle loads of bridges, nor do they indicate the average distance between passing loops on single-track railway lines. The cost of using the transport links is also an important measurement. As will be shown, the mere indication of a link is not sufficient if freight rates are so high that economic development of the area traversed is inhibited.

Transport in the economy of developing countries

The level of economic development, as we have just seen, will be in part controlled by the level of investment in the transport sector. This will be inadequate, just as investment in the economy as a whole is inadequate. Because of this economic development is limited, and thus the demand for transport in relation to the area and population of the country is also limited. This is one of the several vicious circles which must be broken if the country is to reach the point of economic *take-off*.

Ghana, in spite of recent economic difficulties, is one of the most economically advanced countries of Tropical Africa and its transport infrastructure is more highly developed than most African countries. In 1967 there were 32,392 km of motorable road, 1 km to 10.9 sq. km superficial area and 206 people. Of this network only 10 per cent had a bitumen surface while 70 per cent was described as all-weather (an elastic term!). This implies that 30 per cent of the road mileage was definitely impassable in the wet season. Also, these latter roads can only accommodate traffic levels of less than 10 vehicles per day. This compares with the British road net, where virtually all public roads have a bitumen or concrete surface, and where there is 1 km of road to 1.9 sq. km and 136 people.

In 1967 there were 48,000 vehicles registered in Ghana. Of these 26,000 were private cars. Ghana thus had one car for every 304 people compared with one car to 5.6 people in Great Britain. There were only 12,000 road-haulage vehicles. Tonne-km and passenger-km produced by lorries and buses would therefore be very much lower per head of population than in an economically advanced country. As to traffic densities, in Ghana in 1967 there were 1.5 vehicles per km of road compared with 33.0 per km in Great Britain.

In Europe, as we have seen, modern transport development seldom creates an entirely new line of communication. The development takes place to meet pre-existing demand. In developing economies, such as those of Tropical Africa, the whole process of transport development can be traced from its very beginnings. Even within the last 20 years, entirely new lines of communication have been created by road-building through areas which have hitherto been entirely without motor transport. For the first time lorries arrive bringing trade goods for sale. Farmers now have both the incentive to sell their crop surplus and the ability to get their previously unsaleable produce to market. In short, a cash economy has been introduced for the first time, and with it the possibility of both economic and social progress.

But the consequences are even more far-reaching. The villages hitherto scattered through the area will be resited on the new road to take advantage of ease of movement and possibility of trade. The land-use pattern will also change. Land near the road will be more intensively cultivated, while the land remote from it will tend to go out of cultivation (until feeder roads are built). New cash crops will be introduced. In addition, there will be important social consequences. The area is brought into closer contact with the outside world. More people will travel away from home and more strangers will arrive. In this way new ideas will reach the area.

The spread of cash-crops can often be traced in terms of transport development. Extensive cash cropping was introduced to the Kano region (Northern Nigeria) when the railway to the navigable Niger and the coast was opened in 1911. Cotton was expected to be the main crop, but soon groundnuts proved more profitable. The existence of mineral deposits will often be the origin of transport development, the new facilities being frequently put to general use. In Eastern Nigeria the existence of coal near Enugu led to the opening in 1916 of the railway thence to Port Harcourt. This new deep-water port, established for coal export, has now become the second largest general cargo port of Nigeria. In West Africa alone, three railways have been built in Liberia to exploit iron-ore deposits, one in Mauritania and one in Sierra Leone, all but the last opened since 1950 and with a combined length of 1,194 km.

Transport is also a vital factor in the industrialisation which all developing countries are seeking to achieve. Maximum extension of the market is necessary to provide as large a base as possible on which to establish manufacturing industries. If the market is restricted, then the particular industry may have to be on too small a scale to be economic.

Yet there is also a negative aspect. High transport costs may impose a natural protection, which allows industrial development in an otherwise high-cost area. Uganda is a landlocked country, and the 1,200 km rail haul from the port of Mombasa (Kenya) to the commercial capital of Kampala greatly increases the cost of imported goods and encourages the establishment of manufacturing within Uganda, particularly of cement and other bulky products.

The real cost of transport

We must always bear in mind the cost of using a line of transport rather than just its physical provision. Inland areas of the developing world, such as Uganda or Northern Nigeria suffer a double cost disadvantage, which imposes a severe handicap on their development compared with the coastal area. Heavy transport costs reduce revenue from exports and at the same time increase the price of the imports which are essential for development.

In 1966 groundnuts were fetching about £65 per tonne on the world market. Those produced in the Kano area were faced with a rail rate to the port of Apapa of £7.60 per tonne. To this was added the cost of lorry transport to railhead. For this the official rate was 1.9p per tonne-km on tarred roads and 3p on dirt roads. Assuming a reasonable distance of 50 km on the latter and 30 km on the former, the total transport costs, only as far as the port, would have been £9.67 or 14.4 per cent of the selling price. On the other hand, the selling price of petrol in Kano was 25 per cent over that charged at Apapa. Inland location thus gives the principal export lower real purchasing power and at the same time increases the cost of imports (White 1963b).

The mere provision of transport is not enough if costs are still too high to encourage movement of people and goods. If this is the case, then not only will the transport facilities be under-used, but the economic development of the area will be held back. It was hoped that the irrigation works on the Niger in Mali would lead to the establishment of widespread cotton-growing. This failed to happen for a number of reasons. Among these was the high cost of transport to the coast, first by river steamer, then a costly transfer to rail at Bamako, and the high rail rates thence to Dakar, the port in Senegal.

Costs can be reduced and the spread of facilities encouraged in proportion to the *flexibility* of the system. There are three ways of looking at this factor of flexibility.

1. The need for investment in transport should be as closely adjusted as possible to traffic growth. Ideally, in the pioneering phase when traffic volumes are small, investment should be as small as possible. As traffic builds up, as far as possible investment should be increased in direct proportion.

   This is why a road system is the most flexible of all transport modes. At the pioneering stage all that is needed is to clear a trace through the natural vegetation and to provide a few culverts over streams. As traffic builds up, first a gravel surface can be provided and then tar-sealing. At the same time culverts and bridges can be strengthened to allow larger and heavier lorries. Unfortunately, as in all countries, road improvements tend to lag behind increases in vehicle numbers. This increases transport costs (perhaps by as much as 18%) by checking the use of larger lorries, by increasing maintenance costs because of damage done by deteriorating surfaces and by decreasing vehicle life.

   Conversely, a railway requires a large capital investment, however limited the traffic expected. As traffic increases it is not only costly to provide for increased carryings (to increase wagon capacity, increased axle loads are needed, involving heavier rails and stronger bridges), but it is particularly expensive to undo initial short cuts taken to reduce initial investment (see p. 35).

2. Flexibility is the ability to pioneer areas hitherto beyond the reach of transport. In many parts of the world, especially the grasslands with their marked dry season, no roads are needed. Lorries are driven across country following tracks of preceding vehicles.

3. It is the ability to cope with rapid changes in volume and direction of traffic. In both these latter senses, road transport is also the most flexible mode.

The provision of the infrastructure

1. Waterways. We have seen how inefficient and costly is human porterage, and to a lesser extent the use of animals (p. 22). These forms of transport still have a restricted role in local circulation (Gould 1960), especially when road systems are inadequate. But the basic transport system of any country must be mechanised.

Natural waterways, where they exist, provide a very suitable transport mode in a pioneering situation. Their advantage lies not only in their moderate operating costs but especially in the relatively low investment needs. There are no track costs (except perhaps for clearing *sudd*, i.e. papyrus and other vegetation, from the Upper Nile), either capital or recurrent. Waterways may also provide a trunk system, even after the pioneering stage. Examples are numerous. In South America the Magdalena River formed the essential trunk of a multi-modal (river–rail–road) transport system of Colombia until the recent completion of a railway system by the linking of isolated lines. Waterways are still virtually the only means of surface transport in the vast Brazilian state of Amazonas. In Africa the Nile provides a trunk for the transport systems of Egypt and Sudan as well as the only surface link between the two countries.

But many rivers are interrupted by rapids, which form an obstacle to navigation. Many early railways in the Tropics were built to link navigable reaches of rivers. Mention has been made of the Madeira–Marmoré railway in Brazil (p. 12). In Africa, isolated lines were constructed to avoid rapids in the Congo. Goods for Burundi imported through Matadi formerly had to be transhipped between rail and steamer no less than five times. The evolution of railways in West Africa is best interpreted as the provision of links between the coast and navigable reaches of the Niger.

The operating costs of these joint river–rail routes are greatly increased by the transhipment costs. These can sometimes be tolerated when traffic levels and wage-rates are low. But as these increase, the high operating costs can be reduced by investing in rail extensions to cut out at least the shorter lengths of river navigation.

2. Roads. Although trails can be used by motor vehicles, they must be improved into roads as soon as traffic becomes at all heavy (p. 23). Eventually a road network, however rudimentary, begins to appear. In any developing country this road net is related to five variables:

1. the level of economic development;
2. the population density;
3. the number of vehicles;
4. the physiography;
5. government policy.

But road patterns are also the result of other factors. Trunk roads are provided as links between areas of higher road densities across regions which would otherwise be roadless. Only a single road links the coastlands of Kenya with the interior highlands, each region having a road network of its own.

In contrast, the lack of bridging points over major rivers and the lack of frontier crossings has a constricting effect. To reach Northern Nigeria from the south the Niger–Benue river system must be crossed. In 1970 there were only three bridge points (two of them road/rail and the other a road across the Kainji dam) along some 1,700 km. Similarly, there are only 12 motorable crossings of all the Ghana frontiers.

Most trunk roads now have a tar-seal (*tarmet* as opposed to *tarmac*). Foundations are poor, but even a bitumen strip is important, for gravel roads become badly corrugated and the consequent vibration severely reduces vehicle life. Secondary roads normally have a gravel surface, culverts and bridges, which allow them to be used through the wet season. Finally there is a large mileage of unsurfaced tracks, impassable after rain, but fulfilling a vital pioneering function.

In developing countries the road net is constantly being extended and improved by the building of new trunk roads and the upgrading of existing ones, by the construction of secondary roads and the addition of long, but often unrecorded, lengths of motorable tracks. The substitution of ferries by bridges over the wider rivers is also an important process as it reduces long and costly delays.

The financing of road systems is from a variety of sources. In West Africa funds for building and upkeep of trunk roads are provided by central governments, mainly from their own resources of taxation, though occasionally foreign aid funds are specifically earmarked for particular road-building projects. The secondary road system is the responsibility of provincial governments and local authorities. The *feeder* roads are provided by:

(a) produce marketing boards;
(b) timber and mining firms;
(c) individual villages on a self-help basis, with or without government aid.

The organisation of road transport, passenger and freight, varies in detail from country to country in the Third World. It is intended to concentrate mainly on conditions to be found in West Africa (White & Gleave 1971: Ch. 9). Here investment in lorries and taxis is one of the few outlets for personal savings. African participation in road transport has thus been the main source of funds for the industry since very early days. Most lorries are owned and operated singly or in very small fleets. In the Anglophone countries an unspecialised vehicle emerged. Locally built bodies with open side and with light roofs are mounted on imported chassis. Planks for passengers are placed across the vehicle, so that the latter can be speedily adapted to carry any combination of load from all-freight to all-passenger.

Partly for ease of identification by patrons, these *mammy-wagons* are often gaily decorated, including slogans, sacred or profane, such as 'Save us, O Lord' or 'Beautiful woman never stay with one man, why?' They lack comfort, but maximum flexibility is combined with minimum cost.

The mammy-wagon is normally confined to the forest and coastal regions. In other parts passengers are carried atop the loads of ordinary lorries. In East Africa and South America rather primitive motor buses are common, equipped with enormous roof-racks for the ample baggage passengers normally take with them.

In West Africa, as main roads improved during the 1950s specialised vehicles emerged, first petrol tankers and then high-capacity lorries for freight transport. With these latter, larger haulage firms came into existence, owned both by African and by foreign firms.

On the passenger side, although some long-distance buses have been introduced, most specialised passenger vehicles are minibuses carrying about 12 passengers. Taxis are also used, not only for town work but on long inter-urban runs. They are not exclusively hired, but are operated as minibuses. This system is widespread in Kenya and in South America, where in Peru the long-distance taxi is the *collectivo* and in Venezuela it is the *por-puesta*.

In many developing countries lorries, buses and taxis outnumber the few private cars, which are mainly concentrated into the capital cities and other large towns. Nevertheless, in the large cities traffic congestion is just as serious a problem as it is in economically developed countries. The Central Business Districts are highly developed, but the provision of public transport lags behind. Buses and trains tend to be uncomfortable and overcrowded and this, coupled with the very low densities of the wealthier suburbs, leads to a high level of car commuting which leads to bad congestion.

3. Railways (Jane's Yearbooks, annual). In the early days railways had a pioneering function, but this ceased with the development of road transport. In most developing countries the latter now accounts for the majority of the traffic carried. In a few areas railways have a residual function as local carriers because no roads have yet been built. But these areas are getting less each year.

On the other hand, railways have an important part to play:

(a) when there is a heavy traffic flow; and/or
(b) where distances are long.

Although some lines (such as those in Sierra Leone) have been closed through loss of traffic, since 1945 there has been a considerable mileage of new railways opened, simply because economies have been developing so fast they have created a demand for heavy transport flows in excess of the existing rail and road links.

As has already been pointed out, minerals usually provide the base load which justifies the building of a new railway. In some cases the lines are built solely for this purpose. In Mauritania a 646 km railway of 4 ft 8½ in gauge (1,435 mm) was opened in 1963 to connect the iron mines at Zoueraté with the port of Nouadhibou. Only iron-ore is carried. Trains are of 18,500 tonnes gross (12,000 tonnes payload) and are controlled from a central office in radio communication with the drivers. In contrast the 213 km Swaziland Railway (1964), built to tap iron-ore resources, also carries petroleum, sugar and miscellaneous freight.

Less frequently, agricultural traffic is sufficient to justify the building of a railway. The land-locked Central African country of Malawi formerly relied entirely for its agricultural exports on a rail outlet to the Mozambique port of Beira, but in 1970 a second link was opened to the port of Moçambique.

In many developing countries there is no railway system as such. A single line, with or without branches, leads inland from a port. There may be several such isolated lines in a single country, sometimes of different gauges. Where a system does exist, as in Colombia or Nigeria, the network is still embryonic in terms of the number of junctions (or traffic nodes) and length of line in relation to area and population.

Because of the poor return on capital, most railways in developing countries were financed by the Government concerned. But a number of lines were built with private finance, either to exploit mineral deposits or under favourable concessions by the Government. In recent years all new construction or improvement of existing lines has been financed either by the particular Government, with or without foreign aid, or by companies concerned with mineral exploitation.

Since with few exceptions railways are government-owned, many governments take steps to protect their assets by regulating the growth of competing road traffic. This may take the form of restricting licences issued to long-distance hauliers on routes parallel to railways. Ghana forbids the carriage of cocoa and timber by road between points where a rail service is provided. Other countries, such as Bénin (formerly Dahomey), made no investment in the very bad roads paralleling rail routes, but instead concentrating on improving roads feeding and extending the lines. On the other hand, many countries, such as Senegal and Nigeria, have in recent years made no attempt to regulate competing road traffic.

4. The air. Where surface transport is poor or even virtually non-existent and consequently costly, the air has a considerable role in internal passenger transport. In the 1950s, in terms of cost per passenger-km, it was cheaper to hire a light plane than a Land Rover and driver in parts of East Africa. In Nigeria, with 13 state capitals and a federal capital, all separated by long distances and poor roads, there is a large official demand for air transport. Apart from its use for passengers and mail, sometimes the air also provides the least-cost method of transport for general freight traffic.

Air transport involves sophisticated equipment compared with motor transport. Consequently, skilled labour is needed to maintain and operate the equipment, even though it has nothing like the complexity associated with airline operation on inter-continental routes and those within the USA and Europe. The greatest development of air transport in a pioneering situation is therefore in the remoter areas of economically advanced countries, areas such as the Canadian Arctic and Tropical Australia.

There is a certain amount of commercial activity by light aircraft in Kenya and many of the larger ranches and plantations have landing-strips, while there are air-taxi firms in Nigeria. But on the whole there is little air activity in Tropical Africa other than scheduled passenger–mail–high-value-cargo services.

On the other hand, in parts of South America the air is used to a greater extent as a pioneering instrument. In Ecuador and Peru the military operate air services for passengers and cargo to serve very remote pioneering airstrips. In Peru on the eastern slopes of the Andes many jungle settlements depend completely on the air for their transport links. One settlement did have a road connection, but this was washed away one rainy season. This was not repaired and the area became completely dependent on the air. Although it was an area of expanding export production, the only adjustment was a shift from rice and bananas to higher value cocoa and coffee.

One difficulty facing the pioneering operators is that small and medium-sized aircraft are now very complex and sophisticated pieces of machinery. There has been no really suitable replacement for the Douglas DC3 (known in Britain as the *Dakota*). This aircraft, which first went into service in 1935, is still at work in Tropical Africa and South America. With a capacity of 21 passengers and a total payload of 3.54 tonnes, it has a cruising speed of 264 kph and a range of 1,280 km. Its two piston engines and its airframe were relatively simple to maintain and were thoroughly reliable. It was the workhorse of the air and almost ideal for pioneering; its role in developing air transport in under-developed countries is incalculable. Most of its successors have proved much less suited for pioneering.

5. *Seaports*. These play a particularly important role in the infrastructure of developing countries (Hoyle & Hilling 1970), which are dependent on increasing the volume of their exports to provide themselves with the necessary foreign exchange to import capital goods and bulky raw materials, such as petroleum, cement and structural steel, to permit the industrial development which will lead to economic and therefore social advance. It is important that there should be sufficient investment in the ports to allow them to handle the expected volume of exports and imports at as low a cost per tonne as possible. In West Africa, during the early 1950s the ports of Ghana were just not able to handle the increased volume of imports demanded as a result of very high cocoa prices. Because imports were thus limited, demand exceeded supply and there was considerable inflation.

On the other hand, it is important to match investment aimed at expanding port capacity with that aimed at expanding the capacity of roads and railways serving the port. During the 1950s expansion in the port of Mombasa and in the capacity of the railway leading inland were seldom in step. Although new berths were provided they could not be used to the full because railway capacity formed a bottle-neck, and vice versa.

Because of their limited capacity, ports in many developing countries become heavily congested. The cost of the subsequent delays to shipping is passed on to the cargo shippers, thus raising the price of exports and imports. As port equipment becomes more sophisticated, to increase capacity involves heavy capital cost. Thus all new equipment would have to be intensively used to make it economic. Accordingly, investment has been concentrated on fewer and larger ports.

Case study – the ports of Ghana

A good example of this trend is provided by the ports of Ghana. There were no natural harbours and trade was conducted through surf-ports. As we have seen (p. 27), working a surf-port is slow and costly, while cargoes are liable to damage by water. In addition, before the First World War land communications were primitive, slow and costly. It cost as much to carry a tonne of mining stores the 40 km from Axim to Tarkwa as it did to ship that quantity from Liverpool to Axim. Therefore, each surf port had a very restricted hinterland and in the early 1900s there were some 30 surf-ports along the 530 km of the Ghana coastline.

Westward from Accra a series of low bluff headlands provide some shelter on their eastern side from the surf, which comes in from the south-west. The authors maintain it is no coincidence that Elmina Castle, built by the Portuguese in 1480, is sited on the headland, in the lee of which is the only beach in Ghana on which an ordinary ship's boat can be landed safely. In later years a number of very fine European castles were built on other headlands to protect the beaches in the lee of the headlands. Among them were three at Accra itself.

Gradually some of the ports were provided with improved communications with the interior. A road (in reality a trail) was provided inland from Cape Coast, while Sekondi and Accra were selected as railway termini. In turn, investment was concentrated on these favoured ports. In later years the road system was focused on the now larger ports of Sekondi and Accra, which meant more port facilities being provided there. Gradually ships ceased to call at the smaller ports.

At first, investment took the form of improving the natural shelter of the headlands by building short moles. In addition, at Accra a small pier with a rail siding and a crane was provided to handle heavier indivisible loads such as railway rolling-stock brought in by the surf-boats. At Sekondi a much larger railway pier was built in the lee of a breakwater so that manganese ore could be loaded into large barges, which could be towed out to the ships.

In the early 1920s economic growth in Ghana was such that investment in an artificial harbour protecting cargo berths was now justified. A site where there was deep water close to the shore was selected at Takoradi, just west of Sekondi. The new port was opened in 1928. Thereafter road transport has focused more and more traffic on Takoradi and Accra. By 1930 only nine ports remained open and by 1955 only five. By 1946 Takoradi was handling 92 per cent by weight of the exports of Ghana and 77 per cent of the imports. As the post-war economy was expanding fast, in 1949 port extensions were put in hand. They were completed in 1955.

Meanwhile attention was focused on the need for a similar deep-water port for the eastern part of the country, a need which would become imperative if the aluminium industry developed in connection with power from the Akosombo dam on the Volta River. Accra was unsuited to further development, so a site was selected at Tema, a small fishing village 24 km to the east. Work started in 1951 and the first ships entered in 1961. By 1967 Tema had already overtaken Takoradi in tonnage handled. In that year it dealt with 87 per cent by weight of the imports and 28 per cent of the exports.

In the 60 years between 1905 and 1965 the 30 primitive surf-ports of Ghana had given way to the two large and well-equipped ports of Tema and Takoradi, which handle a very much greater tonnage of traffic. Neither of these places were numbered in the original 30.

Chapter 12
Geographical change in patterns of transport since 1950

The period since 1950 has been marked by far-reaching technological change in transport, though it must be remembered that many of the changes we shall be examining started before that date. Technological change and the economic changes in cost and price structures that have accompanied it have in turn caused widespread change in the patterns of transport systems.

Passenger transport

The most important geographical change in passenger transport has been brought about by the spread of private car ownership. In Great Britain the number of cars grew from 1.96 m. in 1948 to 14.15 m. in 1980 (British Road Federation), the number having approximately doubled over any ten years during that period. In the latter year there was one car for every 3.5 persons, which was a representative level for Western Europe generally. On the other hand, as early as 1965 there were 75 m. private cars in the USA, about one car to two persons. It has been predicted that this level will eventually be reached in Western Europe by about 1990, though fuel crises and the economic recession of the early 1980s may postpone this date.

Thus, while passenger journeys as a whole have greatly increased, those made by private car have increased even faster, at the expense of all forms of public transport. Between 1960 and 1970 the estimated total of passenger-km in Great Britain rose by 60 per cent. But passenger-km by private car rose by 120 per cent, while passenger-km by bus and coach fell by 23 per cent and by rail by 11 per cent. Over the next decade the trend continued, though at a much reduced rate. Passenger-km rose by a further 16.5 per cent in total, but the private car share rose by 28.7 per cent. The fall in the share of public transport was much smaller, 4 per cent in the case of bus and coach and 2 per cent in that of rail. But by 1980 cars and motor cycles accounted for 80 per cent of the estimated passenger-km.

Many of the consequential geographical changes have already been mentioned (Christensen 1966; Patmore 1971; Rivers 1972; Rae 1971). But they can be usefully summarised here.

In the first place there has been considerable change in the morphology of urban areas, both in town centres and in suburbs. In town centres it has become necessary to separate the various functions that the street system was traditionally expected to perform: namely access by pedestrians and vehicles to premises lining the streets, parking, local circulation by pedestrians and vehicles, and arteries for through vehicular traffic. Separation has involved the construction of outer and inner ring-roads to divert through and local traffic respectively from the central area, and the removal of houses, shops and commercial premises from the main radial roads, grouping them into traffic-free areas such as shopping precincts or housing estates with vehicle access only to the periphery.

This rebuilding of town centres, involving radical alterations in street layout and morphology of buildings, has been partly the response to the relative and absolute decline in the importance of central areas as they lose functions to the suburbs in the Motor Age. For whereas reliance on public transport leads to centralisation, the use of the motor car leads to decentralisation. Thus shopping functions are becoming decentralised to suburban or 'out-of-town' centres. These may have a range of shops and supermarkets, or they may be dominated by a single very large 'hypermarket'. To quote two random examples of out-of-town hypermarkets, there is one at Birchwood, almost mid-way between Manchester and Liverpool, adjacent to the intersection of the M6 and M62 motorways, and one at Barrhill, 9.5 km. from Cambridge on the A604 trunk road to Huntingdon. A very large suburban centre has been created at Brent Cross, at the junction of the M1 and the North Circular Road in North London.

The car has allowed commuters a much wider range of choice in a place of residence in relation to their place of work. This has resulted in extensive migration from urban areas into rural villages. In spite of rising costs the trend is continuing. The Preliminary Report on the 1981 Census of England and Wales reveals an inter-censal decrease of 1.9 per cent in the population of urban areas and a 9.7 per cent increase in that of rural areas. If journeys of up to 60 minutes each way are regarded as being tolerable, no village between the southern boundary of the Lake District and the English Channel is beyond commuting range of a major urban area.

There have also been changes in the pattern of holiday and recreation areas. While the railway was the principal means of transport to the seaside, coastal resort areas were mainly confined to towns, large ones such as Brighton and Blackpool down to small ones, served by wayward branch lines, such as Burnham-on-Sea (Somerset) and Hornsea (Humberside). The car, however, has rendered virtually the whole of the coastline accessible. Coastal villages have expanded and in many areas the gaps between filled by caravan sites.

Similarly, inland recreation areas are becoming increasingly accessible and therefore vulnerable to development to such an extent that the environment is threatened, while local roads become overcrowded at holiday times.

However, the decentralising trends, as far as rural and coastal areas are concerned, are held in check by the planning policies of National and Local Government, which are based on the realisation of the limited amount of land available and the need to preserve the environment. Suburban decentralisation is slowed by pressures to maintain the functions and quality of town centres. Decentralisation has therefore not proceeded as far as in many parts of North America.

The car has also brought about geographical change in the patterns of other transport modes, particularly in rural areas, involving the widespread closure of branch railway lines and of intermediate stations on main lines. By 1980 Gloucestershire had only four stations. There has also been an almost equal contraction of rural bus services (Hibbs 1968; 1975).

Another change of great geographical importance has been the rapid growth of air travel (Sealy 1966). Development in long-haul (inter-continental) operations has been concentrated into the relatively short period since 1945. At first the trend was to reinforce the traditional lines of communication along established sea routes such as those across the North Atlantic and to the Far East via Suez. Along these the air created new traffic and abstracted that formerly going by sea. By 1955 40 per cent of passengers crossing the North Atlantic travelled by air and by 1967 87 per cent. In 1979 of passengers arriving in the UK from North America, 3.5 m. were travelling by air and 14,900 by sea. As far as the North Atlantic is concerned, passenger liners run scheduled services only in summer, while in 1978 passenger sailings from Southampton to southern Africa ceased, while the West African passenger services were withdrawn almost a decade earlier.

In the case of the Far East and of direct flights to the West Coast of North America, the increased reliability of aircraft and extended range and advances in the sciences of navigation and meteorology allowed the inauguration of direct flights over the Arctic along Great Circles. This developed entirely new lines of communication.

In the case of intra-continental transport, because of reduced costs, increased reliability in terms of safety and time-keeping and increased capacity, the air has become extremely important, especially in North America, where it accounts for the majority of inter-city passenger-journeys by public transport as opposed to the car. Travel by rail has been reduced to 1 per cent of the total. Development in Europe has also been considerable, but because of competition from surface transport, especially rail, the proportion carried is not so high.

The impact of air travel within the UK has not been nearly so great, due to short distances, time taken getting to and from airports, and rapid increase in speed by surface modes both by rail and motorway. The exception is where a water crossing gives the air an added advantage. Thus traffic to and from Aldergrove (Belfast) and the Channel Islands airports is much greater in proportion to the size of their catchment areas compared with similar-sized airports on mainland Britain. Air traffic to and from Orkney and Shetland has also greatly increased with the development of the North Sea oilfields.

Freight transport

In the field of freight transport, changes of equal or even greater importance have taken place. For example there has been a spread in the use of the motor lorry parallel with that of the private car. In 1946 there were 560,000 goods vehicles in use in Great Britain. By 1979 numbers had grown more than threefold to 1.7 m. The majority, 68.5 per cent, were vans of less than 1.5 tonnes unladen weight. But of the rest the proportion of heavy lorries is growing. In 1965 there were 24,000 vehicles over 8 tonnes unladen weight, but by 1979 there were 121,100.

All this has resulted in new traffic coming on to the roads and the transfer of existing traffic from rail and water. Between 1960 and 1970 carryings by road rose from 1,216 m. tonnes to 1,703 m., while rail carryings fell from 254 to 209 m. The trend is continuing, though at a reduced rate, especially in longer-distance traffic. This has resulted in widespread change in the location of industrial plants and in patterns of farming (Ch. 8). It has also led to low-cost pioneer transport in underdeveloped areas (Ch. 12).

Before turning to specific studies, a simple classification of the basic methods of freight handling is useful. Freight may be handled in three ways.

1. Break-bulk. This is the traditional method of freight handling. Heterogeneous cargo is packed into cases, cartons, drums, sacks, etc. in an infinite range of shapes and sizes. Each package is handled separately when loaded, off-loaded or transhipped. These mean high levels of labour inputs and therefore high costs. Though developments such as the widespread use of fork-lift trucks have led to marginal change, there has been no basic technological change in this method.

2. Bulk. Bulk cargo consists of homogeneous shipments of single commodities, such as petroleum, vegetable oils, grain, ores, sugar and cement, handled without any form of packaging. Strictly speaking, it need not necessarily mean large traffic flows. But bulking requires heavy investment in specially designed vehicles and in the equipment for loading and unloading. This investment leads to economies of scale and large traffic flows are needed to obtain these.

3. Unit-loads. This term is used when package freight is partially consolidated into larger units of uniform dimensions and which can be easily transferred at low cost from one transport mode to another.

Example 1: Bulk transport of iron ore and coal

During the nineteenth century oil was shipped in wooden barrels (the 'barrel' is still the unit of crude petroleum output). The first oil-tanker went into service in 1884. By 1912 the world tanker fleet amounted to 1.5 m. dwt. But after 1920 tanker tonnage rapidly increased in response to the growth in world consumption of petroleum. Between 1952 and 1956 alone the world tanker fleet rose from 31 to 45 m. dwt. By 1971 nearly 40 per cent of the world's shipping tonnage was accounted for by tankers. With the halting of the increase in world trade after the 1974 oil crisis this proportion has remained constant since then.

Traditionally iron ore was conveyed in unspecialised tramp ships, as likely to carry grain, cotton or general cargo as ore. Specialised ore carriers were first used from 1900 onwards on the North American Great Lakes. But after 1945 their use spread widely in ocean transport at the expense of the tramps. The economies gained from increasing size of vessels were examined on page 26. Because of these, ore carriers have greatly increased in size. The number of bulk carriers over 15,000 dwt increased from 244 in 1961 to 1,443 in 1971. The number over 100,000 dwt has also increased, from 45 in 1970 to 376 in 1980. In recent years the *universal bulk ship* (UBS) has been introduced. This is a multipurpose vessel capable of carrying in bulk a variety of dry and liquid cargoes (Couper 1972).

The consequences of increasing size and range of ocean ore carriers, together with concurrent development in methods of ore carrying over long distances and at low cost by rail (White 1979a,b), can be summarised as follows.

1. There has been a very great increase in both the tonnage of iron ore carried and in the average length of haul (Manners 1967). Figure 12.1 shows something of the extent of these changes. In 1950 long-distance flows were virtually limited to those from Sweden and Algeria to Western Europe and from Sweden, Labrador and Venezuela to the USA. By 1965 large-scale exports had started from many other parts of the world.

In 1960 exports from the three West African countries of Mauritania, Sierra Leone and Liberia amounted to 5.04 m. tonnes, already a great increase over the 1950 figure. But by 1964 they had risen to 24.1 m. tonnes. Rail hauls from interior mines were also involved, the longest being of 650 km in Mauritania. South America also shared in the increased trade, exporting to the USA, Japan and Western Europe. By 1970 8.5 m. tonnes of ore were shipped from Australia to Japan, while smaller quantities were even being shipped to Europe.

2. Because of cost reductions in long-distance transport of iron ore, established steel producers such as the USA, West Germany and the UK, have switched from high-cost indigenous sources of ore to imports. By 1963 the UK was importing a weight of high-grade ore equal to the 19.9 m. tonnes of low-grade home-produced ore. By 1969 home production had fallen to 12.2 m. tonnes and by 1980 it had ceased altogether with the closure of the Corby steel plant.

3. Proximity to ore supplies is no longer necessary to establish a steel industry, and countries without indigenous ore and coal have been able to expand steel production. The supreme example is that of Japan. In 1943, at the height of her war effort, Japanese steel production reached 7.6 m. tonnes. After the war Japan was cut off from her nearby supplies of ore and coal in

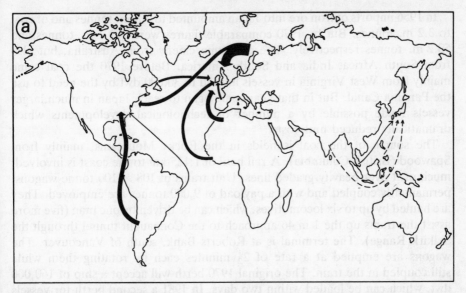

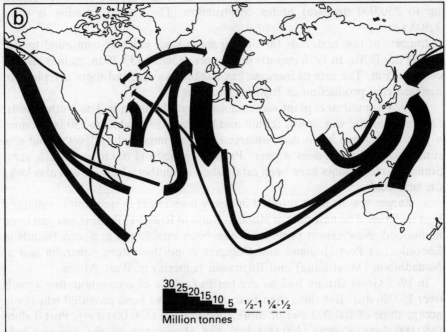

30 25 20 15 10 5   ½-1 ¼-½
Million tonnes

Fig. 12.1 Movement of iron ore by sea: (a) in 1939 (after Manners 1967); and (b) in 1968 (after Couper 1972)

Manchuria, but from the mid-1950s began to rebuild and expand steel-making capacity on the basis of long-range importation of raw materials. By 1970 production reached 85 m. tonnes and by 1975 120 m. tonnes. After that, even Japan felt the consequences of the world recession and the 1980 production was 111.4 m. tonnes.

In 1956 imports of iron ore into Japan amounted to 7.8 m. tonnes and of coal to 3.2 m. tonnes. But by 1970 comparable figures were 102.1 m. tonnes and 50.2 m. tonnes respectively. The ore came chiefly from Australia, but also from South Africa, India and South America. Before 1970 the coal came mainly from West Virginia in vessels limited to 30,000 dwt by the need to use the Panama Canal. But in that year coal began to reach Japan in much larger vessels made possible by a number of technological developments which dramatically reduced unit costs.

The source of the coal is fields in the Rocky Mountains, mainly from Spawood (British Columbia). A rail haul of 1,125 km to the coast is involved, much of it over heavily graded lines. Unit trains of 108 × 100 tonne wagons, permanently coupled and with a payload of 9,000 tonnes are employed. They are hauled by up to six locomotives, which can be driven by one man (five more assist the trains up the 1 in 46 approach to the Connaught tunnel through the Selkirk Range). The terminal is at Roberts Bank, south of Vancouver. The wagons are emptied at a rate of $2\frac{1}{2}$ minutes each by rotating them while still coupled in the train. The original 1970 berth will accept a ship of 160,000 dwt, which can be loaded within two days. In 1981 a second berth for vessels up to 250,000 dwt was under construction. The Pacific crossing is some 7,500 km.

Imports of raw materials for the Japanese steel industry continued to rise during the 1970s. In 1976 imports of iron ore reached 133.75 m. tonnes, and of coal 60.75 m. The rate of increase has slackened since, but there are plans to increase coal production in British Columbia.

In 1924 a small steel plant was established at IJmuiden in The Netherlands. Destroyed in the war, it was rebuilt and by 1952 was producing 550,000 tonnes a year. Since then it has been enlarged several times and by 1969 output was running at 4.3 m. tonnes a year. Present capacity is 6.0 m. tonnes a year. Similarly, steel plants have been established in southern Italy, which also lacks ore and coal.

4. Larger vessels have resulted in heavy investment in new and in enlarged port facilities. The new port of Roberts Bank in British Columbia has just been mentioned. New export ports have also been established at Seven Islands in Labrador, at Port Hedland and Dampier in north-western Australia and at Nouadhibou (Mauritania) and Buchanan (Liberia) in West Africa.

In 1965 Great Britain had no ore berths capable of accommodating vessels over 15,000 dwt. But since then four terminals have been provided which will accept ships of 100,000 dwt or more, Immingham (100,000 dwt), Port Talbot (150,000 dwt), Redcar (150,000 dwt) and Hunterston on the Lower Clyde Estuary (250,000 dwt). Similar improvements have been made at Dunkirk, Rotterdam and other Continental ports and in Japan there are at least five berths which will accept 350,000-tonners.

5. New steel-making capacity in established steel-producing countries is now tending to be located at coastal sites, where ore can be unloaded directly from bulk carriers into the plant, or where very short rail hauls are involved. In the UK plants were established at Port Talbot and Llanwern, the latter using ore imported through Port Talbot. The Anchor Works at Scunthorpe which went

into service in 1973 imports ore through Immingham 32 km. distant by rail. In France a very large plant has been established at Dunkirk (Bird, 1971).

Example 2: Containerisation

Unit-loads take many forms. British Rail now handles the bulk of its parcels traffic by the *British Rail universal trolley equipment* (BRUTEs). These are small trolleys with high sides, which can be loaded at the station with parcels brought in by van, towed by a tractor in trains to the points where they can be pushed into rail vans. Off-loading for transfer or at final destination is just as easy.

But the principal development has been in the use of large *containers*. This has been so rapid since 1965 and the effects have been so far-reaching that people talk of the *container revolution*. The container is essentially a large box which can be loaded with packaged freight and which can be transhipped easily and quickly and therefore cheaply from one transport mode to another. The International Standards Organisation (ISO) has laid down that container sizes should be 8 feet high and 8 feet wide (2.44 × 2.44 m), the length being in modules of 10 feet (3.05 m) from 10 feet (3.05 m) up to 40 feet (12.20 m). The dimensions of containers are still conventionally expressed in feet.

Container operations become economic when the cost savings achieved by their use outweighs the investment in the specialised equipment needed (Johnson & Garnett 1971). On the debit side are:

(a) the cost of containers;
(b) the specialised vehicles or vessels;
(c) equipment for terminal and transhipment points, which includes the large and costly cranes (called *portainers*).

Cost savings include:

(a) the more intensive use of the ships, lorries, rail wagons and aircraft, due to the quicker turn-rounds brought about by speedier loading and unloading;
(b) because of the speed of loading, unloading and transhipment, transit times are speeded up, which reduces the capital sums locked up in goods *in the pipeline*;
(c) the speed and regularity of containerised services reduces the cost of warehousing stocks of goods at the destination;
(d) the greatly reduced demand for labour at ports and other transhipment points;
(e) reduction in breakages and pilfering.

Deep-sea containers

The geographical consequences of the container revolution, as far as ocean shipping is concerned, may be summarised as follows (McKinsey & Co. Inc. 1967).

1. Because it takes so long to load and discharge a conventional cargo vessel, up to a fortnight to turn round a 10,000-ton cargo liner, there is a limit

to the size of such a vessel. Few exceed 15,000 gross registered tons (grt). On the other hand a large container vessel can be turned round in less than 24 hours, so container vessels can be increased in size to 30,000–40,000 grt.. Economies of scale similar to those we have discussed for bulk carriers can thus be obtained. This means that deep-water berths and approaches to them must be provided. Only a few existing general cargo ports are capable of accepting such large ships without radical alteration, and many will never be able to accept them.

2. The rapid turn-round of container ships and consequently their more intensive use, together with their greatly increased capacity, means that the number of vessels required to maintain a particular service will be drastically reduced. It has been calculated that only five large ships will be needed on the UK – USA run to do the work of 50 smaller conventional cargo liners.

3. In a trade such as that between Europe and the West Coast of Africa a cargo liner may make up to 15 calls on the outward leg of a voyage from London to Pointe Noire (Congo) and as many on the homeward leg. On the other hand, in container operations there is a clear trend towards reducing the number of ports of call. In order to increase overall speed (to use the costly vessel as intensively as possible) and to obtain full loads at each port of call, a container ship should not make more than four calls. The ideal is a simple shuttle service between two ports.

4. There could also be a trend towards the reduction of the sea component of a transit, due to the reduction in the cost of the land haul as a consequence of containerisation. This trend has not yet clearly emerged, but it is envisaged that containers from Europe to the Far East could be railed across North America, while Fremantle in Western Australia could develop as the primary container port for the whole country. Already shipments of containers have been made from Great Britain to Japan via the Trans-Siberian Railway, thus involving only two short sea-crossings (*Containerisation International* 1979).

5. The morphology of container berths differs greatly from that of break-bulk berths while the appearance of a container port differs from that of a conventional general cargo port. Whereas a break-bulk berth will have up to six cranes with 5-tonne lifts, a container berth will require one or two very large portainers, each capable of lifting loaded containers weighing 30 tonnes. Behind, a large open stacking area of several hectares replaces the conventional transit sheds. The stacking area must be served by rail lines and roadways and also equipped with portainers. Straddle carriers are used to convey the containers between the stacking area and the quayside.

6. A container berth can handle more cargo in a given time (the *throughput*) than can the most up-to-date break-bulk berth. The former can have a throughput of 720,000 tonnes a year, against one of 150,000 tonnes a year for the latter. On this basis one container berth will replace five conventional ones.

7. This means that the number of berths in any one country will also be greatly reduced. One study (McKinsey & Co. Inc. 1967) estimated that once the UK deep-sea trade is fully containerised, no more than 30 deep-water berths will be needed in 3 or 4 ports. Therefore competition between ports is

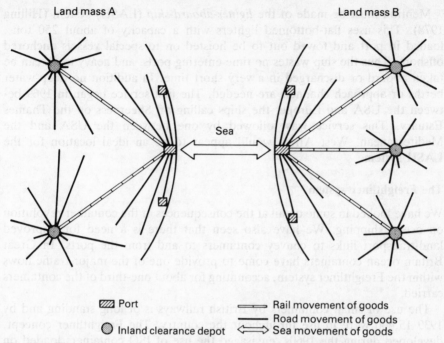

Fig. 12.2 The influence of containerisation on port development. (After Johnson & Garnett 1971)

becoming very acute. Any general cargo port which cannot offer container facilities faces a bleak future, yet if every port does provide them, over-investment will follow.

A good example of enterprise has been set by the small East Coast port of Felixstowe, which was the first in the country to grasp the full significance of the container revolution. In 1960 the port was almost moribund, handling a few thousand tonnes of cargo. But by March 1967 two deep-water berths were in operation and six by 1980. In 1968, 33,800 containers were dealt with, and 70,000 the following year. In 1975 230,400 twenty foot equivalent units (TEU) were handled. Felixstowe was now the second container port in the UK, ex-ceeded only by London which dealt with 260,400 TEU.

8. Figure 12.2 is a theoretical model of the consequences upon ports and links between them and their hinterlands. The nature of these links between a container port and its hinterland are important. It will also be realised that the work of the port will be carried on most efficiently if operations normally associated with ports can be moved elsewhere. Since many export consign-ments are too small to fill a container, small shipments must be consolidated into container-sized lots by agents. These containers should be loaded and unloaded (*stuffed* and *stripped* in the picturesque jargon) and customs examina-tion carried out on all containers as near as possible to the points of origin or destination of goods. *Inland ports* have therefore been established in industrial centres such as Birmingham, Manchester and Leeds.

Mention must be made of the *lighter-aboard-ship* (LASH) system (Hilling 1978). This uses flat-bottomed lighters with a capacity of about 250 tons, loaded in port and towed out to be hoisted on to special vessels anchored offshore. Thus the ship wastes no time entering ports, and heavy loads can be taken aboard or discharged in a very short time. In addition no deep-water berths or approach channels are needed. The first service began in 1969 between the USA and Europe, the ships calling off Sheerness on the Thames Estuary. This service was followed by one between the USA and the Mediterranean. West Africa would appear to be an ideal location for the LASH system.

The Freightliner system

We have looked in some detail at the consequences of the container revolution on ocean shipping. We have also seen that there is a need for improved land-transport links to convey containers to and from the ports. In Great Britain ocean containers have come to provide one of the major traffic flows within the Freightliner system, accounting for about one-third of the containers carried.

The use of small containers by British railways is of long standing and by 1939 15,400 were in use throughout the country. The Freightliner concept, developed during the 1960s, envisaged the use of ISO containers loaded on high-speed trains shuttling between a network of terminals located in industrial areas and ports. The first service, between London and Glasgow, was inaugurated in 1965. After a slow build-up, due largely to trade union opposition, the system expanded rapidly after 1967. Under the 1968 Transport Act the system was transferred to a new company, Freightliners Ltd, owned by the National Freight Corporation (51%) and British Rail (49%), but under the 1978 Transport Act full ownership was returned to British Rail. By 1980 there were 25 terminals owned by Freightliners Ltd and 15 by other bodies, linked by 200 daily services. In 1979 871,000 TEU were carried.

The map (Fig. 12.3) shows the terminals. The shortest length of haul of the services, 107 km, is between Stratford (London) and Harwich, but this is solely concerned with traffic for the ferry services from Harwich to Zeebrugge, Rotterdam, Dunkirk and Esbjerg, which in turn connect with container-train services throughout Western Europe. The longest is 837 km from King's Cross (London) to Aberdeen, a purely domestic service largely concerned with meat traffic. It will be seen from the map that the terminals can be grouped into four types:

1. the Freightliners Ltd terminals, concerned with forwarding and receiving both general domestic, short sea and ocean traffic;
2. British Rail terminals at ferry ports to the Continent and Ireland;
3. terminals owned by Containerbase Ltd, which is a consortium of shipping companies and British Rail. They are located in industrial areas and are terminals of services to ports;
4. private terminals, owned by port authorities, steel plants and motor-car plants handling train-loads of their own traffic.

Freightliner Terminals in operation
31 December, 1980

Terminal operators

- • Freightliners Ltd
- ◉ Port authorities
- ≠ British Rail
- □ Other

Aberdeen

Dundee

Glasgow

Edinburgh

Newcastle

Stockton

Leeds · Hull

Liverpool
Holyhead ≠ · Manchester
Halewood · Sheffield
(Ford)

Nottingham

Birmingham
□ Coventry

≠ Fishguard · Llanwern
(Spencer Works) · □ Stewartby · Felixstowe ≠
Swansea · Harwich ≠

Port Talbot · Tilbury
(Abbey Works) · Cardiff · London ≠
· Bristol

Southampton

Poole

0   150 km

Willesden · Kings X
Park Royal ≠ · Stratford · Barking
London
Tilbury
0   150 km

Fig. 12.3 "Freightliner" terminals. Note: Freightliners Ltd became wholly owned by British Rail in 1979

153

Example 3: Roll-on-roll-off

A loaded lorry or trailer can sometimes be treated as a unit-load by being itself loaded on to another mode of transport. This will obviously reduce transit costs. Loading and off-loading is speedy and turn-rounds of the road vehicles and the other transport units reduced, as is the incidence of damage and pilfering. On the debit side are the cost of specialised loading equipment, of specialised transport units and the fact that the lorry itself is idle. This last factor can be reduced by using a semi-trailer rather than a lorry. The trailer alone is loaded on the other transport unit, while the tractor can be kept in more continuous use.

There are two situations where this system can be used, *short* sea-crossings and *long* rail hauls.

Short sea-crossings

This situation is a logical extension of river-crossings by vehicular ferry. The road vehicles can be driven on and off specially designed ships, the *roll-on-roll-off* or *Ro-Ro* system. However, because the *loadability* of the vehicles is by no means good, obviously much worse than with containers of a standard size, and because of the need to maximise the use of road vehicles, ferry-crossings are normally overnight at the longest.

In the past, of course, because sea transport was cheaper than land transport, the sea component of a journey was maximised. General cargo from Birmingham to Milan would have been sent by lorry to London, thence by sea to Genoa and on by lorry or rail to Milan. But if the lorry were going right through, the cross-Channel ferries, perhaps that from Southampton to Le Havre, would be used.

The first Ro-Ro facilities were provided for tourist cars in the form of a *garage* on one of the decks of the Dover – Dunkirk train ferries, which entered service in 1936. After the last war, aided by the building of a terminal at Dover in 1952, the traffic in tourist cars boomed. At Dover alone, accompanied cars increased from 220,000 in 1956 to 655,000 in 1966 and 1.3 m. in 1979. Commercial vehicles by Ro-Ro began in 1939 between Stranraer and Larne. After the last war a number of other services were started between Great Britain and Northern Ireland on the one hand and the Continent on the other, using tank-landing craft. These were gradually replaced by purpose-built vessels and new routes inaugurated. In addition, commercial vehicles are accepted on many services which are primarily for tourist cars. By 1980 there were 117 Ro-Ro sailings a week from Larne.

Ro-Ro services have been established in many other parts of the world where short sea-crossings are involved. There are services across the Baltic, between Italy and Greece, the North and South Islands of New Zealand and Tasmania and the Australian mainland. *Train-ferries*, of course, are almost as old as railways. From this country there are services between Dover and Dunkirk and between Harwich and Zeebrugge and Dunkirk. They are also highly developed across the Baltic and between the Japanese islands.

It is in the sphere of Ro-Ro that the hovercraft has at present its best future. There are only two cross-Channel services, Dover – Calais and Pegwell Bay (Ramsgate) – Calais operated by four ACVs, yet by 1971 they carried one-third of the tourist car traffic.

Trunk rail hauls

Where very long distances are involved, the costs of road haulage tend to be higher than rail. The exact break-even point is difficult to calculate, but it is probably about 480 km. The *piggy-back* or *trailer-on-flat-car* (TOFC) system was established by US railways in 1954. In 1955 there were 168,150 car-loadings at two trailers per wagon. By 1968 car-loadings had risen to 1,337,149. But to get this into perspective, this accounted for under 5 per cent of total car-loadings. Since 1968, a considerable number of new terminals have been established and car-loadings have increased to 1.9 m. in 1979 (8% of total loadings) although due to the trade recession there was a fall to 1.7 m. in 1980. Among other countries to adopt TOFC are Canada and Australia, while France uses a modified system using special wagons and adapted trailers, the *Kangerou* system.

Example 4: Air-cargo

Cargo (Smith 1974), especially in the form of mail, has been carried in aircraft since scheduled services began about 1920. Between 1950 and 1965 the volume of air-cargo grew extremely fast, at about 15 per cent per year, and by 1967 17 per cent by value of British exports were by air cargo. After that, partly due to containerisation in surface modes, expansion virtually ceased. In the following decade the value of exports by air grew only by some 2 per cent of total exports. By 1977 215,000 tonnes of exports were lifted and 41,000 tonnes of cargo carried on domestic services. Traditionally, due to rates on air-cargo being high in direct comparison with surface rates, commodities shipped by air are of exceptionally high value in proportion to their weight – gold bars, watches, drugs and so on. But to these may be added commodities of lower value, but which are highly perishable. Although transport costs may be high, to get the goods to market quickly and in good condition means higher prices and low wastage. Thus, flowers from the Scillies and the Channel Islands are normally sent by air-cargo to London. In this connection news is a perishable commodity. People are prepared to pay twice or three times the cost of a paper, provided it has been only recently published, by the time it reaches its destination.

In addition, air-cargo is employed for bulky low-value articles to meet an emergency. For example a large spare part for a machine vital to a Fijian sugar factory may be despatched by air so the factory may resume production in hours rather than weeks. In the same way, articles may be despatched by air to meet contract delivery dates.

Obviously, the principal contribution is speed. In 1843, when the official party attending the opening of the Folkestone–Boulogne ferry service arrived at Boulogne at midday, they presented their astonished French hosts with

London papers printed the previous night. In 1967 one of the authors bought a London Sunday paper at midday on the day of publication when he was in Ibadan in Nigeria (128 km from Lagos Airport).

Air-cargo rates may not always be costly in relation to surface routes. In many parts of the world surface transport is slow and costly, or even non-existent. In the outback of Australia large sheep and cattle stations depend on regular aircraft flights for mail and supplies. Aircraft are used widely for prospecting and trading in northern Canada. Finally, a good example of the potential for air-freighting in an underdeveloped area is provided by the building of the 500 km iron ore railway in Labrador from the port of Sept Iles to the mines at Schefferville, which was opened in 1954. All construction plant and supplies to the workers were flown to airstrips built at intervals along the route through roadless country. Even after the railway was open, passengers and light goods traffic was handled by air, the railway operating only as a specialised bulk ore carrier.

Air-cargo is carried by three methods:

1. By combination flights, which are ordinary scheduled passenger flights. The revenue from these is mainly from the passengers. Cargo is used to make up the balance of the payload, mail being given first priority.
2. By all-cargo flights. Though perhaps checked by the use of jumbo jets in combination flights with ample cargo space, all-cargo flights are growing in numbers, but are mainly found where there is a large volume of high-value cargo offering. The principal services are within North America and Europe or across the North Atlantic. All-cargo planes may be standard aircraft, often older ones, with the seats taken out. They may also be specially designed.
3. By charter flights. These are by aircraft chartered for unscheduled special flights, either for a single flight or for a specified number at specific intervals. The machines must be loaded to capacity and, if possible, a return load arranged so that economic rates can be quoted. But a whole range of widely differing aircraft is available and the type most suited to the job can be selected. The whole operation of chartering is similar to that traditionally used for tramp shipping. The Baltic Exchange in London, which arranges ship chartering, also brings airlines and their prospective customers in contact through its member firms of brokers.

The argument for unit-loads apply to air-cargo with as much force as for any other mode of transport. Loading general cargo on pallets or into containers drastically reduces the time an aircraft is on the ground and therefore the cost of the flight.

Conclusion

It will be seen from the examples briefly listed in this chapter that the technology of passenger and freight handling has developed very rapidly, particularly since 1960. This development has resulted in very important and widespread geographical change. To record these changes exhaustively in a textbook of this nature is a waste of time as change is so rapid the information would soon be out of date. But it is important that we should be aware of the trends of these changes. These can best be recorded by regular reference to the journals and annuals listed in the bibliography.

Part III

Selected
Quantitative
Approaches

Chapter 13

Quantitative methods for applied transport geography

Setting the scene

Quantitative methods have played an important role in transport studies for some 25 years, and are symptomatic of a more scientific approach to the subject (Harvey 1969). Garrison and his colleagues at the University of Washington were instrumental in fostering the quantitative revolution in geography generally, and in transport geography in particular (Garrison *et al*. 1959). At the same time a quantitative approach to strategic transport planning was being developed for the first urban transport studies (Detroit Metropolitan Area Traffic Study 1956), and operational research scientists were devoting some attention to the problems associated with transport administration and physical distribution management (e.g. Dantzig & Ramser 1958).

Quantitative studies of transport systems have multiplied since this pioneering work and span a broad spectrum of issues. To comprehend this material in an ordered and coherent fashion we adapt a simple but effective representation of a spatial system used by McLoughlin (1969). Essentially this involves a dissection of the transport system and its environment into **activities** and **stock**, each of which is cross-classified according to whether the activities or stock are associated with a single location or area, or with interrelationships between two or more locations or areas. Activities are classified as either **within-place**, such as employment, residential, shopping and recreational activities, or as **between-place**, namely flows of persons, goods or information arising almost exclusively from the need to perform different within-place activities in different locations (Fig. 13.1). The within-place activities are not only the motivating forces producing between-place activities, but are also responsible directly for their own accommodation in **adapted spaces**, such as houses, factories, shops and parks, and indirectly for **channel spaces** accommodating the between-place activities.

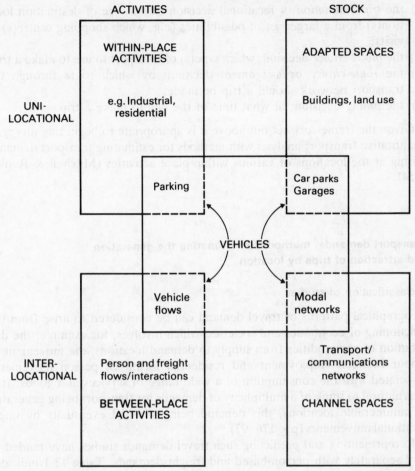

Fig. 13.1 Schematic representation of the transport system and its environment

In terms of this framework the transport system can be thought of as constituting between-place activities with an associated infrastructure, and which operates to service the demands of its environment defined in terms of the within-place activities accommodated in adapted spaces. However, within the transport system there is a special category of mobile stock, namely vehicles, which has intimate connections with the already defined categories of stock and activities. Thus, parking is a within-place activity occurring in adapted spaces, comprising garages and open space car parks. More obviously many flows of persons and goods occur in vehicles, so creating vehicular flows over various modal networks.

The behavioural basis of the above framework is made explicit by identifying the components of trip-making decisions:

(a) the *trip-generation* decision: the frequency with which a trip purpose should be made (e.g. how often to go shopping);
(b) the *vehicle-ownership* decision;

(c) the *trip-destination* or locational decision: the choice of destination location(s) from a larger set of possibilities (e.g. which shopping centre(s) to visit);

(d) the *mode-choice* decision: which type(s) of transport to use to make a trip;

(e) the *route-choice* or assignment decision: by which route through the transport network should a trip be made;

(f) the *timing* decision: at what time of the day to make a trip.

Given the framework set out above it is appropriate to begin this survey of quantitative transport analysis with methods for estimating transport demands arising at the locations of various within-place activities (Mitchell & Rapkin 1954).

Transport demands: methods for estimating the generation and attraction of trips by location

A classification of studies

Geographical patterns of travel demand can be considered to arise from the functioning of economies and societies, which involves, for example: the distribution of commodities from supply to demand locations; the movement of labour between employment and residential locations; person movements associated with the consumption of a wide range of services and goods. It is thus natural to think of a multiplicity of demands for transport being generated at innumerable locations, this demand being satisfied eventually by inter-locational movements (pp. 176–97).

In representing and predicting such travel demands studies have tended to deal separately with person-based and freight demands. Table 13.1 indicates the predominance of regression techniques in both areas, and also draws attention to a crucial distinction related to the scale at which such techniques are applied. The decision-making or behavioural units directly responsible for creating travel demands are households and various 'organisations', such as industrial firms, warehouses, shops, offices and so on. The so-called *disaggre-*

Table 13.1 A classification of techniques for forecasting trip generations and attractions.

	Person trips	Freight trips
Aggregate scale	Zonal regression (e.g. O'Sullivan 1967)	Zonal regression (e.g. Chisholm and O'Sullivan 1973)
Disaggregate scale	(i) Household regression (e.g. Douglas and Lewis, 1971a) (ii) Household category analysis (e.g. Wootton and Pick 1967)	Organisation regression (e.g. Starkie 1967; Watson 1975)

gate behavioural techniques use data applying directly to these individual households or organisations, or at least to behaviourally meaningful groupings of them. *Aggregate* methods, however, deal with data relating to households or organisations grouped together on some areal or zonal basis. The implications of this difference in approach will be brought out shortly, but first the general properties of the much-used regression methods must be considered.

General properties and assumptions of linear regression methods

To gain insight into the reasons for travel demand variations, the widely applicable multiple linear regression model could be used to relate, for example, a measure of household trip generation to plausible explanatory variables such as car ownership, household size and income. In general terms this model relates a dependent variable, Y_u, like trip generation, recorded over a set of observation units, u (which may be households, organisations or zones), to a set of independent variables, $X_u^1, X_u^2 \ldots X_u^l$, measuring various characteristics of these same units which are deemed to explain variations in the value of the dependent variable. This may be specified formally as:

$$Y_u = \alpha^0 + \alpha^1 X_u^1 + \alpha^2 X_u^2 \ldots \alpha^l X_u^l + \varepsilon_u \qquad [1]$$

where α^0 is an intercept parameter, α^1 to α^l are regression coefficients whose values measure by how much the number of generated trips, Y_u, will change as the values of the associated independent variables change by one unit and the ε_u are random error or disturbance terms measuring the deviations of the observed trips, Y_u, from the systematic linear component of the regression. Values of the parameters α^0 to α^l are estimated from sample data, usually by minimising the sum of squared deviations between observed and predicted trip generations, Y_u and $\hat{Y}_u$ respectively.[1]

Although linear regression appears a highly attractive technique for exploring multivariate travel demand situations, its validity is dependent on a set of assumptions which should not be seriously violated (Silk 1979; Johnston 1978):

(a) the independent variables should be measured with negligible error;
(b) the disturbance terms should be normally distributed, with a mean of zero and a constant variance for all values of the independent variables;
(c) the independent variables must not be strongly correlated with each other, otherwise multicollinearity is said to exist – indicating that two or more variables are at least partly explaining the same variation in the dependent variable; unfortunately deciding when multicollinearity is a serious enough problem to warrant attention involves subjective judgement;
(d) the dependent variable should be related linearly to the independent variables; various transformations of either or both types of variable may be employed to produce linearity if it is not exhibited using their actual measurements;
(e) the disturbance terms should be statistically uncorrelated, displaying no systematic trend with respect to: the regression line; the locations of the

observations; nor to any possible explanatory variable not included in the regression equation.

Provided these conditions are met, reasonable confidence can be placed in the results of tests assessing the statistical reliability and accuracy of the regression equation. These include tests of the statistical significance of the independent variables and intercept parameter, measures of goodness-of-fit between model predictions and observations, the construction of confidence intervals and the calculation of residual standard errors.

As will be seen subsequently, some of these general issues have cropped up when applying linear regression methods to travel demand estimation.

Zonal regression analysis

It was common practice until the late 1960s to estimate person trip generations and attractions by applying regression methods to zonal data (O'Sullivan 1967). A typical example relating to all person trips, O_i, generated from residential zones, i, in Reading in 1962 (Downes & Gyenes 1976) is:

$$\hat{O}_i = -39.32 + 2.74P_i - 0.13P_id_i \quad (R = 0.97) \tag{2}$$

where the independent variables are P_i, the population of each zone, and P_id_i, a crude measure of the accessibility of that population in terms of distance, d_i, from the town centre. The numerical values are those of the intercept parameter (-39.32) and the regression coefficients; the latter indicate that a population increase of one generates 2.74 additional trips, whereas an increase of one unit of population-distance, P_id_i, results in a 0.13 decline in trips. The multiple correlation coefficient, R, expresses how well the predicted trip generations, $\hat{O}_i$, compare with the observed ones, O_i.

Zonal regression has also been used to estimate freight generations and attractions by Chisholm and O'Sullivan (1973: Ch. 5) for a study area comprising the whole of Britain divided into 78 zones. An example from this study relating to the amounts of food commodities, D_j, attracted to each of the 78 zones, j, is:

$$\hat{D}_j = 5954.7 + 5.8E_j^{(F)} + 28.4E_j^{(Q)} \quad (R^2 = 0.76) \tag{3}$$

where $E_j^{(F)}$ denotes zonal employment in the agricultural, fishing and forestry industries, and $E_j^{(Q)}$ that in the food, drink and tobacco industries. The squared multiple correlation coefficient or coefficient of determination, R^2, indicates that 76 per cent of the between-zone variation in freight attractions is accounted for by the equation.

Considerable doubts have been voiced about the utility of zonal regression techniques because of inconsistent empirical results. Thus Douglas and Lewis (1970) point to different findings concerning the significance of various independent variables from one study area to another,[2] while other studies which have identified common explanatory variables reveal discrepancies between the magnitudes, and even the signs, of their regression coefficients. Such instability between different study areas is also evident for the same study area at different points in time. Thus Downes and Gyenes (1976) find that the statistically most reliable equation for all residential trip generations in Reading in 1971 is:

$$\hat{O}_i = -3.65 + 1.89P_i + 1.77V_i \quad (R = 0.99) \tag{4}$$

Comparing this with the 1962 equivalent, equation [2], it is observed that the number of cars owned per zone, V_i, replaces the accessibility measure as an explanatory variable, and marked changes have occurred in the magnitudes of the intercept and population regression coefficient. Such results imply that zonal regression may be an unreliable method for making trip generation and attraction forecasts. Somewhat surprisingly, however, Downes and Gyenes found for a series of zonal trip generation regressions that the equations fitted using 1962 data provided forecasts of 1971 trip generations only marginally inferior, in general, to those produced by regression equations fitted using 1971 data.

Nevertheless, there are still sound reasons against using zonal regression techniques if one is not obliged to rely on zonal data from the outset. The chief problem is that zonal regressions can account for only the variation *between* zones and not for any within-zone variation. As each zone's travel demands are the sum of the individual travel demands of household or organisational decision-making units located in the zone, any variation between these households or organisations in trip-generating or trip-attracting characteristics is lost irretrievably in the zone totals of trip generations and attractions. Similarly, within-zone variations in, for example, household car ownership or size of organisation, factors which are important in explaining trip-making, are eliminated by forming zonal aggregates or averages, such as average household car ownership and total zonal employment. All such zonal aggregation of the data is performed prior to the application of regression analysis. Consequently, evidence suggests that zonal regressions explain only a small proportion of the total variability in trip-making. Thus, Downes and Gyenes (1976) quote figures of 2.27 per cent and 3.23 per cent for the percentages of between-zone variation to between-household variation in trip generations in 1962 and 1971 respectively.

It is therefore quite invalid to make inferences about the travel-demand behaviour of households or organisations on the basis of zonal analyses. Nor must one be misled by the typically high values of the correlation coefficient, R, and the coefficient of determination, R^2, into thinking that zonal regressions provide superior fits to reality. That these high R^2 values indicate that a large proportion of the between-zone variation is explained is true, but this leaves the more behaviourally meaningful within-zone variation totally unexplained. We shall have cause to refer to these issues again when discussing household regression in the next section.

To mitigate the severity of the above problems, zone size could be made smaller, thereby increasing the number of zones for a study area; or trips could be categorised according to type of household or organisation. Chisholm and O'Sullivan (1973) employ the latter device by distinguishing between major commodity classes. However, these modifications may have limited effectiveness and may aggravate other problems.

For instance, Fleet and Robertson (1968) calculate sum-of-squares measures of trip generation variability for data relating to 5,255 households and for the same information aggregated to various zonal levels. The percentages of between-zone variation related to between-household variation are 9.8 per cent for 10 zones, rising to only 13.6 per cent for 57 zones, and to a mere 20.4 per cent for 247 zones. Thus a 25-fold increase in the number of zones is required to double the between-zone variation. Moreover, an increased categorisation of trip generations or attractions on a zonal or sector (i.e. household or organisation type) basis may well increase the pressures on data derived from a sample of households or organisations. Smaller numbers of sample observations per zone or sector means less accuracy in inferring the aggregate values of dependent and independent variables, and remember that one of the assumptions of regression analysis is that the independent variables should be measured with negligible error. Because information has to be aggregated to arbitrary zonal areas, zonal regression methods tend to make inefficient use of sample data collected for households or organisations. Furthermore, as the intercept and regression coefficients are specific to a zoning system, the zonal regression is an inflexible tool for forecasting purposes. Unfortunately, in land use and transport planning it may often be desirable to change the zone system to take account of land-use developments.

Disaggregate regression analysis

Disaggregate regression analyses seek to explain the travel demands generated by households and organisations as a function of the characteristics of these decision-making units. Borrowing from the Downes and Gyenes (1976) study of Reading once more, their equations for all home-based trip generations, in 1962 and 1971 respectively, are:

$$\hat{o} = -1.823 + 3.115r + 0.862(\text{one car}) + 1.317(\text{two or more cars}) \qquad [5]$$

$$\hat{o} = -2.154 + 2.929r + 1.183(\text{one car}) + 1.985(\text{two or more cars}) \qquad [6]$$

where $\hat{o}$ denotes predicted trips per household and r household size; households are further classified according to car ownership using dummy variables which are explained later. Downes and Gyenes quote imprecisely a multiple correlation coefficient of 'above 0.5'.

By comparison with zonal regression methods such disaggregate methods capture much more of the true behavioural variation in trip-making and use survey data more efficiently. Because of the relatively large variation in trip generations between households to be explained, the coefficients of correlation and determination tend not to be high, but this does not mean that disaggregate regressions provide fits to reality inferior to those of zonal regression. Fleet and Robertson (1968) present an instructive example where a disaggregate regression equation using 5,255 household observations yielded an R^2 value of 0.36, whereas a zonal regression on the same data previously aggregated to 143 zones gave an R^2 of 0.95. However, as disaggregate regressions are not zone-dependent, they can be used to provide predictions for any desired zoning system. Thus, Fleet and Robertson could insert zonal averages for household size and car ownership in their disaggregate regression and, by multiplying their disaggregate predictions by the number of households per zone, derive estimates of zonal trip generations. The resulting R^2 of 0.94 indicates that disaggregate regressions can be applied at any zonal level and provide trip predictions of equal quality to those from zonal regressions. Moreover, greater confidence can be put in the regression coefficients obtained from disaggregate models as indicators of genuine trip-making responses to any changes in the explanatory variables.

Of course these disaggregate methods are subject to the assumptions of all linear regression techniques, and indeed various problems have emerged in practice. Douglas and Lewis (1971a), for example, used a stepwise build-up procedure to regress trip generations per household, o, against four independent variables: family size, r; employees per household, e; cars per household, v; household income x. Such a procedure constructs what is hopefully the 'best' regression equation according to the statistical significance of the independent variables. Douglas and Lewis quote the following resultant regression equation:

$$\hat{o} = 0.91 + 1.44e + 1.07v \quad (R = 0.62) \tag{7}$$

They discovered, however, that the residual errors, although exhibiting a normally distributed form with a mean value of zero, did not display constant variance for variations in the values of the independent variables. It was conjectured that this problem might be caused by the exclusion of a family size effect from the final regression equation. An associated problem was that trips generated were related non-linearly to family size when the effects of the other independent variables were held constant. This implied that some transformation of the family size variable should have been undertaken to linearise the relationship prior to entering this variable in the stepwise regression procedure.

Starkie (1967) experienced similar problems in his study of commercial vehicle trip generations from manufacturing plants. Graphical plots of vehicle generations against employment and floor-space variables displayed non-linear relationships, indicating that vehicle generations increased at a decreasing rate as the size of manufacturing establishments increased. This was explained in terms of 'scale economies' in trip-making through higher average vehicle loadings. In addition, the observed vehicle generations were not normally distributed. Consequently the values of both dependent and independent variables were transformed into logarithms to satisfy approximately the assumptions of a linear relationship and the normality of the dependent variable. The simple regression equation relating vehicle generations, $\hat{o}(v)$, to floor space, g, for manufacturing plants was:

$$\log \hat{o}(v) = -1.1749 + 0.5714 \log g, \quad (R = 0.7754) \tag{8}$$

This logarithmically transformed regression equation was found to be distinctly superior to the untransformed version in terms of statistical reliability and goodness-of-fit.

167

Another way of tackling the non-linearity problem is to categorise an independent variable and treat each category as a dummy variable. Effectively, this means that each portion of the independent variable is treated as having a separate effect on trip generation. Such a device has already been illustrated in equations [5] and [6], where 'one-car' and 'two-or-more car' household categories are defined. One dummy variable category, in this case zero household car ownership, is always omitted from the regression equation. Each household observation is given the value '1' for the particular category to which it belongs, and '0' for all other categories. Dummy variables are, of course, essential if an independent variable is measured on a nominal or ordinal measurement scale in the first place, as for example with occupational data related to working heads of households.

A less tractable problem with regression analysis is the multicollinearity problem. In household trip-generation studies it is possible to find relatively high correlations between such explanatory variables as household income, car ownership and number of employed persons. If all of these variables were to be included in the regression equation their individual effects on trips generated would likely be obscured. As seen from the Douglas and Lewis (1971a) example, household income was excluded from the regression equation by the stepwise procedure used. Douglas and Lewis have suggested examining the regression coefficients for large changes in magnitude or sign at each stage of the stepwise regression procedure to gauge the effects of multicollinearity. This is something that Chisholm and O'Sullivan (1973) did on finding intuitively unreasonable negative coefficients when regressing freight generations and attractions against employment in certain standard industrial categories. An alternative solution is to reduce a set of intercorrelated independent variables to a smaller set of uncorrelated 'factors' or 'components' using the methods of factor analysis. However, it is important for policy analysis to be able to interpret such 'factors' unambiguously and, for forecasting purposes, to identify one easily projected variable representing each 'factor'.

Category analysis

Category analysis, applied at a household category level, was the technique which superseded zonal regression in the late 1960s for forecasting trip generations and attractions. It was developed first in Britain by Wootton and Pick (1967) for the West Midlands Transport Study (Freeman *et al.* 1968). The central principle is to define trip rates, τ^h, for various trip purposes, for each category, h, of household or organisation. Ideally, such trip rates should be constant over time and space, and household categories should be defined so that within-category variations in trip rates are negligible. The number of zonal trip generations may then be estimated by simply multiplying the appropriate trip rates by the number of households, H_i^h, by category and zone and by summing the products over all household categories:

$$\hat{O}_i = \sum_h \tau^h H_i^h \qquad [9]$$

Although this basic principle seems straightforward, considerable efforts are needed to make it workable. For a start the trip rates have to be established by sample surveys of the trip-making characteristics of households or organizations. Douglas and Lewis (1971b) contend that reliable trip rates ought to be based on samples of 250 to 500 households for each category defined. Given the large number of categories (108) suggested by Wootton and Pick (1967), the total survey would be massive. However, trip rates established in this manner should be more reliable for use in other areas and at other times, subject to some smaller local sampling to check their accuracy.

More problematical is finding the number of households by category type, h. Sample surveys of the present situation are usually expensive, while published census information does not identify directly household types with sufficient categorisation. More importantly, for forecasting purposes, this household information must be projected for future dates if future trip generations are to be predicted. Consequently, much of the ingenuity in devising an operable category analysis procedure went into the estimation of households by category from more aggregate, more readily available and more easily projected variables, such as zonal totals of households, population, employed residents and household car ownership. Here it is only possible to offer a brief verbal and diagrammatic description of the household categorisation procedures as the mathematics is rather cumbersome. More detailed expositions are given in Douglas and Lewis (1971b) and Senior (1975).

The aim of the household categorisation procedure is to determine the probabilities, p^h, of households being in each of the h categories. For Wootton and Pick's (1967) 108 categories these probabilities are constructed from three component probabilities representing the three major dimensions of the proposed categorisation, namely household car ownership, household income level and household structure.

First the probabilities, $p(v|x)$, of households being in one of three car-ownership groups (zero, one and two or more cars), conditional on their income level x, are derived from probability distributions of gamma form.

Formally:

$$p(v|x) = a_0^v x^{a_1^v} \exp(-a_2^v x) \tag{10}$$

where income, x, is treated as a discrete variable comprising the median incomes of the six income classes used by Wootton and Pick (1967). The parameters a_0^v, and a_1^v and a_2^v are used to control the shape of the probability distributions so that they can be fitted to observed car ownership–income distributions. Figure 13.2 provides an illustration of this, using the parameter values obtained in the West Midlands Transport Study. Subsequent developments of the category analysis procedure (Pick & Gill 1970) have made car ownership conditional not only on income but also on residential density. This latter variable acts as a crude indicator of the likely adequacy of public transport which empirical investigations have shown to exert an independent influence on car ownership.

Secondly, household incomes are assumed to display a gamma distribution form (Fig. 13.3). The probabilities, $p(x)$, of households being in the six income

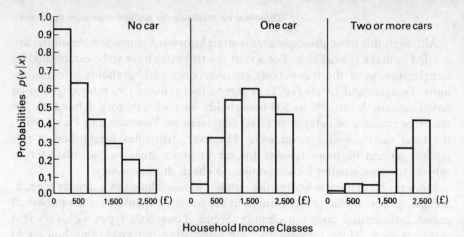

Household Income Classes
(based on 1966 incomes and car prices)

Fig. 13.2 Probabilities of households being in three car-ownership categories given their incomes

$$\text{Gamma function} = \frac{\alpha^{m+1}}{\Gamma(m+1)} x^m \exp(-\alpha x)$$

$$\text{where: } m = 1.636 \text{ in examples; } \alpha = \frac{m+1}{\bar{x}}$$

$$\bar{x} = \text{mean household income}$$

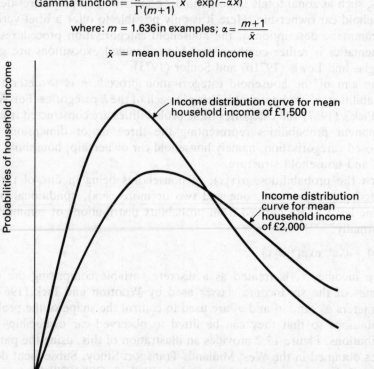

Income distribution curve for mean household income of £1,500

Income distribution curve for mean household income of £2,000

Notes: (i) the parameter α determines the distribution of income around the mean household income $\bar{x}$;
(ii) the household income group probabilities $p(x)$, are calculated from the areas under the appropriate income curve

Fig. 13.3 Example distributions of household income summarised by gamma functions

classes are found by calculating the appropriate areas under such probability distributions, as income is treated as a continuous variable in this case. Again, implementation of such calculations requires empirically derived parameter values controlling the precise shapes of the probability distributions, plus a mean household income for each zone. However, as such income data are not available from British censuses, it may be necessary to derive household income probabilities indirectly, using the previously discussed car ownership–income relationships. Household car ownership by zone becomes the required data input, and such data are usually more readily available. It is then possible to pursue a trial-and-error process to determine mean zonal household incomes consistent with the observed zonal information on household car ownership. This consistency is assessed by using the income probabilities in connection with the car ownership–income relationships.

Finally, there are the six household structure categories defined according to the number of persons, r, in a household and the number of them, e, who are employed. The required probabilities are produced from a combination of two component probability distributions. First the probabilities, $p(r)$, of households having r members are given by a Poisson distribution which requires data on average household size per zone. Secondly, the conditional probabilities $p(e|r)$, that e members of a household containing r members are employed, are derived from a binomial distribution which utilises information on the proportion of employed residents to total population found in each zone. Illustrative examples of these distributions are displayed in Fig. 13.4.

It then remains to combine these separate probabilities, taking into account the conditional dependences of car ownership on income and of employed members on household size, to produce the composite probabilities of being in each of the 108 household categories:

$$p^h = p(v|x)p(x)p(r)p(e|r) \tag{11}$$

On multiplying these composite probabilities by the number of households in each zone, H_i, the required estimates of households by category, H_i^h, are produced.

Summary evaluation of methods

Douglas and Lewis (1971b) have provided a most useful comparative summary of the above methods. On balance it would appear that disaggregate regression analysis has the edge on category analysis. The main advantage of the latter method is its avoidance of assumptions about the shape of functional relationships between trips generated and various explanatory variables. Also, intercorrelation between such independent variables may be less of a problem than in regression analysis. Yet category analysis also has distinct disadvantages *vis-à-vis* household regression. It is not possible to test the statistical significance of the explanatory variables used to define the categories; the technique is also relatively inflexible when it comes to adding new variables which create another dimension of categorisation; and computer programs are

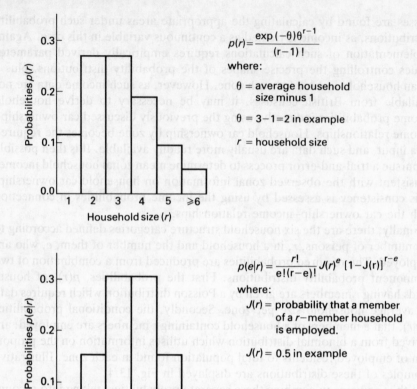

Fig. 13.4 (a) Poisson probability distribution of household size; (b) binomial probability distribution of employed household members conditional on household size

much less readily available. In any event it is possible to specify the category analysis model in a household regression format by treating the categories as dummy variables.

Temporal and spatial forecasting of vehicle ownership

In the previous section it was seen that vehicle ownership cropped up as an important variable for explaining trip generations. What was less evident was that the category analysis procedure can be used to predict household car ownership, as a function of income and possibly residential density, if assumptions are made about the growth of real incomes and trends in car prices. In this section some other methods of forecasting vehicle ownership are reviewed.

Extrapolation methods

The extrapolation method is a device for projecting a known trend into the future. So time series data on the past levels of car ownership per head of population, v, are plotted against time, t. If a systematic trend in these data can be detected, this may be approximated by a mathematical expression or trend line expressing car ownership as 'a function of' (f) time:

$$v = f(t) \qquad [12]$$

This trend line is then allowed to 'run on' beyond the latest date for which car-ownership information is available to give car-ownership predictions for future points in time.

A modified version of this general extrapolation procedure has been used until recently by the British Government's Department of Transport as part of its traffic-forecasting techniques for the assessment of inter-urban road projects (Department of Transport 1978: Ch. 2). The precise form of the general vehicle–time function [12] is specified as an S-shaped logistic curve (Fig. 13.5), which can be stated mathematically as:

$$v = \frac{s}{1 + \exp(a + bt)} \qquad [13]$$

where s is the saturation, or absolute maximum, level of car ownership per head; a is the intercept parameter, giving the car ownership level at the beginning of the time series ($t = 0$); and b is the parameter reflecting the extent to which car ownership changes over time.

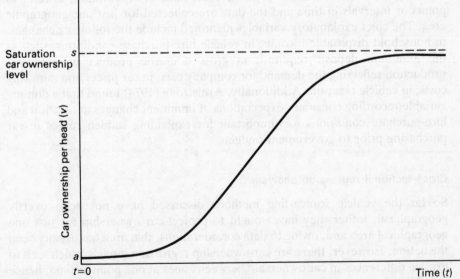

Fig. 13.5 Logistic curve representing car-ownership growth over time. (Adapted from: Department of Transport 1978: 9)

In the standard logistic form s, a and b are all constants so that car ownership is 'explained' by only one variable, namely time. However, time has no genuine explanatory power and merely stands as a composite proxy variable for all the unidentified variables that really do influence car-ownership changes over time. In systems theory terms, extrapolation is a 'black box' technique, for it conceals rather than illuminates these true causal variables. If these latter variables are stable over past and future time intervals then accurate forecasting may be possible, but this is a strong assumption to make and one that is not often valid in practice. The Department of Transport, however, has introduced the effects of changes in income and motoring costs on vehicle ownership by adjusting the value of the constant b outside of the extrapolation model [13]. This has the effect of adjusting car-ownership growth rates in the short to medium term, but in the long run the saturation level, s, dominates the car-ownership forecasts, and this is unsatisfactory because saturation is not dependent on either income or motoring costs. As long-term vehicle forecasts are highly sensitive to changes in saturation level, it is vital to determine the latter's value accurately. Unfortunately, the methods for estimating s are crude and produce values ranging from 0.34 to 0.66 cars per head of population (Department of Transport 1978)! It is therefore hardly surprising that this technique is much criticised despite its practical advantage of ease of use.

Economic time series regression analysis

A more truly explanatory method of projecting vehicle ownership trends involves so-called 'econometric' models, relating, for example, new vehicle registrations to various economic series which vary over time (Armstrong 1974; Silberston 1963). The relationships are often specified in the basic multiple regression format of equation [1], where the units of observation, u, refer to points or intervals in time and the data are collected for just one geographic area. The chief explanatory variables identified include the following changes: in household disposable income; in vehicle hire-purchase conditions, such as the minimum deposit required; in gross domestic product or industrial production reflecting the demand for company cars; in car prices and motoring costs; in vehicle taxation. Additionally, Armstrong (1974) found that a dummy variable recording consumer expectations of imminent changes in taxation and hire-purchase conditions was important for explaining sudden surges in car purchasing prior to government budgets.

Cross-sectional regression analyses

So far the vehicle forecasting methods discussed have not been overtly geographical; rather they have sought to project car ownership for just one geographical area and, owing to data considerations, that area has usually been the nation. However, there are car-ownership regression models which seek to explain differences in car ownership between zones at one point in time, hence justifying the description 'cross-sectional'. Such zonal regression techniques are subject to the same problems as their trip-generation counterparts (see pp. 164–66) by obscuring some variation in car ownership between house-holds. Button (1973) has explored some of these aggregation effects, and has suggested using the fairly readily available small area census data on car ownership as a reasonable alternative to conducting a household car-ownership survey.

The example of a cross-sectional zonal regression reviewed here is taken from Fairhurst (1975). He examined variations in car ownership between 149 districts in London, paying particular attention to the effects of access to public transport upon the ownership decision. First, he hypothesised that the most important variables affecting spatial variations in car ownership are: household size, which is deemed to be an important index of the benefits derivable from owning a car; household income which affects the ability to buy; the relative attractiveness of public transport. He argues, too, that household income and size are likely to be highly correlated with other possible explanatory variables such as socio-economic group, age of heads of households and the number of employed household members. Therefore, before applying the regression model he ruled out the use of some independent variables which might give rise to multicollinearity problems. By inspecting graph plots of the relationships between the probabilities of not owning a car and the chosen explanatory variables he suspected non-linear associations which required logarithmic transformations of all variables to approximate linearity. His version of the multiple regression model had the following general specification:

$$\log \left(\frac{p_i^v}{1 - p_i^v} \right) = \alpha_0 + \alpha^1 \log X_i^1 + \alpha^2 \log X_i^2 \ldots + \varepsilon_i \qquad [14]$$

where the dependent variable denotes the probability of a household in zone i not owning a car, p_i^v, divided by the probability of it owning one $(1 - p_i^v)$.

Fairhurst then proceeded to construct his regression equation in stages. A simple regression between the dependent variable and household income explained 40 per cent of the interzonal variation in car ownership. On adding household size as a second independent variable the variation explained increased to 72 per cent. Moreover, household size had a low correlation with household income in this study so multicollinearity was not a serious problem. Public transport accessibility indexes, one for bus services the other for rail, were then introduced to the regression equation, increasing the explained car-ownership variation to 80 per cent. However, not only were the accessibility indexes highly correlated with each other, but also each one was highly correlated with household size. Although the accessibility indexes were found to be statistically significant explanatory variables, their inclusion in the regression equation meant that household size, which was previously a highly statistically significant variable, became only marginally significant.

Further experiments involved the addition of a residential density variable, but this aggravated the multicollinearity problem and increased the explained variation in car ownership by a trivial 1 per cent. Moreover, it rendered the household size variable statistically insignificant. Omitting household size and both accessibility variables, but retaining household income and residential density as independent variables, causes the explained variation to fall only slightly to 78 per cent. Although this eases the statistical problem of multicollinearity, the resulting equation is not considered to be satisfactory from a behavioural standpoint. In fact regression equations using residential density as an explanatory variable, in preference to household size and accessibility measures, have been found to underpredict changing car-ownership levels over time. It is therefore concluded by Fairhurst that household size and accessibility variables should be retained in the final regression equation, as being more sensitive and direct indicators of changes in car ownership than the crude residential density proxy measure. Of course, this does raise the dilemma that the statistical requirements of reducing multicollinearity are in conflict with the theoretical requirements of incorporating genuine causal or explanatory variables. This difficult problem is further discussed by Harris (1970).

Finally, it should be noted that a cross-sectional car-ownership model is inevitably deficient for forecasting purposes, because it omits variables which vary over time but very little over space. In this context this is possibly best illustrated by car prices. However, in forecasting exercises this deficiency might be overcome by relating income to car prices to produce a measure of car-purchasing ability.

Modelling transport flows

Introduction

It is at this juncture that attention is turned to what many geographers will consider to be one of the core components of the transport system – namely transport flows. What has gone before in this chapter will help to emphasise that transport flow activities are connected inextricably with activities pursued at their starting and terminating locations. However, the features of the transport system which appear to be more overtly spatial in character are transport interactions themselves and the networks accommodating them. It is therefore not surprising that these features of the transport system have attracted much more attention from geographers than have trip-generation, vehicle-ownership and transport-mode-choice aspects.

Two techniques have dominated the representation and forecasting of transport flows in geography – the **transportation problem of linear programming** and various forms of **gravity model**. It is easy to pick up the impression from the geographic literature (for example, Chisholm & O'Sullivan 1973) that these two models are distinct and competing alternatives for representing spatial interactions. However, it should be stressed here and now that the solution of a transportation problem can be obtained from a certain type of gravity model (Evans, 1973). Further details are presented later (pp. 195–7), but readers should bear in mind that the predicted transport flows derived from a transportation problem solution can be viewed as one particular and specialised set of flows from a whole range of sets of transport flows which can, in principle, be predicted by gravity models.

The transportation problem

Statement of the general problem

The **transportation problem** is concerned with a general supply and demand situation operating in a spatial setting. 'Suppliers', who could be one of a variety of types of private or public organisation such as warehouses or hospitals, provide goods or services for 'consumers', who could again be private or public organisations, like retail outlets, or sectors of the general population, such as those in need of medical care. Transport flows of persons and goods arise as suppliers based at locations denoted i, are usually spatially separated from consumers at locations j. The fundamental feature of the transportation problem is the assumption that *all* those responsible for making transport flow decisions in this context act homogeneously to minimise the total 'costs' of spatial separation. As a result of this transport-cost-minimising behaviour a rather limited set of transport flows is predicted, because each supplier seeks to serve only his nearest customers, while the latter try to buy from or visit only their nearest suppliers. Depending on the type of supply – demand problem being considered, suppliers may be responsible for delivering goods or services to consumer locations by use of either an independent transport agency or their own vehicles; or consumers may be responsible for arranging the collection of goods purchased, or may need to visit the supply locations to avail themselves of services offered there.

Formally, the transportation problem is specified as follows. The objective of minimising all transport flow costs, C, can be expressed as:

$$\text{minimise: } C = \sum_i \sum_j T_{ij} c_{ij} \qquad [15]$$

where T_{ij} denotes the flow quantity, such as amount of freight or number of person trips, between each pair of supply and demand locations; and c_{ij} denotes the corresponding travel cost for each unit of flow, such as per tonne of freight or per person. The $\sum\sum_{ij}$ symbols indicate that transport costs are summed over all possible $i - j$ spatial interactions in the area studied. The ability to minimise transport costs is limited by the existence of constraints which typically require that the demands of consumers, D_j, are fully satisfied, and that suppliers can 'dispose of' all their 'stocks' of goods or services O_i. Such conditions are represented formally as:

$$\sum_j T_{ij} = O_i \qquad [16]$$

which guarantees that the sum of all transport flows originating from each supply location exhausts available supplies there; and

$$\sum_i T_{ij} = D_j \qquad [17]$$

which likewise ensures that the sum of all transport flows terminating at each demand location meets the requirements there exactly. Taken together, these two conditions imply that there is an overall balance of supply and demand in the study area:

$$\sum_i O_i = \sum_j D_j \qquad [18]$$

177

Finally, to find the transport-cost-minimising set of transport flows, the common-sense condition that flows cannot be negative is imposed:

$$T_{ij} \geqslant 0 \qquad [19]$$

The above specification of supply and demand constraints may be varied if either supplies are not fully utilised or demands are not completely met. For example, consider the commodity flow problem in the Portbury study (Ministry of Transport 1966) where export supplies from the British regions, O_i, could be sent to a range of ports, j, with export capacities, D_j. This could easily be formulated as a transportation problem, but the 'demand' constraint equation [17] would need modification, as it is unlikely that all ports fully utilise their export capacity, D_j. Thus, to allow for under-utilisation at some ports and full utilisation at others the 'demand constraint' must be written with the inequal-ity–equality option sign:

$$\sum_i T_{ij} \leqslant D_j \qquad [20]$$

Osayimwese (1974) provides another example of this very problem, in his case related to the export of groundnuts through three major ports in Nigeria (see also Hay 1977 for comments on this article).

It is also possible to deal with transportation problems where the supply condition [16] is less restrictive. Maxfield (1969) presents such variants of the transportation problem for the case of exports of hard red spring-wheat from the north-central states of the USA. Essentially, the demand for such wheat from 10 world markets must be satisfied, as specified by equation [17], but the export quantities by region, O_i, are identified by the solution of the transporta-tion problem. In this simple case, Maxfield effectively dispenses with supply constraint [16] altogether, but in other variants of his problem, he sets a maximum export supply for each region:

$$\sum_j T_{ij} \leqslant O_i \qquad [21]$$

which is intended to reflect the effects of domestic competition for the wheat. In addition, Maxfield experiments with the objective function [15] by adding wheat prices at the farms to transport costs. This has the effect of taking into account spatial variations in agricultural production costs.

Maxfield further makes use of the *dual transportation problem* which provides measures of the comparative locational advantages of wheat-producing areas in relation to export points. Duality will be illustrated in greater detail in the next section. However, it should be noted at this stage that the mathematical formulation given above is the allocation approach to the transportation problem, commonly known as the *primal* problem. Such allocations involve, at least implicitly, a pricing or valuation of the 'resources' allocated. Allocation in the transportation problem means designating particu-lar supply locations, i, to serve particular demand locations, j, with certain amounts of goods or services. The corresponding dual pricing mechanism places values on the relative locational advantages of having units of supply and demand in one location rather than another. Thus, with respect to the spatial pattern of demands, the supply dual variables, μ_i, value the locational advantage of having a marginal unit of commodity or service at each supply location relative to all other supply locations. Likewise, with respect to the spatial pattern of supply, the demand dual variables, γ_j, measure the locational value of having a marginal unit of demand at each consumer location relative to other consumer locations. The μ_i may be interpreted as excess profits to suppliers and are thus direct measures of comparative locational advantage. However, the γ_j have a natural interpretation as delivered prices to customers, and so there is an inverse relationship with relative locational advantages which decline as the γ_j values increase.

The formal specification of the dual transportation problem is to maximise the sum of all delivered prices and to minimise (= maximises the negative of) the sum of all excess profits. Effectively, this involves the *minimisation of relative locational advantages*, even though the dual transportation problem is specified formally as a maximisation problem:

$$\text{maximise: } \sum_j \gamma_j D_j - \sum_i \mu_i O_i \qquad [22]$$

subject to:

$$\gamma_j - \mu_i \leqslant c_{ij} \qquad [23]$$

The latter constraint prevents, for every supply – demand pair, the consumer's delivered price less the supplier's excess profits from exceeding the transport costs.

A numerical illustration and interpretation of the transportation problem

Consider a simple, hypothetical example of three warehouses at locations $i(= 1, 2, 3)$, with the following supplies (in tonnes) of a commodity: $O_1 = 20$; $O_2 = 60$; $O_3 = 40$. They supply four customers at locations $j(= 1, 2, 3, 4)$ having the following demands: $D_1 = 30$; $D_2 = 20$; $D_3 = 40$; $D_4 = 30$. By summing these two sets of figures it can be seen that supply balances demand as a whole. This supply and demand information can be represented as the row and column sums respectively of the transport flow matrix, T_{ij} (see Table 13.2); indeed, constraints [16] and [17] insist that the transport flows to be found must sum to these row and column totals. The travel costs per tonne of flow, c_{ij}, are also given in the bottom right-hand corners of the cells of the matrix. An optimal (i.e. transport-cost-minimising) set of flows T_{ij} may be found by some suitable procedure, such as the stepping-stone method illustrated by Haggett, Cliff and Frey (1977: Ch. 15). For this example, more than one optimal solution exists, so Table 13.2 presents just one of the solutions with the blank cells indicating no interactions between corresponding supply – demand location pairs.

The solution illustrates the limited number of non-zero transport flows predicted, a feature intrinsic to the transportation problem. Out of 12 possible supply – demand interactions only 6 have non-zero flows. In fact it is possible to state that for all transportation problems the number of non-zero flows is at most equal to the number of independent constraints. In this example there are three supply and four demand constraints, but one of these seven constraints is

Table 13.2. A numerical illustration of the transportation problem with an optimal solution

Suppliers at locations i	Consumers at locations j				Supply Quantities O_i	Supplier dual variables μ_i
	$j=1$	$j=2$	$j=3$	$j=4$		
$i=1$	– 5	– 8	$T_{13}=20$ 3	– 6	$20=O_1$	$\mu_1=5$
$i=2$	$T_{21}=30$ 4	– 9	$T_{23}=20$ 8	$T_{24}=10$ 11	$60=O_2$	$\mu_2=0$
$i=3$	– 6	$T_{32}=20$ 2	– 4	$T_{34}=20$ 5	$40=O_3$	$\mu_3=6$
Demand quantities D_j	$D_1=30$	$D_2=20$	$D_3=40$	$D_4=30$		
Consumer dual variables γ_j	$\gamma_1=4$	$\gamma_2=8$	$\gamma_3=8$	$\gamma_4=11$		

redundant because total supplies equal total demands, leaving six independent constraints.

Using the 'map' of these supply and demand locations (Fig. 13.6) it is possible to attempt interpretations of this optimal solution (cf. Stevens 1961). The transportation problem could be taken as representing a **competitive** situation with suppliers vying with one another to serve customers, and the latter competing with one another to 'patronise' suppliers. No matter who is responsible for transport costs, both supplier and customer will seek to minimise them. From the supplier's viewpoint transport costs add to the delivered cost, and thus to the delivered price needed to make reasonable or 'normal' profits. Clearly, high transport costs can affect the relative competitiveness of suppliers in terms of who can deliver goods or services to the customer at the lowest price. The customer is just as anxious to obtain goods or services at the lowest price given that his demand is assumed to be inelastic with respect to price, and so he too wishes to minimise the transport cost component of the delivered price. Given this situation, then it is logical for

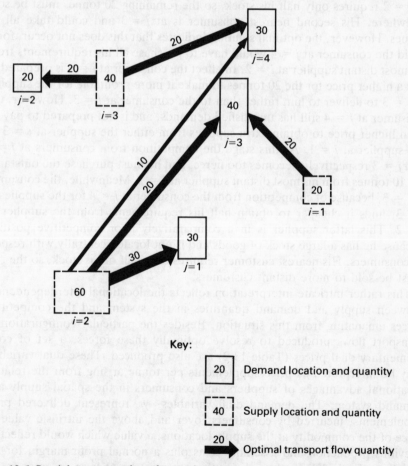

Key:

20	Demand location and quantity
40	Supply location and quantity
➡ 20	Optimal transport flow quantity

Fig. 13.6 Spatial representation of an optimal transportation problem solution (refer to Table 13.2)

suppliers to try to dispose of all their goods or services to their nearest consumers subject to competition from fellow suppliers, while consumers attempt to obtain all their requirements from their nearest suppliers subject to competition from fellow consumers.

Applying these general principles to the hypothetical example, it is observed that the supplier at $i = 1$ sells all his stock to his nearest customer (at $j = 3$), and consumers at $j = 1$ and $j = 2$ purchase all their requirements from their nearest suppliers (at $i = 2$ and $i = 3$ respectively). This supplier and these consumers are particularly competitive in the spatial system because they face favourable balances of supply and demand within local areas involving relatively low transport costs. Thus the supplier at $i = 1$ is fortunate that the customer at $j = 3$ has a relatively high demand which absorbs all his stock. Conversely, consumers at $j = 1$ and $j = 2$ have relatively low demands compared with the available stock of their nearest suppliers.

The supplier located at $i = 3$ is also well located to sell all his stock as he is reasonably close to consumers at $j = 2, 3$ and 4. However, his nearest customer at $j = 2$ requires only half his stock, so the remaining 20 tonnes must be sold elsewhere. His second nearest consumer is at $j = 3$ and could take all 20 tonnes. However, the optimal solution indicates that this does not occur, for if it did the consumer at $j = 4$ would have to purchase all his requirements from his most distant supplier at $i = 2$. In effect the consumer at $j = 4$ is prepared to pay a higher price for the 20 tonnes to make it more profitable for the supplier at $i = 3$ to deliver to him rather than to the consumer at $j = 3$. However, the consumer at $j = 4$ still has unsatisfied demands, and is not prepared to pay an even higher price to obtain extra supplies from either the supplier at $i = 3$ or the supplier at $i = 1$. At this stage the competition from consumers at $j = 2$ and $j = 3$ respectively becomes too fierce, and he must purchase the outstanding 10 tonnes from his most distant supplier at $i = 2$. Meanwhile, the consumer at $j = 3$, because of competition from the consumer at $j = 4$ for the supplies at $i = 3$, finds it cheaper to obtain half his requirements from the supplier at $i = 2$. This latter supplier is in a comparatively poor competitive position because he has a large stock of goods and is not located centrally with respect to consumers. His nearest customer requires only half of his stock, so the rest must be sold to more distant customers.

This rather intricate interpretation reflects the locational interdependences between supply and demand quantities in the system and the competitive forces emanating from this situation. Besides the particular configuration of transport flows produced to resolve optimally these forces, a set of complementary dual prices (Table 13.2) are also produced. These dual variables may be interpreted as price supplements per tonne arising from the relative locational advantages of suppliers and consumers in the spatial supply and demand system. The demand dual variables, γ_j, represent delivered price supplements, incurred by consumers, over and above the intrinsic value or price of the commodity at the supply locations, a value which would reflect all previous production and assembly costs plus a normal profit margin for the suppliers. Each delivered price supplement must be at least as great as the largest transport cost incurred by the consumer in question. Delivered price premiums in excess of the largest transport cost might arise where a competitively located supplier has two or more potential customers who are competing for his limited supply. This occurs in the example for the supplier at $i = 3$ in his dealings with the consumer at $j = 2$. The delivered price premiums, γ_j, less the transport costs, c_{ij}, give the extra profits accruing to each supplier because of his relative locational advantage with respect to other suppliers. Such 'excess' profits are measured by the other set of dual variables, μ_i.

The dual values of Table 13.2 indicate that the most competitive consumer is located at $j = 1$, his delivered price premium of 4 cost units being equal to the transport costs he incurs. Consumers at $j = 2$ and $j = 3$ face delivered price supplements of 8 units because they experience strong competition from the consumer at $j = 4$. This competition forces the consumer at $j = 3$ to meet some of his requirements by buying from the supplier at $i = 2$ at a transport cost of 8 units per tonne. For the consumer at $j = 2$ this competition is met by offering a higher price, 6 units in excess of the transport costs of 2, to the supplier at $i = 3$. If this is not done this consumer must purchase goods from his second nearest supplier at $i = 1$, incurring transport costs of 8 units. Consequently, it is worth his while to offer to pay a delivered price premium of up to 8 cost units to his nearest supplier at $i = 3$ to outcompete the rival consumer at $j = 4$. The latter is shown to be the most uncompetitive consumer suffering the highest delivered price premium.

The delivered price premium is constant for each consumer, although he may be receiving goods from more than one supplier. Thus, the customer at $j = 4$ obtains goods from suppliers at $i = 2$ and $i = 3$ with a delivered price premium of 11 units in both cases. For the supplier at $i = 2$ this premium just covers his transport costs, and he earns zero excess profit; but for the supplier at $i = 3$, once the transport costs of 5 units are paid, there is an excess profit of 6 units per tonne. These excess profit dual variables, μ_i, have been interpreted as location rents by Stevens (1961), meaning a monetary valuation of comparative locational advantage. Such excess profits may ultimately accrue as rents to the owners of land on which supply and demand facilities are constructed, or as taxes to some local or central government institution.

The above interpretation is all very well for a private sector competitive situation, but the same spatial supply and demand problem could occur within one **centrally controlled** private or public organisation, such as a multiplant manufacturing firm or a regional health authority. In such cases the transportation problem solution is useful for assessing the efficiency of transport flows. For example, the manufacturing firm may be keen to keep its distribution costs from production points to regional distribution centres to a minimum; whereas the health authority may be interested in defining population catchment areas for hospitals, which minimise access time for patients and minimise ambulance running costs. In both cases, the dual variables may prove useful indicators of where future investment in facilities should be concentrated.

Applications and extensions of the transportation problem

So far the interpretation of the transportation problem has involved a hypothetical but manageable commodity flow example. Actual applications to freight studies include Henderson (1958) and Land (1957) on the distribution of coal; Morrill and Garrison (1960) on the wheat and flour trade; Chisholm and O'Sullivan (1973) on interregional flows of a variety of commodities in Britain; and O'Sullivan and Ralston (1974) on flows of food and animal products. Some of this more recent work makes comparisons between the transportation problem and gravity models. Unfortunately, making such comparisons is not as straightforward as, say, Chisholm and O'Sullivan (1973) would have us believe. The interested reader should refer to the papers by Pitfield (1978; 1979) which provide the most satisfactory technical discussion of this issue so far produced.

Some of the most novel geographical applications of the transportation problem involve person trips to public or private service facilities. One of the earliest was Yeates's (1963) study of school districts. Students identified by zone of residence i were allocated to schools at locations j to minimise transport costs. From the solution Yeates drew up optimal school catchment areas which he used to assess the efficiency of actual school districts. Such information is of importance to education authorities who may be responsible for the cost of transporting students to and from school. However, it could be argued that this problem is oversimplified given the desirability of some parental freedom to choose a school and the differences in school characteristics.

Another example which extends the use of the transportation problem is the Gould and Leinbach (1966) study of hospital locations in Guatemala. Essentially, this involves repeated use of a transportation problem to solve a small-size *location–allocation* problem, involving the choice of three out of five possible locations for the construction of three hospitals, and the subsequent allocation of patients to them so as to minimise distance travelled. By using the combinatorial formula it is easily shown that there are ten different ways of locating three hospitals at five possible locations:

$$\frac{5!}{3!(5-3)!} = \frac{5!}{3!2!} = \frac{5. \, 4. \, 3. \, 2. \, 1}{3. \, 2. \, 1. \, 2. \, 1} = 10 \qquad [24]$$

Gould and Leinbach solved the transportation problem for each of the ten sets of three locations, each time obtaining the minimum distance for the allocation of patients to the prespecified hospital locations. From these ten optimal solutions for the allocation problems they were then able to select the optimal set of locations for the three hospitals, namely that set of locations minimising the total distance travelled by patients. Clearly, such a procedure becomes increasingly laborious and infeasible for increasingly large location-allocation problems. However, during the 1970s there has been a significant expansion in the location–allocation literature (Scott 1971; Lea 1973) with the result that more manageable methods for solving such problems have come to the attention of geographers (see, for example, Rushton, Goodchild and Ostresh 1973).

A similar use of the transportation problem, in this case for a private firm seeking to locate a branch manufacturing plant to improve its distribution to an expanding national market, has been summarised by Smith (1971: Ch. 20). Here it would be appropriate to expand the basic transportation problem, as

Beckmann and Marschak (1955) first suggested, by recognising three cost components for each potential branch plant location: the costs of transporting inputs from the firm's suppliers; production costs; distribution costs to markets. In this way a more comprehensive approach to branch plant location would result. Casetti (1966) has used this type of formulation to determine the optimal location of steel mills in the Great Lakes – St Lawrence Seaway area.

Gravity models

Components and relationships of the Newtonian gravity model

As its name suggests, the gravity model is derived from physics by analogy with Newton's law of gravitation. This states that the magnitude, T, of the attractive force between any two objects, i and j, is related directly to their masses, O_i and D_j, and inversely to the squared distance, d_{ij}^2, between them. Formally,

$$T_{ij} = G \, O_i D_j d_{ij}^{-\beta} \quad \text{(where } \beta = 2\text{)} \qquad [25]$$

where G is a constant and $d_{ij}^{-\beta}$ is a convenient way of writing $1/d_{ij}^{\beta}$.

In a transport context T_{ij} measures flow quantities (i.e. number of person or vehicle trips or amount of freight) between i–j origin–destination location pairs. The 'mass' terms, O_i and D_j, are measures of the trip-generating and trip-attracting power of origin and destination locations respectively. The particular variables chosen to represent these mass terms fall into two broad classes. *Proxy measures*, as their name suggests, are relatively crude, but readily available indicators deemed to correlate adequately with the actual amount of interaction likely to originate from or be attracted to a location. Thus, population is a favourite variable used to index both origin and destination mass terms in gravity models ranging in coverage from migration (Flowerdew & Salt 1979), through telephone calls (Smith 1963) to airline passenger traffic (Taaffe & Gauthier 1973). By contrast, *precise measures* are exact measures of the amount of travel produced at or attracted to locations. The trip generations and attractions estimated by the models of pp. 162–72 are of this type. Alternatively, for journey-to-work flows, employed residents and occupied jobs could be used as precise mass terms provided it can be assumed that commuters make one return work journey per working day. Because such mass variables are precise measures of origin and destination travel demands, it is only to be expected that they should relate consistently to the interaction quantities T_{ij} predicted by the gravity model.

The impedance effect of spatial separation on transport flows is handled by the d_{ij} terms which might measure distances, costs, times or even intervening opportunities. The latter measure implies that, for example, shopping trips from residential area, i, to shopping centre, j, could have terminated at a retail centre between i and j. These measures may also be combined to produce more sophisticated impedance effects. Thus, in many urban transport studies undertaken in the 1960s and 1970s, use is made of 'generalised costs' for each mode of transport k. Thus, in the SELNEC (South-East Lancashire North-East

Cheshire) study (Wilson *et al.* 1969) these generalised costs, c_{ij}^k, are defined as:

$$c_{ij}^k = a_1 t_{ij}^k + a_2 w_{ij}^k + a_3^k d_{ij} + q_j^k + \delta^k \qquad [26]$$

where:

t_{ij}^k denotes travel time, including parking time for the car mode and walking time associated with public transport usage;

a_1 denotes the value of a unit of travel time to trip-makers;

w_{ij}^k denotes excess time, namely waiting times in the public transport system;

a_2 denotes the value of a unit of excess time;

d_{ij} denotes distance through a network;

a_3^k denotes either fare per mile for public transport or operating costs per mile for private transport;

q_j^k denotes parking charges at destinations for private transport;

δ^k is a modal penalty – incorporating other attributes, such as comfort and convenience, which affect the relative attractiveness of private and public transport.

The structural relationships between these components of the gravity model suggest that transport flows increase at a constant rate with increases in either *one* of the mass terms, O_i or D_j, but at an increasing rate with simultaneous increases in both O_i and D_j. Thus, in a shopping trip example, an increase in population by residential district, *i*, *or* an increase in shopping centre size would increase trips at a constant rate, other things being equal. However, if population and shopping centre size doubled simultaneously, trips would increase four-fold! This does not seem a very reasonable hypothesis and we shall return to this issue shortly.

The relationship between transport flows and spatial separation is represented in the Newtonian gravity model by a negative power function, $d_{ij}^{-\beta}$. Geographers have not usually pre-set the value of β, as in the physical gravity law, where it was deduced to have a value of 2. Instead, a value of β is determined empirically to provide the closest 'fit' between predicted and observed flows. Figure 13.7 indicates that flows, although decreasing steeply at first, decrease less steeply as spatial separation increases. In other words the gradient of this transport flow–spatial separation relationship decreases with increasing spatial separation. Moreover, it can also be inferred from Fig. 13.7 that, as β becomes smaller and approaches zero, increasing spatial separation becomes less of a deterrent to trip interactions.

Applications and modifications of the Newtonian gravity model

A wide-ranging set of applications of the gravity model by geographers and other social scientists are dealt with in Olsson (1965), Taylor (1975) and Tocalis (1978). Such applications usually proceed by converting the model into a form suitable for the use of linear regression analysis to estimate the parameters G

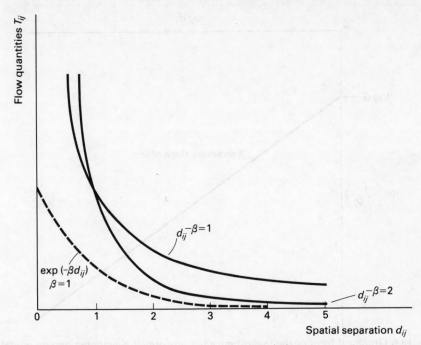

Fig. 13.7 Some alternative ways of representing the relationship between flow quantities and spatial separation

and β. This is achieved by first rearranging equation [25] as follows:

$$\frac{T_{ij}}{O_i D_j} = G\, d_{ij}^{-\beta} \tag{27}$$

and then taking logarithms of all variables throughout:

$$\log\left(\frac{T_{ij}}{O_i D_j}\right) = \log G - \beta \log d_{ij} \tag{28}$$

The graphical form of this transformed relationship is shown in Fig. 13.8. As the values of the dependent variable, $T_{ij}/O_i D_j$, are typically less than unity their logarithms are negative; hence, the functional relationship lies below the axis of the independent variable, $\log d_{ij}$.

Much interest has centred around the values of β as a measure of the frictional effects of spatial separation on the intensity of transport flows. Naturally, geographers wish to know the extent to which this 'distance deterrence' parameter is stable from one area to another and the extent of its variation over different types of transport flow. However, such issues are by no means easily resolved, and indeed this particular topic has generated much debate as to whether β reflects the frictional effects of distance alone, or whether its value is determined partly by the locational or map pattern of the opportunities at potential destinations confronting trip-makers. Readers wishing to pursue this debate might consult Johnston (1976) and Sheppard (1979) as pointers to a wider literature.

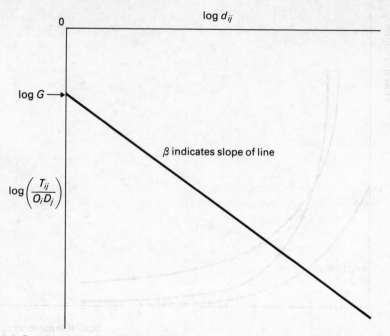

Fig. 13.8 Graphical form of the logarithmically transformed Newtonian gravity model. (Source: Senior 1979: 183)

A second feature of interest is how well the Newtonian gravity model replicates various observed transport flows and, in particular, whether modifications to its form are necessary for applications in a social science context. Such modifications are of two types (Olsson 1965). First, various experiments have been tried with alternatives to the Newtonian negative power impedance term, $d_{ij}^{-\beta}$. Figure 13.7 shows that this latter function may predict unrealistically large flows for very small values of the spatial separation variable, d_{ij}. Wilson (1970a) has suggested that this negative power function may be most appropriate for the study of longer distance flows, such as inter-urban freight and passenger interactions, whereas a negative exponential function, $\exp(-\beta d_{ij})$, represented by the broken line in Fig. 13.7, might be more suitable when modelling trips at an intra-urban scale as its prediction of flows remains strictly finite even at zero distance, whereas the negative power functions suggests trips tend to infinity as distance approaches zero. If necessary, of course, multi-parameter impedance terms may be used to provide more accurate representations of the distance – decay effect. In this connection the generalised distribution function discussed by March (1971), which combines power and exponential functions into a gamma distribution form, might be worth serious consideration.

A second type of modification to the Newtonian model is to append exponents, which may be denoted by ϕ and ψ, on the mass terms to give a generalised gravity model of the form:

$$T_{ij} = G\, O_i^{\phi} D_j^{\psi} d_{ij}^{-\beta} \qquad\qquad [29]$$

These exponents are treated like β as parameters to be estimated by comparing predicted and observed transport flows. By taking logarithms of all the variables in this modified model it is possible to derive all parameter values by multiple regression methods:

$$\log T_{ij} = \log G + \phi \log O_i + \psi \log D_j - \beta \log d_{ij} \qquad [30]$$

Although such exponents must improve the gravity model's ability to reproduce an observed set of transport flows more accurately, they do raise problems of interpretation. Indeed, when 'proxy' variables are used for the mass terms, it could be argued that these exponents merely compensate for the lack of precision of these variables as indicators of trip generations and attractions. The use of such exponents when the mass terms are precise measures of trip generations and attractions, as in the commuting study of Rahmatullah and O'Sullivan (1968) where O_i is measured as employed residents and D_j as jobs, and in the freight study of Chisholm and O'Sullivan (1973) where these mass terms are direct measures of freight tonnages generated and attracted, could be taken as a sign that the gravity model suffers from more serious structural deficiencies when applied in a geographical context. Indeed, transport geographers have much to learn from their counterparts in transport planning when it comes to applying and modifying the Newtonian gravity model.

Fundamental properties and weaknesses of the Newtonian gravity model

With the emergence from the mid-1950s of transportation studies to assist transport planners in their attempts to grapple with increasingly serious urban transport problems, gravity models became part of the armoury of systematic methods used to forecast the impact of transport policies on trip-making behaviour. This trip-making behaviour is commonly taken as a composite of four interrelated decisions, namely:

1. the decision to make a trip and how often (i.e. trip generation and attraction as exemplified on pp. 162–72);
2. the locational choice of a trip destination, known as 'trip distribution', which is the general concern on pp. 176–97;
3. the choice of transport mode, known as 'modal split' (pp. 197–201);
4. the choice of a route through a modal transport network, known as 'route split' or 'assignment' (pp. 201–5).

Transport analysts have used the methods discussed on pp. 162–72 to represent type (1) decisions, thereby deriving forecasts of trip generations, O_i, and trip attractions, D_j. Such forecasts have been subsequently used as mass terms in gravity model representations of type (2) destination choice decisions, as reflected in the predicted transport flows, T_{ij}. Clearly, as these estimates of O_i and D_j are 'precise' rather than 'proxy' measures of travel demands by location, common sense suggests that the transport flows output by gravity models should relate to the input values of trip generations and attractions, O_i and D_j, in a consistent manner. In effect there should be some simple accounting conditions, for if predicted transport flows, T_{ij}, are summed over all destination choices, j, an independent estimate of trip generations by origin location, i, should be obtained and this should equal exactly the input value of O_i; so formally:

$$\sum_j T_{ij} = O_i \qquad [31]$$

Likewise, summing transport flows over all origin zones for each destination location should lead to an independent estimate of trip attractions, which should equal exactly the input value of D_j:

$$\sum_i T_{ij} = D_j \qquad [32]$$

Unfortunately, neither the Newtonian gravity model of equation [25] nor the modified form of equation [29] can guarantee to satisfy either of these two accounting constraints. Consequently, when 'precise' trip generation and/or trip attraction measures are used as the mass terms in Newtonian gravity models, the ludicrous situation arises that the predicted transport flows are inconsistent with the mass values used in their prediction. A numerical illustration of this is presented in Senior (1979).

An intimately related problem is that estimated changes in trip generations and attractions will tend to exaggerate changes in transport flows. This is easily demonstrated by use of a highly simplified numerical example. Imagine some steel town facing the prospects of a declining number of jobs and a consequent decline in the number of persons in employment. Assume that at the present time the town has 10,000 occupied jobs available in a zone labelled j, and that the 10,000 workers employed in these jobs reside in zone i. These workers make the usual one return home – work journey per day and travel on average a distance of 2 km on each leg of the return journey. These commuting trips are easily represented by the Newtonian gravity model, as work trip generations O_i are 10,000 and so are work trip attractions D_j, and the spatial separation term d_{ij} has a value of 2. Clearly the observed transport flow between residence and employment zones is 10,000 trips, and this information may be used to find the best values of the parameters with, say, β having a value of 1 and G of $1/5,000$. In this simplistic example we obtain a perfect fit of predicted and observed trips:

$$T_{ij} = \frac{G\, O_i D_j}{d_{ij}^{\beta}} = \frac{1 \cdot 10,000 \cdot 10,000}{5,000 \cdot 2^1} = 10,000 \qquad [33]$$

Assume that employment is expected to fall by 1,000 in a year, so that work trip generations and attractions will each be 9,000, but average distance travelled to work will still be 2 km. Now it is obvious that an intuitive forecast of 9,000 commuting trips in one year's time can be made. Yet what forecast would the previously parameterised gravity model give? It is easily seen that the answer to this question is:

$$T_{ij} = \frac{1 \cdot 9,000 \cdot 9,000}{5,000 \cdot 2^1} = 8,100 \text{ trips} \qquad [34]$$

which is quite clearly a nonsensical forecast, exaggerating the effect of a declining job supply and labour force. Similar simplified illustrations can be found in Taylor (1975) and Senior (1979). It should be emphasised that although these simplistic examples make this forecasting property of the Newtonian gravity model blatantly obvious, in more realistic applications, using numerous origin and destination locations, such a dubious property of the model may be far less readily apparent from the mass of transport flow predictions produced.

A family of constrained gravity models with applications

Transport planners found it relatively easy to overcome the limitations of the Newtonian gravity model by introducing so-called *balancing factors* to make the predicted transport flows, T_{ij}, satisfy such constraints as [31] and [32]. By pursuing this line of development it is possible to construct a family of gravity models with systematic and intuitively logical variations in detailed structure. However, all the gravity models presented conform to the following general form:

$$\text{transport flow} = \frac{\text{balancing factor (s)} \times \text{mass terms}}{\text{spatial separation term}}$$

To understand this family of models it is necessary to appreciate that gravity models predict not only transport flows, T_{ij}, but three aggregates of the transport flow matrix, namely,

1. $\Sigma_j T_{ij}$, which are predictions of the trips originating at each location i irrespective of their destination; if it is desirable to make such predictions consistent with input values of the origin mass term, O_i, then a set of balancing factors, denoted A_i, are introduced into the gravity model to enforce constraint [31];
2. $\Sigma_i T_{ij}$, which are estimates of the trips terminating at each destination j irrespective of their origin; if it is required to make these estimates match the input values of the destination mass term, D_j, then balancing factors denoted B_j become a feature of the gravity model and ensure that constraint [32] is satisfied;
3. $\Sigma_i \Sigma_j T_{ij}$, which is a prediction of the total trips in the system; if neither of conditions [31] and [32] is operative it may be necessary to ensure that this predicted trip total corresponds with a known or independently estimated trip total, N:

$$\sum_i \sum_j T_{ij} = N \tag{35}$$

in which case a single balancing factor, K, is required in the gravity model.

The use of particular balancing factors to enforce consistency between transport flows and mass terms depends on the type of interaction problem under investigation, and the way it is interpreted and the variables defined. It is therefore up to the model user to justify use of a particular member of the gravity model family. Various examples are presented below to illustrate the range of constrained gravity model forms available.

The most highly constrained member of the gravity model family is the *production – attraction constrained* form, which has been extensively employed in urban transportation planning studies for various kinds of person trip, but especially for home – work interactions. This version of the gravity model assumes a numerical balance between total demand for travel generated at all origins and the total trips attracted to all destinations:

$$\sum_i O_i = \sum_j D_j = \sum_i \sum_j T_{ij} \tag{36}$$

Thus, for the journey to work there is an implied balance between trips generated by the resident labour force and trips attracted by the available job opportunities in the study area; or, interpreted another way, there is a balance between trips generated by the workforce at all job locations and the trips attracted by the available housing stock in the area. Transport planners have devoted very little attention to the interpretation of the production–attraction constrained model in terms of job, residential, or other types of location choice. Instead this gravity model is used in a more pragmatic manner for forecasting transport flows consistent with the independently estimated trip generations and attractions. The main interest then is how these transport flows are split among various transport modes and routes, and what this implies for congestion on various links of the road network, for the viability of public transport and so on. Thus the destination or locational choice implications of the gravity model have traditionally been subordinated to interests in the modal and network flow characteristics of the transport system, and in the trip-generating and attracting powers of the land-use system. To a transport geographer at least the gravity model, used as part of the larger transport planning model package, will no doubt be seen as a rather oversimplified representation of locational choices, especially for home–work flows.

The production–attraction constrained model is specified as:

$$T_{ij} = A_i B_j O_i D_j d_{ij}^{-\beta} \tag{37}$$

where the A_i and B_j balancing factors are calculated to ensure that conditions [31] and [32] are not violated. By substituting for T_{ij} in these latter constraints from equation [37] and rearranging terms, it can be shown that A_i and B_j may be calculated as:

$$A_i = \frac{1}{\sum_j B_j D_j d_{ij}^{-\beta}} \tag{38}$$

$$B_j = \frac{1}{\sum_i A_i O_i d_{ij}^{-\beta}} \tag{39}$$

In a transport planning situation, concerned, say, with commuting trips, anticipated changes in the land-use system would be expected to produce changes in commuter trip generations, O_i, and in trip attractions, D_j, to employment locations. These land-use-induced changes, accompanied by policy-induced changes in the transport system affecting values of the spatial separation term, d_{ij}, are input to the production – attraction constrained gravity model, which in turn predicts the new set of journey-to-work flows which are consistent with the input commuter generation and attraction estimates. In fact it is common to use a somewhat more sophisticated version of this gravity model than the one presented in equation [37], which involves identifying trip-makers by car ownership or car availability.

Whereas the production–attraction constrained model is used particularly to investigate the impacts of transport policies on transport flows, a second member of the gravity model family, the *production constrained* version, finds greater application where locational policies are to be assessed. A classic example of such an application was the study by the Ministry of Transport (1966) of the proposed investment policy of locating extra dock capacity at the port of Bristol at Portbury. To assess the likely viability of this scheme it was decided to forecast the amounts of export freight from various regions of Britain which might be attracted to the expanded port of Bristol, relative to the amounts destined for other British ports. The justification for using a gravity model in the first place was established by analysing the available information on export freight flows which showed a marked distance – decay effect around each port.

The production constrained model used to represent this situation can be written as:

$$T_{ij} = A_i O_i D_j d_{ij}^{-\beta} \tag{40}$$

where T_{ij} was the freight tonnage shipped from region i to port j, and where O_i was the independent forecast of export tonnage originating from each region. The A_i balancing factors exist to ensure that the total freight exports originating from each region, as predicted by the gravity model, sum to these O_i values. Thus, constraint equation [31] is satisfied in this case, and substituting from model equation [40] into this constraint gives the necessary expression for A_i as:

$$A_i = \frac{1}{\sum_j D_j d_{ij}^{-\beta}} \tag{41}$$

By substituting this formulation for A_i back into equation [40] a more complete and useful specification of the production constrained model is obtained:

$$T_{ij} = O_i \left[\frac{D_j d_{ij}^{-\beta}}{\sum_j D_j d_{ij}^{-\beta}} \right] = O_i p_{ij} \tag{42}$$

It is now more clearly observed that each region's exports are 'shared' among ports according to the relative attractiveness of each port as compared with all other competing ports. The attractiveness of each port is defined by $D_j d_{ij}^{-\beta}$, where D_j is its handling capacity and d_{ij} is the distance exports have to travel between region and port. This composite attractiveness for each port is divided by the combined attractiveness of all ports in the model, so that the term in square brackets in equation [42] represents the relative attractiveness of each port in the system and also the probability, p_{ij}, of the exports of region i being attracted to that port. Although the D_j mass term is measured as handling capacity, this variable might be thought a suitable proxy for other port attributes that may be attractive to regional exporters. For example, it may be the case that the greater the handling capacity the less likely that exports will be delayed, and the more likely is the port to have a greater number and variety of shipping services.

Production constrained models are characterised by the existence of origin constraints, but the absence of destination ones. To impose such destination constraints in this port problem would be nonsensical, because they would automatically imply that the amounts of exports attracted to ports would always fully utilise handling capacities and thus any port investment scheme to expand such facilities would be viable. In fact the production constrained model represents the attraction of exports to ports free from all restrictions at the destinations. This may, of course, lead to predictions of export flows exceeding port capacities. If this is realistic then delays at some ports would be implied; if not, modifications of the model are possible (see Wilson 1970b, section 5.4 for an analogous residential capacity problem). In any event the model results for the Portbury study suggested that the requisite increase in exports needed to justify the planned expansion at Bristol would not be forthcoming, and on this and further evidence the Minister of Transport refused to sanction the proposed investment.

Another popular application of the production constrained model concerns shopping interactions. Normally interactions would be defined as consumer trips, but Lakshmanan and Hansen (1965) have established a tradition of measuring interactions as money flows. Thus, T_{ij} is defined as the amount of money consumers from residential area i spend at shopping centre j. The origin mass term, O_i, is now a precise measure of the retail spending power of the population in area i, to which the money flows are related consistently via the A_i values. The ability of competing shopping centres to attract this money is again measured partly in terms of travel distance and partly according to shopping centre size, D_j, perhaps defined as number of shops or retail floor area. Such a model can be used to assess shopping centre viability. An example might be the proposed development of an out-of-town shopping complex, where interest focuses not only on its own viability, but on its effects in drawing custom away from neighbouring suburban centres and the Central Business District.

Brief mention should also be made of further applications of the production constrained model. In a journey-to-work context it can be used to predict the job location choices of persons whose residential locations are known or, conversely, the residential choices of those with known employment locations. It is particularly used in the latter capacity within a Lowry model (Lowry 1964; Batty 1976), where the labour force is first residentially located with respect to basic employment. Subsequently, a production constrained shopping or service model forecasts the demand for services by this residential population and locates the required service activities. Then the residential gravity model is called into play again to locate those employed in these service activities.

The final member of the constrained gravity model family reviewed here is the rarely used *total interaction constrained* model. Such a model is applicable in situations where only the total flow in the system, N, is known or estimated independently, and the gravity model is being used to predict trip origins and trip attractions as well as the transport flows T_{ij}. For example, imagine a situation where N denotes the national demand for inter-urban passenger travel, and the total interaction constrained gravity model is used to predict inter-urban passenger trips plus the totals of such trips originating and terminating at each urban centre. If these predictions are to be consistent with the national inter-urban travel demand, then constraint equation [35] must be enforced, and this is achieved in the total interaction constrained model:

$$T_{ij} = K \, O_i D_j d_{ij}^{-\beta} \tag{43}$$

Although this model is structurally identical to the Newtonian gravity model of equation [25], K is the balancing factor which ensures that the model's predictions sum to N. Again by substituting for T_{ij} from equation [43] into constraint equation [35], it is found that K is defined as:

$$K = \frac{N}{\sum_i \sum_j O_i D_j d_{ij}^{-\beta}} \tag{44}$$

A note on entropy maximising methods

All the gravity models developed so far have derived ultimately from the analogy with Newton's gravitational law. This is an unsatisfactory state of affairs, for if gravity models have some validity in transport geography it should be possible to derive them without recourse to laws developed in physics. One such non-physical derivation involves the use of the *entropy concept* of information theory, where entropy is a measure of the analyst's uncertainty, in this case about the travel behaviour of individuals. The procedure is to maximise this uncertainty so as to minimise the analyst's bias, subject to any known information about transport behaviour usually measured at a more aggregate level. This entropy maximising method is discussed and illustrated from first principles in Senior (1979) and Haggett, Cliff and Frey (1977).

Relating gravity models to the transportation problem

Evans (1973) has demonstrated that the production – attraction constrained gravity model of equation [37], but with a negative exponential 'cost' term, exp $(-\beta d_{ij})$, replacing the negative power one, $d_{ij}^{-\beta}$, will predict transport flows, T_{ij}, which are increasingly closer approximations to the cost-minimising flows of an optimal transportation problem solution as the value of the β parameter tends to infinity. Moreover, if β is varied in the opposite direction towards a value of *minus infinity*, a cost-maximising set of flows will be approximated. Therefore, for any given set of trip origins, O_i, and trip attractions, D_j, to which the predicted T_{ij} flows must always sum, an infinite number of sets of transport flows can in principle be derived from the gravity model as β is allowed to vary continuously from plus to minus infinity, and this in turn will imply a systematic rise in the total transport costs incurred by these flows (see Fig. 13.9).

It has been observed previously that the transportation problem solution is characterised by a limited number of positive T_{ij} transport flows, the rest being zero. By contrast, gravity models with finite β values predict all possible T_{ij} interactions to be positive. However, for large positive β values the gravity

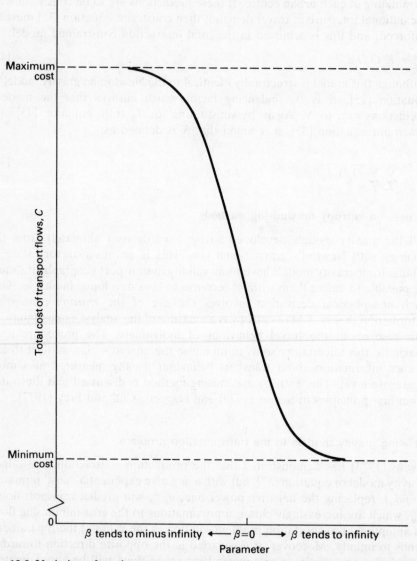

Fig. 13.9 Variation of total transport costs as β varies from minus to plus infinity in a production-attraction constrained gravity model. (Adapted from: Evans 1973: 42)

model flows will differ little from the transportation problem interactions, as the size of β indicates that transport decision-makers are on average very sensitive to travel costs and thus will select destinations to minimise them. Consequently, a few flows will be relatively large for $i-j$ interactions where costs tend to be low, whereas the remaining flows will often be trivially small.[3] As the value of β tends to zero sensitivity to travel costs decreases and the variation in the size of the T_{ij} flows will diminish. For β equal to zero travel cost has no influence whatsoever on the pattern of transport flows, while a negative β value implies that decision-makers favour more costly interactions. Clearly, these latter two situations are likely to remain of theoretical interest only.

Modelling the choice of transport mode

Alternative representations of mode choice in the trip decision process

There are a variety of models for estimating the modal choices of trip-makers, which may be classified according to their relationships with other components of the trip decision, especially trip frequency and trip destination choices. At least four variants in the structure of mode choice models can be identified.

Integrated trip frequency and mode choice models predict trip generations by transport mode directly. They include the types of method reviewed on pp. 162–72 with a transport mode element incorporated. For example, in the West Midlands Transport Study (Freeman *et al.* 1968) a mode choice dimension was incorporated in the category analysis procedure by defining trip rates by mode as well as household type and journey purpose. However, this representation implies that only the household characteristics of income, size and car ownership determine mode choices, but not any of the characteristics of the transport system itself such as those items included in the generalised modal travel cost expression [26]. It is thereby further implied that any transport policies altering the relative attractiveness of competing transport modes, such as restraints on car parking, will have no influence on shifting demand from one mode to another. This has obvious deficiencies, especially for large cities, where the differential attractiveness of travel by private and public transport may be relatively small, and where switching from one mode to another is likely to be most noticeable. Attempts to incorporate transport system influences on mode choice were thus built into the modal category analysis used for home-based trip generations in the second phase of the London Traffic Survey (Freeman *et al.* 1966). This was done by classifying households into rail and bus accessibility categories according to the districts in which they lived.

Integrated trip destination and mode choice models became increasingly fashionable in the British urban transport studies of the early 1970s (Coventry City Council 1973; Greater London Council 1973). Armed with predictions of trip generations, O_i^n, by car-ownership type, n, the aim was to predict the number of trips, T_{ij}^{nk}, destined for each location, j, by each transport mode k. By defining M_{ij}^{nk} as the probability, or 'market share', of type n trip-makers at origin locations i choosing destination j *and* mode k, as it were, 'jointly' (Manheim 1973; Williams 1977), this model can be written in the general form:

$$T_{ij}^{nk} = O_i^n \, M_{ij}^{nk} \qquad [45]$$

The problem is then to specify a suitable equation to explain these mode – destination choice probabilities. Both aggregate and disaggregate versions of such models are possible (cf. pp. 162–3). The aggregate development of model equation [45] put forward by Wilson (1970b) is recognisable as a production – attraction constrained gravity model (cf. equation [37]):

$$T_{ij}^{nk} = A_i^n \, B_j \, O_i^n D_j \, \exp \, (-\beta^n c_{ij}^k) \qquad [46]$$

with A_i^n and B_j as the balancing factor terms ensuring that trips, T_{ij}^{nk}, sum to the trip generations, O_i^n, and to the trip attractions, D_j respectively, and c_{ij}^k is the type of generalised cost of travel by mode k defined in equation [26]. The single set of parameters, β^n, reflect the sensitivity of both trip-makers' destination *and* mode choices to changes in these generalised costs.

The *pre-distribution mode choice models*, in a sense, lie between the trip-generation models (pp. 162–72) and the trip-distribution models (pp. 191–5). In other words they utilise trip generations, O_i^n, as inputs and they output, for a subsequent trip-distribution model, the number of trip generations by mode, T_i^{nk}. They have the general form:

$$T_i^{nk} = O_i^n \, M_i^{nk} \qquad [47]$$

where M_i^{nk} denotes the market share or probability of trip-makers of type n at origin location i choosing to travel by mode k. An aggregate example of this class of models is given by Williams and Senior (1977), where these probabilities are specified as:

$$M_i^{nk} = \frac{\exp(-\lambda^n c_i^{nk})}{\sum\limits_k \exp(-\lambda^n c_i^{nk})} \qquad [48]$$

The c_i^{nk} 'cost' terms are related inversely to a common measure of accessibility suggested by Hansen (1959) which in turn measures, for each origin location i, the relative ease of getting to all destination opportunities in the system by each mode. To some geographers this type of accessibility index will perhaps be better known as a measure of potential (see Abler, Adams and Gould, 1971: 216–221). Equation [48] defines the mode choice probabilities by relating the attractiveness of one particular mode k to the combined attractiveness of all modes available to the trip-maker, where attractiveness increases (decreases) as 'costs', c_i^{nk}, fall (rise).

In the combined trip destination – mode choice models a single set of parameters, β^n, implied that trip-makers were equally likely to change mode as destination in response to changes in transport costs. Now, in the pre-distribution model a separate set of parameters, λ^n, measures mode choice sensitivity only and, according to the choice theory propounded by Williams

(1977), this type of model is valid only when trip-makers are more likely to switch their trip destination than their transport mode when faced with changing transport costs. This particular assumption is perhaps most likely to be valid for some recreational and shopping trips.

Finally, the *post-distribution mode choice models* deal with the probabilities, M_{ij}^{nk}, of trip interactions destined for locations j going by modes, k. Such probabilities are thus multiplied by predictions of trip interactions by person type, T_{ij}^{n}, derived from an associated trip distribution model, and so the general model form may be written as:

$$T_{ij}^{nk} = T_{ij}^{n} M_{ij}^{nk} \qquad [49]$$

An example of an aggregate model of these probabilities comes from the SELNEC Transportation Study (Wilson *et al.* 1969):

$$M_{ij}^{nk} = \frac{\exp(-\lambda^n c_{ij}^k)}{\sum_k \exp(-\lambda^n c_{ij}^k)} \qquad [50]$$

Clearly, this has a similar structure to the pre-distribution model of equation [48], but now generalised travel costs by mode to specified destinations j are used. These c_{ij}^k terms are identical to those used in the integrated trip destination and mode choice model of equation [46], but now λ^n parameters, reflecting separately the mode choice sensitivity of trip-makers, should have values greater than those β^n parameters measuring destination choice sensitivity. This implies that trip-makers are more likely to change mode than destination in response to transport cost changes. Such an assumption should prove particularly appropriate for the journey-to-work trip purpose as, on average, commuters are more likely to change mode than job location in the event of changing transport costs. However, applications of this post-distribution mode choice model in its aggregate form have caused problems in terms of obtaining realistic values of these mode and destination sensitivity parameters (Williams and Senior 1977).

General remarks on mode choice models

Three general points about mode choice models need to be made here. First, in terms of the above fourfold classification, it is the combined trip frequency and mode choice models which stress the effects of household characteristics on mode choice. For the other three classes of model it has been common practice with aggregate models to define trip generations by the car ownership or car availability of trip-makers, and then let the characteristics of the transport system, as measured via generalised modal transport costs, play a prominent role in determining mode choices. However, it is possible to employ a finer categorisation of trip-makers, according to their personal and household attributes, and thereby allow the values of the mode choice sensitivity parameter to vary with these attributes (Southworth 1975).

A second general point is that the modal choice probabilities of the pre- and post-distribution models of equations [48] and [50], plus those implicit in the integrated trip destination and mode choice model of equation [46], may be rewritten as logistic functions (cf. pp. 173–4). Thus, for choices between two modes of transport, say private and public, equation [50], for example, may be transformed to:

$$M_{ij}^{nk=\text{private}} = \frac{1}{1 + \exp[-\lambda^n(c_{ij}^{k=\text{public}} - c_{ij}^{k=\text{private}})]} \quad [51]$$

This formulation facilitates interpretation of such models, as the share of trip interactions going by each mode is a function of the differences in generalised travel costs between the modes. Thus the proportion of trips by private transport increases as public transport becomes more expensive relative to the private mode (see Fig. 13.10).

Third, and finally, the types of mode choice model identified above can be developed at the disaggregate level of individual households or organisations instead of at the zonal level. Indeed such 'behavioural' models have become increasingly popular since the pioneering work of Warner (1962). However, disaggregate models do not explain mode choices in terms of pre-specified and composite generalised travel costs. Instead they deal directly with the individual component variables making up the generalised costs, such as travel times, waiting times and so on, and derive values of the parameters, such as values of time, associated with these component variables. In fact the generalised travel costs, like c_{ij}^k, used in the aggregate models rely for their formation on available estimates of these value of time parameters from disaggregate studies. Domencich and McFadden (1975) provide examples of

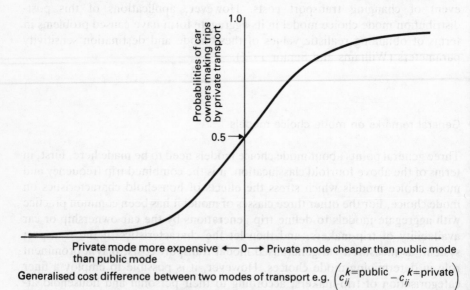

Fig. 13.10 Choice of transport mode related to modal cost differences using the logistic curve

disaggregate mode choice models for the journey to work based on the logistic function, like equation [51], but transformed into a linear logit form for estimation of the parameters:

$$\log\left(\frac{p_u}{1 - p_u}\right) = -4.76 + 0.147z_u^{\text{public}} - 0.0411\,(t_u^{\text{private}} - t_u^{\text{public}})$$
$$- 2.24\,(m_u^{\text{private}} - m_u^{\text{public}}) + 3.78v_u \qquad [52]$$

where p is the probability of an individual commuter, u, choosing to travel to work by the private mode; z_u denotes his access time to the public transport system; t_u signifies his travel and transfer times for each mode; m_u denotes the money outlays which would be incurred on each mode; and v_u is the number of cars per worker in his household.

Network analysis for travel demand forecasting

Introduction

The description and analysis of transport networks has commanded considerable attention in geography (for example, see Kansky 1963; Haggett and Chorley 1969; Hay 1973; Taaffe and Gauthier 1973; and, for optimising aspects, Scott 1971). However, relatively little interest has been displayed in those aspects of network analysis associated with travel demand forecasting. It is appropriate to concentrate on such aspects here, for they are in keeping with the applied, planning-oriented tone of this chapter.

Three features need to be considered. Firstly, it has been seen already that transport flow and mode choice models use as explanatory variables various spatial separation measures, such as travel costs and times. These measures are derived from a knowledge of the characteristics of transport networks. Secondly, trip-makers will have a route choice decision to make as part of their wider trip-making decision. Thirdly, these route choice decisions will produce various flows on the network which will, in turn, alter various network characteristics, most obviously travel times, for a given network supply.

Network description and shortest paths

Transport networks are defined by sets of links and nodes, the latter representing the junctions identified in the networks. Numbering of each node permits the identification of each link by two node numbers, and this provides a referencing system for information on link characteristics. The level of detail at which a network is represented depends on the particular problem in hand. For a very localised policy, such as the pedestrianisation of a shopping street, all roads, however minor, may be included in the analysis. For more strategic transport problems minor roads and very local access links are likely to be omitted. For studies dealing with interzonal transport flows there is the problem of linking zonally generated and attracted trips to the defined networks. Consequently, zone 'centroids', each representing the 'average' location of travel demands spread throughout a zone, have to be defined. It is unlikely that all zone centroids will lie very close to nodes in the networks. Therefore, fictitious centroid connectors are appended to appropriate nodes. For private vehicle users these connectors are proxies for the local road network not explicitly identified, say in the vicinity of homes or jobs. Also, at the destination end of a private vehicle trip, any excess time involved in parking a car and walking to the final destination location can be associated with them, as can car-parking charges. For public transport users these connectors may be used to represent access time to the network of public transport services, and possibly time spent waiting for the next bus or train. Very careful choices of centroid connectors must be made, as their locations could produce spurious effects on subsequent attempts to predict trip-makers' route choices. Other notional links needed in networks are those representing transfer times between public transport services.

Once information on the characteristics of these real and fictitious links (e.g. length, capacity, travel time and so on) has been collected, a shortest path algorithm (see Scott 1971 for a simple illustration) can be employed to find the minimum generalised cost routes between all pairs of zones. Summing all the relevant 'cost' components for the links of these shortest routes gives the generalised travel costs, c_{ij}^k, as defined in equation [26]. Particular care may be needed in determining shortest routes when fares on public transport are not linearly related to travel distance, which is often the case (Bonsall 1976).

These costs, which are used in trip distribution and mode choice models, must be calculated initially without any knowledge of the level of transport flows on the road network. However, as these transport flows affect speeds, and therefore travel times, on routes, there is an *interdependence* between travel demands and transport costs. To understand how this interdependence can be dealt with, it is first necessary to review methods for assigning traffic to routes in the networks.

Assigning traffic to transport networks

There are various methods available for representing how trip-makers select routes in transport networks. The most obvious one is the *all-or-nothing* assignment based on the assumption that all trip-makers travelling between origin locations, i, and destination locations, j, will use the previously identified shortest routes. Although this seems an eminently sensible assumption, given that the travel costs on these shortest routes have been used to predict trips by mode, the results of an all-or-nothing assignment may prove unrealistic. In the first place the method produces very 'lumpy' assignments to certain routes, and if two or more selected routes have common links, the amount of traffic assigned to these key links could be unrealistically high. In effect, the method makes very strong assumptions about the route choice behaviour of trip-makers, suggesting that *all* trip-makers between i and j perceive route costs identically and *all* choose the same minimum cost route, even if an alternative route is only marginally more costly.

Such homogeneity of behaviour is unlikely on at least two grounds. First, trip-makers' perceptions of the costs involved will probably be imperfect, and the degree of misperception is likely to vary among trip-makers. Second, trip-makers may have different preferences regarding the various factors that go to make up the generalised cost of travel on routes, implying that the generalised cost on the shortest route is an average cost for trip-makers making a particular $i - j$ interaction. Taking these trip-makers individually, it will thus be quite possible for some of them to perceive and prefer alternative routes as being less costly to themselves. Moreover, the locational approximation, which has interzonal trips originating and terminating only at zonal centroids, is more likely to produce error in route choice with the all-or-nothing assignment. It is thus quite feasible for two trip-makers, travelling between zones i and j, to identify accurately different minimum cost routes solely because of their different locations within one or both zones. An all-or-nothing method is incapable of mitigating the possibly arbitrary effects of the zonal centroid assumption on route choice.

A major alternative to this method is some form of *multiple routeing* procedure (Burrell 1968; Dial 1971). Burrell's method treats the measured generalised costs on network links as average costs for all tripmakers, around which are distributed the *expected* costs of individual trip-makers. As argued above this variation in expected costs may result from the varying perceptions and preferences of trip-makers. Instead of the all-or-nothing assumption that all trip-makers will perceive the cost of particular links identically, it is now assumed that perceived costs may differ between trip-makers from different origin zones. The identification of shortest expected routes and the calculation of their expected generalised costs is performed using sets of expected link costs selected randomly for each origin zone, from the assumed cost distributions for each network link. This does mean that all trips between i and j are assigned to the same minimum expected cost route, but the procedure makes it less probable that trips originating from neighbouring zones, and bound for a common destination, will follow routes with common links. It has been suggested (Lane, Powell & Prestwood-Smith 1971) that this technique be extended to obtain multi-routeing within each set of $i - j$ transport flows. This could be achieved by dividing up each set of flows into arbitrary segments and allowing expected route costs to vary between these segments. In this respect the likely reality that perceived route costs will vary with the location of a trip-maker within a zone may be accommodated.

This possibility of dividing up each set of $i - j$ flows, and assigning each of the groups so defined separately, is used in the *incremental loading* assignment method. In effect this is a sequential all-or-nothing assignment process which can produce multi-routeing of trips, because travel times or links are adjusted after the assignment of each increment of trips to take account of changing travel speeds on links as traffic is assigned to them. This raises the issue of the balance between transport demands and the route capacity supplied by the network.

Network demand and supply

Up to this point the generalised costs of travel on network links have been taken as fixed and given, and such costs have played a part in explaining trip-makers' destination, mode and route choices. However, the travel time component of these generalised costs is dependent on the relationships between the volume of flows and the capacities of network links, which determine traffic speeds. It is, therefore, likely that the predicted transport flows cannot be accommodated by the network at the traffic speeds implied by the travel times, as the latter were initially set for each link in the absence of link flow information. Thus the current loadings of traffic on the links will imply different travel times, which in turn implies different generalised costs, possibly relating to different shortest routes, which further implies some changes in trip-makers' choices of route, mode, destination and possibly trip frequency. Thus a circular process is set up which requires the balancing of predicted travel demands against the supply capacities of the network links.

To initiate this circular process, new link travel times have to be calculated which are consistent with the link traffic loadings produced by the assignment procedure. These times are derived from speed – flow curves, whose precise forms vary according to the type of link and its environment (for example, whether it is a single-lane street in a town centre or a dual carriageway in the suburbs). However, Fig. 13.11 portrays their general features. Up to a cer-

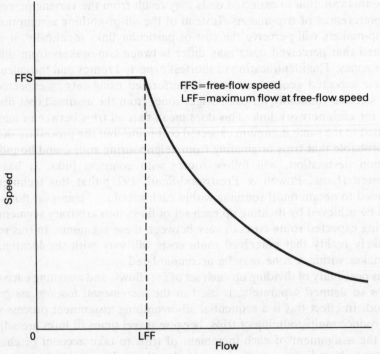

Fig. 13.11 Example of a speed-flow curve for network links. (Adapted from Wilson, A. G., Rees, P. H. and Leigh, C. M. (eds), 1977, *Models of Cities and Regions*, Wiley, Chichester, 480)

tain level of flow, denoted LFF, a roughly constant and maximum free-flow speed (FFS) can be sustained, so in the range 0 to LFF travel times will be independent of flow quantities. Eventually, however, increases in flow will begin to reduce speeds progressively, and thereby increase travel times, and as flows increase the probability of queuing delays will increase. Knowledge of the flows per unit of time and of the appropriate speed – flow curves allows the new speeds to be determined, and then these can be converted into travel times. These revised travel times are then fed back to the techniques predicting travel demands, and so the process goes on until an acceptable convergence is obtained between the demands placed on network links and their supply capacities.

As a final point it should be mentioned that it is most natural to think of capacity restraints operating in a road network context. However, public transport services are also subject to capacity limits, and any overcrowding of buses and trains, as may well occur during peak periods, adds certain costs of comfort and convenience to users. Unfortunately, such costs are difficult to measure. What can be taken into account, however, is the effects of road congestion on the operation of bus services through its impact on waiting times and travel times, and thus on service reliability generally.

Transport geography and the study of transport systems

This chapter has focused on the more applied quantitative studies of transport systems, especially the representation and forecasting of travel demands. It is clearly an area where the transport geographer will find his interests overlapping with transport planners, civil engineers and transport economists, and it is perhaps because of this lack of distinct demarcation of interest that relatively few geographers have ventured into this field. Yet the spatial element is often of fundamental interest in transport studies, and there is a growing literature by non-geographers concerned with a more serious examination of locational decisions in relation to trip-making behaviour. Ironically, these developments may percolate into geography via the back-door route of statistical analysis given the currently growing interest by geographers in the analysis of categorical data (Wrigley 1979). There are at least two vital implications for transport geographers associated with these wider developments in the quantitative analysis of travel behaviour: first, there is the shift from studying zonally or spatially aggregated trip-making to the study of the behaviour of individual transport decision-makers; and, second, there is an increasing reliance on theories of choice behaviour as a foundation for the development of quantitative models (Domencich and McFadden 1975; Williams 1977). Unfortunately, it is probable that such developments will meet resistance from many geographers given their traditional concern with zonal analyses and their suspicion of theories assuming that decision-makers make economically rational choices.

Notes

1. When presenting regression models a circumflex sign ($\hat{}$) over a variable will indicate that reference is being made to values of that variable predicted by the regression, and that these should be distinguished from the observed values for the same variable.
2. A word of caution must be added here. Different findings regarding the significance of explanatory variables may result from variations in data availability and possibly from the type of regression procedure used, especially in the case of stepwise methods.
3. It is impossible to restrict gravity model predictions of the flows, T_{ij}, to integer values, and therefore fractional flows right down to zero can be obtained. This is no problem if continuous transport flow quantities, like freight tonnage, are under investigation, but rounding flows to the nearest integer values is clearly obligatory for predictions of person or vehicle trips.

Further reading

To gain a broader perspective on the type of material covered in this chapter, geography undergraduates could consult, with profit, some general texts in transport planning and transport economics.

It would be advisable to commence with a text like **Bruton's** (1975) *Introduction to Transportation Planning*, and then supplement this with **Lane, Powell and Prestwood Smith's** (1971) *Analytical Transport Planning*. For a broader approach stressing transport policy making **Starkie's** (1976) *Transportation Planning, Policy and Analysis* is useful, while transport forecasting and economic evaluation is dealt with in the relatively advanced text by **Jones** (1977), *Urban Transport Appraisal*.

Chapter 14

Conclusion – the place of transport geography in transport studies

Transport exists for the purpose of bridging spatial gaps, though these gaps can be expressed not only in terms of distance but also of time and of cost. It is the means by which people and goods can be moved from the place where they are at the moment to another place where they will be at a greater advantage; goods can be sold at a higher price, people can get a better job, or live in the sort of house they prefer, or go for a holiday at the seaside. In short, people and goods are transported from one place where their utility is lower to another place where it is higher. Transport as a fundamental human activity may thus be effectively studied in spatial terms: geographical methods are basic to such study and are of practical relevance to the solution of many of the problems associated with the transport industry and with its activities.

But, in addition, transport has numerous secondary consequences which themselves have spatial implications. Upon the level of transport systems, from pack-horse trails to the road–rail–air system of today, depends other spatial patterns: the structure and layout of cities and their suburbs; the location and distribution of industrial activities; of farming systems and of their associated rural land use; the distribution of population.

For the geographer, one of whose principal concerns is the causes and consequences of the distribution in space of Man's activities, transport is of both direct and indirect interest. Conversely, since each individual transport line and node is unique in that it has a specific location which is not shared by any other line or node, the environment of each line or node is different and therefore their relations with that environment differ. Appreciation of these spatial variables is thus basic to the understanding of transport problems, therefore geography should be one of the basic disciplines in transport studies.

Transport geography is concerned with the patterns of transport as they exist at any particular moment of time, present, past or future, not only with the patterns of the transport network, the roads and railway lines and other aspects of the infrastructure, but with the patterns created by the flow of traffic through the network, with the factors influencing the development of these patterns and with the consequences of transport upon other human activities. This study can best be approached by regarding transport as a system. Obviously the whole gamut of transport activities is far too complex for meaningful study as a single system. We must simplify things either by looking at a single mode or at the complete transport facilities of a geographical region. In each of these cases the single mode or the complete facilities provided by two or more modes can be taken as the system. The concept of the system, with its interrelated factors and its inputs and outputs is familiar enough to the geographer – who talks of an agricultural system or an ecological system.

We are also interested in comparisons between modes and between the transport systems of different regions. This again is a familiar geographical method.

Thus, for example, we are not only interested in the pattern of roads in relation to such factors as physical feature, distribution of population, settlement patterns and industrial development. We are also concerned with the flow of the vehicles using the road. But we are equally concerned with the volume, the origins and the destinations of the passengers and freight carried by the vehicles. The roads, vehicles, passengers and freight form the system, for without any of these three groups of factors the other two would be useless or stationary.

In the same way, within a particular geographical area, a conurbation for instance, we should look at the complete transport facilities, together with what they carry, as a system. Thus, within our hypothetical conurbation, the road network, the network of bus routes, the flow of private cars and lorries, the railway network, together with all the passengers and goods carried, all this can be considered as being a system. We can, however, think of the railways and their traffic separately as a separate sub-system. But we must not forget this sub-system is part of a greater whole. In the past it has been far too common an error on the part of planners and decision-makers to think of the rail sub-system of a conurbation as something complete in itself and apart from other transport modes. In the same way roads have been thought of as separate from and unaffected by other transport modes concerned with the carrying of commuters.

We must also be aware of the reciprocal relationships between the transport system and its environment – physical, economic and social. In our conurbation we must study the transport system in relation to the patterns of land use – residential, commercial, industrial, etc. These environmental factors have been listed in the book as historical, technological, physical, economic, political and social. All these are of fundamental importance and to neglect the influence of any one of them will lead to an incomplete answer to a particular problem.

Finally, it must be stressed that, though we have been talking for convenience about transport geography, what is really meant is the geographical study of transport patterns and associated problems. We cannot talk of transport geography as a special branch of geography in the same way as we can (whether we *ought* is a separate issue) talk of human and physical geography, of systematic and regional and of historical and economic. We are first and foremost geographers with a specialised training in methods of spatial analysis and a particular approach to the study of human and physical phenomena. This means the geographer has a special contribution to make to the study of any human activity, a contribution which is no less and no greater than that made by the other major disciplines.

One such activity is transport. This, because of its direct and indirect consequences, is one of the more basic of Man's activities. It is important that geographers should, with their particular approach, make a full contribution to the understanding and development of this basic activity. But in turn geographers must learn from the other disciplines which are basic to transport studies. As Vidal de la Blache wrote in 1913: 'that which geography, in exchange for the help it receives from other sciences, can offer to the common treasure, is the aptitude not to break up what nature brings together, [and] to understand the correspondence and correlation of facts.' This is particularly applicable to the transport system and its reciprocal relationship with its environment.

Bibliography

Abler, R., Adams, J. S. and Gould, P. (1971) *Spatial Organization: The Geographer's View of the World*, Prentice-Hall, Englewood Cliffs, New Jersey.

Albert, W. (1972) *The Turnpike Road System in England, 1663–1840*, CUP, London.

Aldcroft, D. H. (1968) *British Railways in Transition: The Economic Problems of Britain's Railways since 1914*, Macmillan, London.

Aldcroft, D. H. (1975) *British Transport Since 1914: An Economic History*, David & Charles, Newton Abbot.

Allen, G. F. (1968a) Closures and grant aid, *Mod. Rlys.*, **25**, 22–6.

Allen, G. F. (1968b) Social service grants: how they will work, *Mod. Rlys.*, **25**, 564–8.

Allen, G. F. (1969) Railroads give Toronto a new heart, *Mod. Rlys.*, **26**, 610–15.

Appleton, J. H. (1956) The railway geography of South Yorkshire, *Trans. Inst. Brit. Geogs.*, **22**, 159–70.

Appleton, J. H. (1960) The communications of Watford Gap, Northamptonshire, *Trans. Inst. Brit. Geogs.*, **28**, 215–24.

Appleton, J. H. (1962) *The Geography of Communications in Great Britain*, University Press, Hull.

Appleton, J. H. (1965) A morphological approach to the geography of transport, *Occasional Papers in Geography*, **3**, University of Hull.

Appleton, J. H. (1967) Some geographical aspects of the modernisation of British Railways, *Geography*, **52**, 357–76.

Armstrong, A. G. (1974) *The Demand for Cars: An Econometric Model for Short-term Forecasting*, National Economic Development Committee, London.

Barker, T. C. and Robbins, M. (1963/74) *A history of London Transport: Vol. 1 The Nineteenth Century* (1963); *Vol. 2 The Twentieth Century to 1970* (1974) Allen & Unwin, London.

Barker, T. C. and Savage, C. I. (1974) *An Economic History of Transport*, Hutchinson, London.

Barwell, F. T. (1973) *Automation and Control in Transport*, Pergamon, Oxford.

Batty, M. (1976) *Urban Modelling: Algorithms, Calibrations, Predictions*, CUP, Cambridge.

Bayliss, B. T. (1965) *European Transport*, Mason, London.

Beaver, S. H. (1936) Geography from a railway train, *Geography*, **21**, 265–70.

Beaver, S. H. (1967) Ships and shipping: the geographical consequences of technological change, *Geography*, **52**, 133–56.

Beckmann, M. J. and Marschak, T. (1955) An activity analysis approach to location theory, *Kyklos*, **8**, 125–41.

Best, R. H. and Gasson, R. M. (1966) The changing location of intensive crops, *Studies in Rural Land Use*, **6**, University of London, Wye College, Kent.

Bird, J. (1963) *The Major Seaports of the United Kingdom*, Hutchinson, London.

Bird, J. (1971) *Seaports and Seaport Terminals*, Hutchinson, London.

Bonsall, P. W. (1976) Tree building with complex cost structures – a new algorithm for incorporation into transport demand models, *Transportation*, **5**, 309–29.

British Railways Board (1963) *The Reshaping of British Railways* (Beeching Report), BRB, London.

British Railways Board (1978) *Measuring Cost and Profitability in British Rail*, BRB, London.

British Road Federation (*passim*) *Basic Road Statistics*, BRF, London.

Bruton, M. J. (1975) *Introduction to Transportation Planning*, 2nd edn, Hutchinson, London.

Buchanan, C. D. (1963) *Traffic in Towns* (Buchanan Report) HMSO, London.

Buchanan, C. D. (1981) *No Way to the Airport*, Longman, London.

Buchanan & Partners (1969) *Report to Tracked Hovercraft Ltd*, Buchanan & Partners, London.

Burrell, J. E. (1968) Multiple route assignment and its application to capacity restraint, paper presented at the Fourth International Symposium on the Theory of Traffic Flow, Karlsruhe, W. Germany.

Button, K. J. (1973) Motor car ownership in the West Riding of Yorkshire: some findings, *Traffic Engineering and Control*, **15**, 76–8.

Casetti, E. (1966) Optimal location of steel mills serving the Quebec and southern Ontario steel market, *The Canadian Geographer*, **10**, 27–39.

Chisholm, M. (1957) Regional variations in road transport costs, *Farm Economist*, 30–38.

Chisholm, M. (1962) *Rural Settlement and Land Use* (Ch. 2), Hutchinson, London.

Chisholm, M. (1970) *Geography and Economics*, Bell, London.

Chisholm, M. and Manners, G. (1971) *Spatial Policy Problems of the British Economy*, CUP, London.

Chisholm, M. and O'Sullivan, P. (1973) *Freight Flows and Spatial Aspects of the British Economy*, CUP, London.

Chaloner, W. H. (1973) *The Social and Economic Development of Crewe, 1780–1923*, University Press, Manchester.

Christensen, D. E. (1966) The auto in America's landscape and way of life, *Geography*, **51**, 339–48.

Copeland, J. (1968) *Roads and their Traffic, 1750–1850*, David & Charles, Newton Abbot.

Corbett, D. (1965) *Politics and the Airlines*, Allen & Unwin, London.

Couper, A. D. (1972) *The Geography of Sea Transport*, Hutchinson, London.

Coventry City Council (1973) *Coventry Transportation Study. Report on Phase Two. Technical Reports*, Coventry.

Crossley, J. C. (1971) The River Plate countries, Ch. 9 in **Blakemore, H. and Smith, C. T.** (eds) *Latin America: Geographical Prospects*, Methuen, London.

Dantzig, G. B. and Ramser, J. H. (1958) The truck dispatching problem, *Management Science*, **6**, 80–91.

Day, A. (1963) *Roads*, Mayflower, London.

Department of Transport (1978) *Report of the Advisory Committee on Trunk Road Assessment*, HMSO, London.

Department of Transport (1979) *Transport Statistics, Great Britain: 1967–1977*, HMSO, London.

Detroit Metropolitan Area Traffic Study (1956) *Part II: Future Traffic and Long Range Expressway Plan*, Detroit.

Dial, R. B. (1971) A probabilistic multipath assignment model which obviates path enumeration, *Transportation Research*, **5**, 83–111.

Domencich, T. A. and McFadden, D. (1975) *Urban Travel Demand: A Behavioural Analysis*, North-Holland, Amsterdam.

Douglas, A. A. and Lewis, R. J. (1970) Trip generation techniques 2. Zonal least-squares regression analysis, *Traffic Engineering and Control*, **12**, 428–31.

Douglas, A. A. and Lewis, R. J. (1971a) Trip generation techniques, 3. Household least-squares regression analysis, *Traffic Engineering and Control*, **12**, 477–9.

Douglas, A. A. and Lewis, R. J. (1971b) Trip generation techniques, 4. Category analysis and summary of trip generation techniques, *Traffic Engineering and Control*, **12**, 532–5.

Downes, J. D. and Gyenes, L. (1976) Temporal stability and forecasting ability of trip generation models in Reading, *Laboratory Report*, **726**, Transport and Road Research Laboratory, Crowthorne, Berkshire.

Drake, J., Yeadon, H. L. and Evans, D. I. (1969) *Motorways*, Faber, London.

Edwards, S. L. and Bayliss, B. T. (1971) *Operating Costs in Road Freight Transport*, Dept. of the Environment, London.

Estall, R. C. and Buchanan, R. O. (1966) *Industrial Activity and Economic geography*, Hutchinson, London.

Evans, S. P. (1973) A relationship between the gravity model for trip distribution and the transportation problem in linear programming, *Transportation Research*, **7**, 39–61.

Fairhurst, M. H. (1975) The influence of public transport on car ownership in London, *Journal of Transport Economics and Policy*, **9**, 193–208.

Fisher, C. A. (1948) Economic geography in a changing world, *Trans. Inst. Brit. Geogs.*, **14**, 71–85.

Fleet, C. R. and Robertson, S. R. (1968) Trip generation in the transportation planning process, *Highway Research Record*, No. **240**, 11–27.

Flowerdew, R. and Salt, J. (1979) Migration between labour market areas in Great Britain, 1970–1971, *Regional Studies*, **13**, 211–31.

Foster, R. T. (1969) Pipeline development in the U.K., *Geography*, **54**, 204–10.

Freeman, Fox, Wilbur Smith and Associates (1966) *London Traffic Survey, Vol. II*, Greater London Council, London.

Freeman, Fox, Wilbur Smith and Associates (1968) *West Midlands Transport Study*, Birmingham.

Fuller, G. J. (1953) The development of roads in the Surrey–Sussex Weald and coastlands between 1700 and 1800, *Trans. Inst. Brit. Geogs.*, **19**, 37–53.

Garrison, W. L., Berry, B. J. L., Marble, D. F., Nystuen, J. D. and Morrill, R. L. (1959) *Studies of Highway Development and Geographic Change*, Seattle, University of Washington Press.

Gauthier, H. L. (1970) Geography, transportation and regional development, *Econ. Geog.*, **46**, 612–9.

Gould, P. R. (1960) Transportation in Ghana, *Studies in Geography* **5**, Northwestern University, Evanston.

Gould, P. R. and Leinbach, T. R. (1966) An approach to the geographic assignment of hospital services, *Tijdschrift voor Economische en Sociale Geografie*, **57**, 203–6.

Greater London Council (1973) GLTS Models: The state-of-the-art, *Greater London Transportation Survey*, Note **71**, London.

Grimshaw, P. N. (1972) Bulk cement movements in the British Isles: a review of 1966–1972, *Cement, Lime & Gravel*, **47**, No. 5, May.

Grinling, C. H. (1903) *The History of the Great Northern Railway, 1845–1902*, London.

Griswold, W. S. (1963) *A Work of Giants: Building the First Transcontinental Railroad (The Union Pacific–Central Pacific)*, Muller, London.

Gwilliam, K. M. and Mackie, P. J. (1975) *Economics and Transport Policy*, Allen & Unwin, London.

Haggett, P., Cliff, A. D. and Frey, A. (1977) *Locational Analysis in Human Geography*, (2nd edn) Edward Arnold, London.

Haggett, P. and Chorley, R. J. (1969) *Network Analysis in Geography*, Edward Arnold, London.

Hailey, W. M. (Baron) (1957) *An African Survey*, OUP, London.

Hansen, W. G. (1959) How accessibility shapes land use, *Journal of the American Institute of Planners*, **25**, 73–6.

Harris, B. (1970) Change and equilibrium in the urban system, mimeographed paper, Institute for Environmental Studies, University of Pennsylvania, Philadelphia.

Harvey, D. (1969) *Explanation in Geography*, Edward Arnold, London.

Hatley, V. A. (1959) Northampton re-vindicated, *Northamptonshire Past and Present*, **2**.

Hay, A. (1973) *Transport For The Space Economy: A Geographical Study*, Macmillan, London and Basingstoke.

Hay, A. (1977) *Linear Programming: Elementary Geographical Applications of the Transportation Problem. Concepts and Techniques in Modern Geography*, No. **11**, Geo. Abstracts, Norwich.

Henderson, J. M. (1958) *The Efficiency of the Coal Industry: An Application of Linear Programming*, Harvard UP, Cambridge, Mass.

Hibbs, J. (1967) Common Market transport policy, *Mod. Rlys*, **24**, 348.

Hibbs, J. (1968) *The History of British Bus Services*, David & Charles, Newton Abbot.

Hibbs, J. (1970) *Transport studies: An Introduction*, John Baker, London.

Hibbs, J. (1971) *Transport for Passengers*, Hobart Paper **23**, Institute of Economic Affairs, London.

Hibbs, J. (1975) *The Bus and Coach Industry: Its Economics and Organisation*, Dent, London.

Hilling, D. (1968) Politics and transportation – the problems of West Africa's land-locked states, Ch. 14 in **Fisher, C. A.** (ed.), *Essays in Political Geography*, Methuen, London.

Hilling, D. (1978) *Barge Carrier Systems: Inventory and Prospects*, Benn, London.

Hindley, G. (1971) *A History of Roads*, P. Davies, London.

Hoover, E. M. (1948) *The Location of Economic Activity*, McGraw-Hill, New York.

Hoyle, B. S. (ed.) (1973) *Transport and Development*, Macmillan, London.

Hoyle, B. S. and Hilling, D. (eds) (1970) *Seaports and Development in Tropical Africa*, Macmillan, London.

Hubbard, M. (1967) *The Economics of Transporting Oil*, Maclaren, London.

Ibbotson, D. (1954) All windows open (the Madeira–Marmoré Rly), *J. Stephenson Locomotive Soc.*, **30**, 389–91.

Innes, H. (1972) *A History of the Canadian Pacific Railway*, David & Charles republished, Newton Abbot.

Jackson, A. A. (1973) *Semi-detached London*, Allen & Unwin, London.

Jane's Yearbooks (annual): *All the World Aircraft: Freight Containers: Surface*

Skimmers: World Railways and Rapid Transit Systems, Jane's Yearbooks, London.

Jannelle, D. G. (1968) Spatial re-organisation: a model and concept, *Annals Assoc. American Geogs.*, **58**, 348–64.

Jenkinson, D. (1973) *Rails through the Fells: A Railway Case Study*, Peco, Seaton (Devon).

Johnson, K. M. and Garnett, H. C. (1971) *The Economics of Containerisation*, Allen & Unwin, London.

Johnston, R. J. (1976) On regression coefficients in comparative studies of the frictions of distance, *Tijdschrift voor Economische en Sociale Geografie*, **67**, 15–28.

Johnston, R. J. (1978) *Multivariate Statistical Analysis in Geography: A Primer on The General Linear Model*, Longman, London.

Jones, I. S. (1977) *Urban Transport Appraisal*, Macmillan, London and Basingstoke.

Joy, S. (1973) *The Train that Ran Away*, Ian Allen, Shepperton.

Kalla-Bishop, P. M. (1972) *Future Railways: An Adventure in Engineering*, Dorset House, London.

Kansky, K. J. (1963) Structure of transport networks: relationships between network geometry and regional characteristics, *University of Chicago, Department of Geography, Research Paper* **84**.

Klapper, C. F. (1970) Tracked hovercraft: the Buchanan Report, *Mod. Rlys.*, **28**, 64–8.

Lakshmanan, T. R. and Hansen, W. G. (1965) A retail market potential model, *Journal of the American Institute of Planners*, **31**, 134–43.

Lambert, R. S. (1934) *The Railway King 1800–1871: A Study of George Hudson and the Business Morals of His Time*, Allen & Unwin, London.

Land, A. H. (1957) An application of linear programming to the transport of coking coal, *Journal of the Royal Statistical Society*, **A120**, 308–19.

Lane, R., Powell, T. J. and Prestwood Smith P. (1971) *Analytical Transport Planning*, Duckworth, London.

Lea, A. C. (1973) Location–allocation systems: an annotated bibliography, *Discussion Paper* **13**, Department of Geography, University of Toronto.

Leahy, E. P. (1973) Trans-Amazonia: the rain forest route, *Geog. Mag.*, **45**, 298–303.

Lowry, I. S. (1964) A model of metropolis, RM-4035-RC, RAND Corporation, Santa Monica.

McKinsey & Co. Inc. (1967) *Containerisation, the Key to Low Cost Transportation*, Report to British Transport Docks Board, McKinsey.

McLoughlin, J. B. (1969) *Urban and Regional Planning: A Systems Approach*, Faber and Faber, London.

Manheim, M. L. (1973) Practical implications of some fundamental properties of travel demand models, *Highway Research Record*, No. **422**, 21–38.

Manners, G. (1967) Transport costs, freight rates and the changing economic geography of iron ore, *Geography*, **52**, 260–79.

March, L. (1971) Urban systems: a generalised distribution function, in Wilson, A. G. (ed.), *Urban and Regional Planning*, Pion, London.

Maxfield, D. W. (1969) An interpretation of the primal and the dual solutions of linear programming, *Professional Geographer*, **21**, 255–63.

Miller, C. (1972) *The Lunatic Express (the Kenya and Uganda Rly)*, Futura Publications, London, 1972.

Milne, A. M. and Laight, J. C. (1963) *The Economics of Inland Transport*, Pitman, London.

Ministry of Transport (1966) *Portbury*, HMSO, London.

Mitchell, R. and Rapkin, C. (1954) *Urban Traffic – A Function of Land Use*, Columbia UP.

Morrill, R. L. and Garrison, W. L. (1960) Projections of interregional patterns of trade in wheat and flour, *Economic Geography*, **36**, 116–26.

Munby, D. L. (ed.) (1968) *Transport: Selected Readings*, Penguin, Harmondsworth.

Munby D. L. (1978) *Inland Transport Statistics, Great Britain, 1900–1970, Vol. 1*, Clarendon, Oxford.

O'Dell, A. C. and Richards, P. W. (1971) *Railways and Geography*, Hutchinson, London.

Olsson, G. (1965) *Distance and Human Interaction: A Review and Bibliography*, Regional Science Research Institute, Philadelphia.

Osayimwese, I. (1974) An application of linear programming to the evacuation of groundnuts in Nigeria, *Journal of Transport Economics and Policy*, **8**, 58–69.

O'Sullivan, P. (1967) Review (and list) of home trip estimating equations derived from traffic surveys in U.K., pp. 27–27*i* in *Trip End Estimation*, Proceedings of a PTRC Seminar, PTRC, London.

O'Sullivan, P. and Ralston, B. (1974) Forecasting intercity commodity transport in the USA, *Regional Studies*, **8**, 191–5.

Parris, H. (1965) *Government and Railways in Nineteenth Century Britain*, Routledge & Kegan Paul, London.

Patmore, J. A. (1971) *Land and Leisure*, David & Charles, Newton Abbot.

Pick, G. W. and Gill, J. (1970) New developments in category analysis, pp. 31–35 in *Urban Traffic Model Research*, Proceedings of a PTRC Symposium, PTRC, London.

Pitfield, D. E. (1978) Freight distribution model predictions compared: a test of hypotheses, *Environment and Planning*, **A10**, 813–36.

Pitfield, D. E. (1979) Freight distribution model predictions compared: some further evidence, *Environment and Planning*, **A11**, 223–6.

Ponsonby, G. J. (1969) *Transport Policy: Co-ordination Through Competition*, Hobart Paper **49**, Institute of Economic Affairs, London.

Rae, J. B. (1971) *The Road and the Car in American Life*, Cambridge, Mass.

Rahmatullah, M. and O'Sullivan, P. (1968) The journey-to-work between local authorities on Merseyside from 1921 to 1966, Discussion Paper No. **12**, Graduate School of Geography, London School of Economics.

Rivers, P. (1972) *The Restless Generation*, Davis-Paynter, London.

Roth, G. (1965) *Parking Space for Cars: Assessing Demand*, CUP, London.

Roth, G. (1967) *Paying for Roads: The Economics of Traffic Congestion*, Penguin, Harmondsworth.

Roskill Report (1971) *Commission on the Third London Airport, Papers, Proceedings and Report, 1968–71*, HMSO, London.

Rushton, G., Goodchild, M. F. and Ostresh, L. M. (1973) *Computer Programs For Location–Allocation Problems*, Monograph **6**, Department of Geography, University of Iowa.

Rütz, W. (1969) *Die Alpenquerungen*, Wirtschaft und Sozial-geographische Arbeiten No. **10**, Friedrich Alexander Universität, Nürnberg.

Savage, C. I. (1966) *An Economic History of Transport*, Hutchinson, London.

Schaeffer, K. H. and Sclar, K. (1975) *Access for All: Transportation and Urban Growth*, Penguin, Harmondsworth.

Scott, A. J. (1971) *Combinatorial Programming, Spatial Analysis and Planning*, Methuen, London.

Sealy, K. R. (1966) *The Geography of Air Transport*, Hutchinson, London.

Sealy, K. R. (1976) *Airport Strategy and Planning*, OUP, London.

Senior, M. L. (1975) A category analysis trip end model: Base year results and performance for the West Yorkshire Area, Working Paper **67**, Institute For Transport Studies, University of Leeds.

Senior, M. L. (1979) From gravity modelling to entropy maximizing: a pedagogic guide, *Progress in Human Geography*, **3**, 175–210.

Sharp, C. (1965) *The Problem of Transport*, Pergamon, Oxford.

Sharp, C. (1967) *Problems of Urban Passenger Transport*, University Press, Leicester.

Sharp, C. and Jennings, T. (1976) *Transport and the Environment*, University Press, Leicester.

Sheppard, E. S. (1979) Gravity parameter estimation, *Geographical Analysis*, **11**, 120–32.

Silberston, A. (1963) Hire purchase controls and the demand for cars, *Economic Journal*, **73**, 32–53.

Silk, J. (1979) *Statistical Concepts in Geography*, Allen & Unwin, London.

Smith, D. A. (1963) Interaction within a fragmented state, *Economic Geography*, **39**, 234–44.

Smith, D. M. (1971) *Industrial Location: An Economic Geographical Analysis*, Wiley, London.

Smith, P. S. (1974) *Air Freight: Operations, Marketing and Economics*, Faber, London.

Southworth, F. (1975) A highly disaggregated modal split model, Working Paper **58**, Institute for Transport Studies, University of Leeds.

Stamp, L. D. (1943) *Kent*, Vol. 85 in **Stamp, L. D.** (ed.) *The Land of Britain*, Longmans, London.

Stamp, L. D. and Beaver, S. H. (1971) *The British Isles*, Longman, Harlow.

Starkie, D. N. M. (1967) *Traffic and Industry: A Study of Traffic Generation and Spatial Interaction*, Geographical Paper **3**, London School of Economics; published by Weidenfeld and Nicholson, London.

Starkie, D. N. M. (1976) *Transportation Planning, Policy and Analysis*, Pergamon, Oxford.

Stevens, B. H. (1961) Linear programming and location rent, *Journal of Regional Science*, **3**, 15–26.

Stubbs, P. C., Tyson, W. J. and Dalvi, M. Q. (1979) *Transport Economics*, Allen & Unwin, London.

Taaffe, E. J., Morrell, R. L. & Gould P. R. (1963) Transport Expansion in Underdeveloped Countries: A Comparative Analysis, *Geog. Review*, **53**, 503–29.

Taaffe, E. J. and Gauthier, H. L. (1973) *Geography of Transportation*, Prentice-Hall, Englewood Cliffs, New Jersey.

Tapner, H. (1967) *Air Cargo*, Cassell, London.

Tarrant, J. R. (1974) *Agricultural Geography*, David & Charles, Newton Abbot.

Taylor, P. J. (1975) *Distance Decay in Spatial Interactions. Concepts and Techniques in Modern Geography*, No. 2, Geo. Abstracts, Norwich.

Thompson, J. M. (1970) *Motorways in London*, Duckworth, London.

Tocalis, T. R. (1978) Changing theoretical foundations of the gravity concept of human interaction, pp. 65–124 in **Berry, B. J. L.** (ed.), *Perspectives in Geography 3: The Nature of Change in Geographical Ideas*, N. Illinois UP, De Kalb, Illinois.

Tolley, R. S. (1973) New technology and transport geography: the case of the hovercraft, *Geography*, **58**, 227–36.

Townroe, P. M. (ed.) (1974) *The Social and Political Consequences of the Motor Car*, David & Charles, Newton Abbot.

Tupper, H. (1965) *To the Great Ocean: Siberia and the Trans-Siberian Railway*, Secker & Warburg, New York.

Vance, J. E. (1966) Housing the worker: the employment linkage as a force in urban structure, *Econ. Geog.*, **42**, 294–323.

Wagner, P. L. (1960) *The Human Use of the Earth*, Free Press, New York.

Warner, S. L. (1962) *Stochastic Choice of Mode in Urban Travel: A Study in Binary Choice*, Northwestern University Press, Evanston, Illinois.

Warnes, A. M. (1969) Changing journey to work patterns: an indicator of Metropolitan change, in **Carter, H.** (ed.) *Techniques in Urban Geography*, Proceedings of the 1968 Salford Conference, Urban Studies Group, Inst. of Brit. Geogs., Aberystwyth.

Warnes, A. M. (1970) Early increase of the journey to work and the urban structure of Chorley, *Trans. Hist. Soc. Lancs & Cheshire*, **122**, 105–35.

Watson, P. L. (1975) *Urban Goods Movement: A Disaggregate Approach*, Lexington Books, D. C. Heath, Lexington, Mass.

Watts, D. G. (1970) Milford Haven and its oil industry, *Geography*, **55**, 64–72.

Wheatcroft, S. (1956) *The Economics of European Air Transport*, Michael Joseph, London.

Wheatcroft, S. (1964) *Air Transport Policy*, Michael Joseph, London.

White, H. P. (1963a) The re-shaping of British Railways: a review, *Geography*, **43**, 335–7.

White, H. P. (1963b) The movement of export crops in Nigeria, *Tijdschrift voor Economische en Sociale Geografie*, **54**, 248–53.

White, H. P. (1964) London's rail terminals and their suburban traffic: a geographical appraisal of the commuter problem. *Geog. Review*, **54**, 347–65.

White, H. P. (1969) (1971) *A Regional History of the Railways of Great Britain, Vol. 2: Southern England* (1969), *Vol. 3: Greater London* (1971) David & Charles, Newton Abbot.

White, H. P. (1970) The ports of West Africa: a morphological study, Ch. 2 in **Hoyle B. S. and Hilling, D.** (see above).

White, H. P. (1978) High speed rail pulls in the passengers, *Geog. Mag.*, **50**, 601–4.

White, H. P. (1979a) Unit trains – technology and changing accessibility, *Geography*, **64**, 46–50.

White, H. P. (1979b) Transport moves with technology, *Geog. Mag.*, **51**, 793–9.

White, H. P. (1980) Transport and development in West Africa, *African Research & Documentation*, **24**, 2–9.

White, H. P. and Gleave, M. B. (1971) *An Economic Geography of West Africa*, Bell, London.

White, P. R. (1976) *Planning for Public Transport*, Hutchinson, London.

White Papers – *Transport Policy*, June 1966, Cmnd 3057; *Railway Policy*, November 1967, Cmnd 3439; *The Transport of Freight*, November 1967, Cmnd 3470; *Public Transport and Traffic*, November 1967, Cmnd 3481; *Transport Policy*, June 1977, Cmnd 6836; *Airports Policy*, February 1978, Cmnd 7084.

Williams, H. C. W. L. (1977) On the formation of travel demand models and economic evaluation measures of user benefit, *Environment and Planning*, **A9**, 285–344.

Williams, H. C. W. L. and Senior, M. L. (1977) Model-based transport policy assessment 2. Removing fundamental inconsistencies from the models, *Traffic Engineering and Control*, **18**, 464–9.

Wilson, A. G. (1970a) Advances and problems in distribution modelling, *Transportation Research*, **4**, 1–18.

Wilson, A. G. (1970b) *Entropy in Urban and Regional modelling*, Pion, London.

Wilson, A. G., Hawkins, A. F., Hill, G. J. and Wagon, D. J. (1969) Calibration and testing of the SELNEC transport model, *Regional Studies*, **3**, 337–50.

Wilson, G. (1967) Road and rail productivity compared, *Mod. Rlys.*, **24**, 64–5.

Wootton, H. J. and Pick, G. W. (1967) A model for trips generated by households, *Journal of Transport Economics and Policy*, **1**, 137–53.

Wrigley, N. (1979) Developments in the statistical analysis of categorical data, *Progress in Human Geography*, **3**, 315–55.

Yeates, M. H. (1963) Hinterland delimitation: a distance minimizing approach, *Professional Geographer*, **15**, 7–10.

The following journals provide useful sources for up-to-date information: *Coaching Journal; Commercial Motor; Containerisation International; Dock and Harbour Authority; Fairplay; Flight International; Modern Railways; Modern Transport; Railway Gazette International.*

Annual Reports: British Rail; London Transport; The Passenger Transport Executives; National Bus Company; National Freight Corporation; British Airports Authority.

Index